SECRET

PROCEEDINGS AND DEBATES

OF THE

FEDERAL CONVENTION.

SECRET
PROCEEDINGS AND DEBATES

OF THE

CONVENTION

ASSEMBLED AT PHILADELPHIA, IN THE YEAR 1787, FOR THE PURPOSE OF FORMING THE

CONSTITUTION

OF

THE UNITED STATES OF AMERICA

FROM NOTES TAKEN BY THE LATE ROBERT YATES, ESQUIRE, CHIEF JUSTICE OF NEW YORK, AND COPIED BY JOHN LANSING, JUN. ESQUIRE, LATE CHANCELLOR OF THAT STATE, MEMBERS OF THAT CONVENTION.

INCLUDING

"THE GENUINE INFORMATION,

LAID BEFORE THE LEGISLATURE OF MARYLAND,

By *LUTHER MARTIN, Esquire,*

THEN ATTORNEY-GENERAL OF THAT STATE AND MEMBER OF THAT CONVENTION.

ALSO

OTHER HISTORICAL DOCUMENTS, RELATIVE TO THE FEDERAL COMPACT OF THE NORTH AMERICAN UNION.

University Press of the Pacific
Honolulu, Hawaii

Secret Procedings and Debates of the Constitutional Convention 1787

Compiled by
Robert Yates
John Lansing

ISBN: 1-4102-0363-8

Reprinted from the 1986 edition

University Press of the Pacific
Honolulu, Hawaii
http://www.universitypressofthepacific.com

PREFACE

THE historians of kings, with a religious care, collect the first words, the first sentiments, and the first acts of their infancy ; in the age of innocence, those great personages have not yet acquired the art of disguise ; and philosophy, more than once, has prognosticated, what they would be on the throne, by what they have been in the nursery.

The historians of free nations ought not to be less attentive to collect whatever may throw light on the origin of their government, on the principles which have guided their legislators, and on the seeds of disease from which human prudence has never been able to guard entirely human institutions. The exhibition of such facts impresses the mind with clear and achromatic ideas of the nature, action, and power of those political bodies, much better than the most elaborate dissertations.

It is to increase that source of public instruction, that a friend of American history, who long ago

a *

had secured in his portfolio the original notes of Mr. Yates of the secret proceedings of the convention that framed the present Constitution of the United States, has thought that it would be useful to give publicity to those authentic documents; especially at a period when improvements and alterations in the local constitution of one of the main pillars of the North American union, are about to be undertaken. These documents may serve to show the constitutional lines drawn by the true spirit of 1776, and patriotically defended by the old republicans of 1787; and account, in many respects, for a succession of events which are the natural, if not the necessary results of a preëxisting order of things.

Congress has lately caused to be published the journal of the formal proceedings of the federal convention; but, if we are allowed to repeat what has previously been observed on that subject, in the proposals circulated for publishing the present collection, that official journal has left history in the dark as to the views of the legislators and the principles upon which they acted; and it is in reality nothing but a diplomatic skeleton, deprived of its vital parts. Messrs. Hamilton, Jay, and Madison, in the numbers so well known under the title of the *Federalist*, which made their appearance previous to the interpolation of the ten declaratory and restrictive amendments, so fortunately insisted on by the States, have, it is true, entered into ample discussions and elaborate comments to assist the public judgment in the investigation of the plan of constitution presented to the consideration of the States. But discussions and comments are not history; and history is never more attractive than when it presents to us on the scene, the actors of great transactions; opens, as it were, the doors of their most secret councils to the curiosity of the reader, and procures him, without the compulsion of a literary *dictatorat*, the pleasing task of judging for himself of public men and public measures.

It is to be regretted, that Mr. Yates left the convention before the draft of the Constitution was completed; but he left it after all the basis urged by the promoters of the favored plan had been adopted by a majority of the representatives of the States; and what he did not hear, has not escaped the vigilance of Mr. Luther Martin, whose report is inserted before the notes of Mr. Yates, because it embraces a more general view of the subject, and may serve as a key to discriminate the several interlocutors mentioned in the Debates.

We possess no other testimony concerning the secret proceedings of the federal convention. It is said, that Mr. Madison has also, during the sittings of that body, made his memorandums of the controversies which have arisen in debating the merits of the Constitution, and that he intends to publish them. It will be an additional diffusion of radiant matter on a system of government admirably well calculated for the general and local administration of extensive free countries, — a system, whose excellence and brilliant success have rendered it, not only the pattern, but also the centre of gravity and the point of rest of the several confederacies forming themselves every day on this immense continent, with more rapidity than Herschel has discovered his new constellations. The talents and the veracity of Mr. Madison insure the belief, that his memoirs will enrich our annals, and that his paternal feelings for the *Federalist* will not affect the rigidity of his narratives as an historian.

THE EDITOR.

CONTENTS.

APPENDIX.

SECRET PROCEEDINGS

OF THE

FEDERAL CONVENTION.

To the HON. THOMAS COCKEY DEYE, *Speaker of the House of Delegates of Maryland.*

SIR,

I FLATTER myself the subject of this letter will be a sufficient apology for thus publicly addressing it to you, and through you to the other members of the House of Delegates. It cannot have escaped your or their recollection, that, when called upon, as the servant of a free State, to render an account of those transactions in which I had had a share, in consequence of the trust reposed in me by that State, among other things, I informed them, "that some time in July, the honorable Mr. Yates and Mr. Lansing of New York, left the convention; that they had uniformly opposed the system, and that, I believe, despairing of getting a proper one brought forward, or of rendering any real service, they returned no more." You cannot, Sir, have forgot, for the incident was too remarkable not to have made some impression, that, upon my giving this information, the zeal of one of my honorable colleagues in favor of a system, which I thought it my duty to oppose, impelled him to interrupt me, and, in a manner which I am confident his

1

zeal alone prevented him from being convinced was not the most delicate, to insinuate pretty strongly, that the statement which I had given of the conduct of those gentlemen, and their motives for not returning, were not candid.

Those honorable members have officially given information on this subject, by a joint letter to his Excellency Governor Clinton. It is published. Indulge me, Sir, in giving an extract from it, that it may stand contrasted in the same page with the information I gave, and may convict me of the want of candor of which I was charged, if the charge was just. If it will not do that, then let it silence my accusers.

" Thus circumstanced, under these impressions, to have hesitated would have been to be culpable; we, therefore, gave the principles of the constitution, which has received the sanction of a majority of the convention, our decided and unreserved dissent. We were not present at the completion of the new constitution; but, before we left the convention, its principles were so well established as to convince us, that no alteration was to be expected, to conform it to our ideas of expediency and safety. A persuasion, that our further attendance would be fruitless and unavailing, rendered us less solicitous to return."

These, Sir, are their words. On this I shall make no comment; I wish not to wound the feelings of any person, I only wish to convince.

I have the honor to remain, with the utmost respect, your very obedient servant,

LUTHER MARTIN.

Baltimore, January 27th, 1788.

THE GENUINE INFORMATION, DELIVERED TO THE LEGISLATURE OF
THE STATE OF MARYLAND, RELATIVE TO THE PROCEEDINGS OF
THE GENERAL CONVENTION, HELD AT PHILADELPHIA, IN 1787, BY
LUTHER MARTIN, ESQUIRE, ATTORNEY-GENERAL OF MARY-
LAND, AND ONE OF THE DELEGATES IN THE SAID CONVENTION.

Mr. MARTIN, when called upon, addressed the House
nearly as follows:

Since I was notified of the resolve of this honorable House, that we should attend this day, to give information with regard to the proceedings of the late
convention, my time has necessarily been taken up
with business, and I have also been obliged to make a
journey to the Eastern Shore. These circumstances
have prevented me from being as well prepared as I
could wish, to give the information required. However, the few leisure moments I could spare, I have
devoted to refreshing my memory, by looking over the
papers and notes in my possession; and shall, with
pleasure, to the best of my abilities, render an account
of my conduct.

It was not in my power to attend the convention
immediately on my appointment. I took my seat, I believe, about the 8th or 9th of June. I found that Governor Randolph, of Virginia, had laid before the convention certain propositions for their consideration,
which have been read to this House by my honorable
colleague, and I believe he has very faithfully detailed
the substance of the speech with which the business of
the convention was opened; for, though I was not there
at the time, I saw notes which had been taken of it.

The members of the convention from the States,
came there under different powers; the greatest number, I believe, under powers nearly the same as those

of the delegates of this State. Some came to the convention under the former appointment, authorizing the meeting of delegates merely to regulate trade. Those of Delaware were expressly instructed to agree to no system, which should take away from the States that equality of suffrage secured by the original articles of confederation. Before I arrived, a number of rules had been adopted to regulate the proceedings of the convention, by one of which, seven States might proceed to business, and consequently four States, the majority of that number, might eventually have agreed upon a system, which was to affect the whole Union. By another, the doors were to be shut, and the whole proceedings were to be kept secret; and so far did this rule extend, that we were thereby prevented from corresponding with gentlemen in the different States upon the subjects under our discussion; a circumstance, Sir, which, I confess, I greatly regretted. I had no idea, that all the wisdom, integrity, and virtue of this State, or of the others, were centred in the convention. I wished to have corresponded freely and confidentially with eminent political characters in my own and other States; not implicitly to be dictated to by them, but to give their sentiments due weight and consideration. So extremely solicitous were they, that their proceedings should not transpire, that the members were prohibited even from taking copies of resolutions, on which the convention were deliberating, or extracts of any kind from the journals, without formally moving for, and obtaining permission, by a vote of the convention for that purpose.

You have heard, Sir, the resolutions which were brought forward by the honorable member from Virginia; let me call the attention of this House to the conduct of Virginia, when our confederation was entered into. That State then proposed, and obstinately contended, contrary to the sense of, and unsupported by the other States, for an inequality of suffrage founded on numbers, or some such scale, which should give her, and certain other States, influence in the Union over the rest. Pursuant to that spirit which then characterized her, and uniform in her conduct, the very second resolve is calculated expressly for that purpose, to give her a representation proportioned to her numbers; as if the want of that, was the principal defect in our original system, and this alteration the great means of remedying the evils we had experienced under our present government.

The object of Virginia, and other large States, to increase their power and influence over the others, did not escape observation; the subject, however, was discussed with great coolness, in the committee of the whole House (for the convention had resolved itself into a committee of the whole, to deliberate upon the propositions delivered in by the honorable member from Virginia). Hopes were formed, that the farther we proceeded in the examination of the resolutions, the better the House might be satisfied of the impropriety of adopting them, and that they would finally be rejected by a majority of the committee; if, on the contrary, a majority should report in their favor, it was considered, that it would not preclude the members from bringing forward and submitting any other system to the consideration of the convention; and accordingly, while those resolves were the subject of discussion in the committee of the whole House, a number of the members, who disapproved them, were preparing another system, such as they thought more

1*

conducive to the happiness and welfare of the States.
The propositions originally submitted to the convention having been debated, and undergone a variety of
alterations, in the course of our proceedings, the committee of the whole House, by a small majority, agreed
to a report, which I am happy, Sir, to have in my
power to lay before you ; it was as follows:

" 1. *Resolved*, That it is the opinion of this committee, that a *national* government ought to be established, consisting of a supreme legislative, judiciary,
and executive.

" 2. That the legislative ought to consist of *two
branches.*

" 3. That the members of the first branch of the national legislature ought to be elected by the people of
the several States, for the term of three years, to receive fixed stipends, by which they may be compensated for the devotion of their time to public service,
to be paid out of the national treasury, to be ineligible
to any office established by a particular State, or under
the authority of the United States, except those particularly belonging to the functions of the first branch,
during the term of service, and under the national government, for the space of one year after its expiration.

" 4. That the members of the second branch of the
legislature ought to be chosen by the individual legislatures ; to be of the age of thirty years at least ; to hold
their offices for a term sufficient to insure their independency, namely, seven years, one third to go out
biennially ; to receive fixed stipends, by which they
may be compensated for the devotion of their time to
public service, to be paid out of the national treasury ;
to be ineligible to any office by a particular State, or
under the authority of the United States, except those
peculiarly belonging to the functions of the second

branch, during the term of service, and under the national government, for the space of one year after its expiration.

" 5. That each branch ought to possess the right of originating acts.

" 6. That the national legislature ought to be empowered to enjoy the legislative rights vested in Congress by the confederation, and, moreover, to legislate in all cases to which the separate States are incompetent, or in which the harmony of the United States may be interrupted, by the exercise of individual legislation; to negative all laws passed by the several States, contravening, in the opinion of the legislature of the United States, the articles of union, or any treaties subsisting under the authority of the Union.

" 7. That the right of suffrage in the first branch of the national legislature, ought not to be according to the rule established in the articles of confederation, but according to some equitable rate of representation, namely, in proportion to the whole number of white, and other free citizens and inhabitants of every age, sex, and condition, including those bound to servitude for a term of years, and three-fifths of all other persons not comprehended in the foregoing description, except Indians not paying taxes, in each State.

" 8. That the right of suffrage in the second branch of the national legislature, ought to be according to the rule established in the first.

" 9. That a national executive be instituted, to consist of a single person, to be chosen by the national legislature for the term of seven years, with power to carry into execution the national laws, to appoint to offices in cases not otherwise provided for, to be ineligible a second time, and to be removable on impeachment and conviction of malpractice or neglect of duty;

to receive a fixed stipend, by which he may be compensated for the devotion of his time to public service, to be paid out of the national treasury.

" 10. That the national executive shall have a right to negative any legislative act which shall not afterwards be passed, unless by two third parts of each branch of the national legislature.

" 11. That a national judiciary be established, to consist of one supreme tribunal, the judges of which, to be appointed by the second branch of the national legislature, to hold their offices during good behaviour, and to receive punctually, at stated times, a fixed compensation for their services, in which no increase or diminution shall be made, so as to affect the persons actually in office at the time of such increase or diminution.

" 12. That the national legislature be empowered to appoint inferior tribunals.

" 13. That the jurisdiction of the national judiciary shall extend to cases which respect the collection of the national revenue ; cases arising under the laws of the United States; impeachments of any national officer, and questions which involve the national peace and harmony.

" 14. *Resolved*, That provision ought to be made for the admission of States lawfully arising within the limits of the United States, whether from a voluntary junction of government, territory, or otherwise, with the consent of a number of voices in the national legislature less than the whole.

" 15. *Resolved*, That provision ought to be made for the continuance of Congress, and their authority and privileges, until a given day after the reform of the articles of union shall be adopted, and for the completion of all their engagements.

" 16. That a republican constitution, and its existing laws, ought to be guarantied to each State by the United States.

" 17. That provision ought to be made for the amendment of the articles of union whensoever it shall seem necessary.

" 18. That the legislative, executive, and judiciary powers, within the several States, ought to be bound by oath to support the articles of the Union.

" 19. That the amendments which shall be offered to the confederation by this convention, ought, at a proper time or times, after the approbation of Congress, to be submitted to an assembly or assemblies, recommended by the legislatures, to be expressly chosen by the people, to consider and decide thereon."

These propositions, Sir, were acceded to by a majority of the members of the committee; — a system by which the large States were to have not only an inequality of suffrage in the first branch, but also the same inequality in the second branch, or Senate. However, it was not designed the second branch should consist of the same number as the first. It was proposed that the Senate should consist of twenty-eight members, formed on the following scale; Virginia to send five, Pennsylvania and Massachusetts each four, South Carolina, North Carolina, Maryland, New York, and Connecticut two each, and the States of New Hampshire, Rhode Island, Jersey, Delaware, and Georgia each of them one; upon this plan, the three large States, Virginia, Pennsylvania, and Massachusetts, would have thirteen senators out of twenty-eight, almost one half of the whole number. Fifteen senators were to be a quorum to proceed to business; those three States would, therefore, have thirteen out

of that quorum. Having this inequality in each
branch of the legislature, it must be evident, Sir,
that they would make what laws they pleased, however injurious or disagreeable to the other States; and
that they would always prevent the other States from
making any laws, however necessary and proper, if
not agreeable to the views of those three States.
They were not only, Sir, by this system, to have
such an undue superiority in making laws and regulations for the Union, but to have the same superiority in the appointment of the President, the
judges, and all other officers of government. Hence,
these three States would in reality have the appointment of the President, judges, and all the other officers.
This President and these judges, so appointed, we
may be morally certain would be citizens of one of
those three States; and the President, as appointed
by them, and a citizen of one of them, would espouse
their interests and their views, when they came in
competition with the views and interests of the other
States. This President, so appointed by the three
large States, and so unduly under their influence, was
to have a negative upon every law that should be
passed, which, if negatived by him, was not to take
effect, unless assented to by two thirds of each branch
of the legislature, a provision which deprived ten
States of even the faintest shadow of liberty; for if
they, by a miraculous unanimity, having all their
members present, should outvote the other three, and
pass a law contrary to their wishes, those three large
States need only procure the President to negative it,
and thereby prevent a possibility of its ever taking
effect, because the representatives of those three States
would amount to much more than one third (almost

one half) of the representatives in each branch. And, Sir, this government so organized, with all this undue superiority in those three large States, was, as you see, to have a power of negativing the laws passed by every State legislature in the Union. Whether, therefore, laws, passed by the legislature of Maryland, New York, Connecticut, Georgia, or of any other of the ten States, for the regulation of their internal police, should take effect and be carried into execution, was to depend on the good pleasure of the representatives of Virginia, Pennsylvania, and Massachusetts.

This system of slavery, which bound hand and foot ten States in the Union, and placed them at the mercy of the other three, and under the most abject and servile subjection to them, was approved by a majority of the members of the convention, and reported by the committee.

On this occasion the House will recollect, that the convention was resolved into a committee of the whole ; of this committee Mr. Gorham was chairman. The honorable Mr. Washington was then on the floor, in the same situation with the other members of the convention at large, to oppose any system he thought injurious, or to propose any alterations or amendments he thought beneficial. To these propositions, so reported by the committee, no opposition was given by that illustrious personage, or by the President of the State of Pennsylvania. They both appeared cordially to approve them, and to give them their hearty concurrence ; yet this system I am confident, Mr. Speaker, there is not a member in this House would advocate, or who would hesitate one moment in saying it ought to be rejected. I mention this circumstance, in compliance with the duty I owe this

honorable body, not with a view to lessen those ex-
alted characters, but to show how far the greatest
and best of men may be led to adopt very improper
measures through error in judgment, State influence,
or by other causes, and to show, that it is our duty
not to suffer our eyes to be so far dazzled by the
splendor of names, as to run blindfolded into what
may be our destruction.

Mr. Speaker, I revere those illustrious personages
as much as any man here. No man has a higher
sense of the important services they have rendered
this country. No member of the convention went
there more disposed to pay a deference to their opinions ; but I should little have deserved the trust this
State reposed in me, if I could have sacrificed its
dearest interests to my complaisance for their sentiments.

When, contrary to our hopes, it was found, that a
majority of the members of the convention had in
the committee agreed to the system I have laid before
you, we then thought it necessary to bring forward
the propositions which such of us as had disapproved the plan before had prepared. The members
who prepared these resolutions were principally of
the Connecticut, New York, Jersey, Delaware, and
Maryland delegations. The honorable Mr. Patterson,
of the Jerseys, laid them before the convention ; of
these propositions I am in possession of a copy, which
I shall beg leave to read to you.

These propositions were referred to a committee
of the whole House ; unfortunately the New Hampshire delegation had not yet arrived, and the sickness
of a relation of the honorable Mr. McHenry obliged
him still to be absent ; a circumstance, Sir, which I

considered much to be regretted, as Maryland thereby
was represented by only two delegates, and they un-
happily differed very widely in their sentiments.

The result of the reference of these last propositions to a committee was a speedy and hasty determination to reject them. I doubt not, Sir, to those
who consider them with attention, so sudden a rejection will appear surprising ; but it may be proper
to inform you, that, on our meeting in convention, it
was soon found there were among us three parties,
of very different sentiments and views.

One party, whose object and wish it was to abolish
and annihilate all State governments, and to bring
forward one general government, over this extensive
continent, of a monarchical nature, under certain restrictions and limitations. Those who openly avowed
this sentiment were, it is true, but few ; yet it is
equally true, Sir, that there was a considerable number, who did not openly avow it, who were by myself, and many others of the convention, considered
as being in reality favorers of that sentiment ; and,
acting upon those principles, covertly endeavouring to
carry into effect what they well knew openly and
avowedly could not be accomplished.

The second party was not for the abolition of the
State governments, nor for the introduction of a
monarchical government under any form ; but they
wished to establish such a system, as could give their
own States undue power and influence in the government over the other States.

A third party was what I considered truly federal
and republican ; this party was nearly equal in number with the other two, and was composed of the
delegations from Connecticut, New York, New Jer-

sey, Delaware, and in part from Maryland; also of some individuals from other representations. This party, Sir, were for proceeding upon terms of federal equality; they were for taking our present federal system as the basis of their proceedings, and, as far as experience had shown us that there were defects, to remedy those defects; as far as experience had shown that other powers were necessary to the federal government, to give those powers. They considered this the object for which they were sent by their States, and what their States expected from them; they urged, that, if, after doing this, experience should show that there still were defects in the system (as no doubt there would be), the same good sense, that induced this convention to be called, would cause the States, when they found it necessary, to call another; and, if that convention should act with the same moderation, the members of it would proceed to correct such errors and defects as experience should have brought to light. That, by proceeding in this train, we should have a prospect at length of obtaining as perfect a system of federal government, as the nature of things would admit. On the other hand, if we, contrary to the purpose for which we were intrusted, considering ourselves as master-builders, too proud to amend our original government, should demolish it entirely, and erect a new system of our own, a short time might show the new system as defective as the old, perhaps more so. Should a convention be found necessary again, if the members thereof, acting upon the same principles, instead of amending and correcting its defects, should demolish that entirely, and bring forward a third system, that also might soon be found no better than either of the former; and thus we might always remain young in government, and always suffering the inconveniences of an incorrect, imperfect system.

But, Sir, the favorers of monarchy, and those who wished the total abolition of State governments, well knowing, that a government founded on truly federal principles, the basis of which were the thirteen State governments, preserved in full force and energy, would be destructive of their views; and knowing they were too weak in numbers openly to bring forward their system; conscious also that the people of America would reject it if proposed to them, — joined their interest with that party, who wished a system, giving particular States the power and influence over the others, procuring in return mutual sacrifices from them, in giving the government great and undefined powers as to its legislative and executive; well knowing, that, by departing from a federal system, they paved the way for their favorite object, the destruction of the State governments, and the introduction of monarchy. And hence, Mr. Speaker, I apprehend, in a great measure, arose the objections of those honorable members, Mr. Mason and Mr. Gerry. In every thing that tended to give the large States power over the smaller, the first of those gentlemen could not forget he belonged to the Ancient Dominion, nor could the latter forget, that he represented Old Massachusetts. That part of the system, which tended to give those States power over the others, met with their perfect approbation; but, when they viewed it charged with such powers, as would destroy all State governments, their own as well as the rest, — when they saw a president so constituted as to differ from a monarch scarcely but in name, and having it in his power to become such in reality when he pleased ; they being republicans and federalists, as far as an attachment to their own States would permit them, they warmly and zealously opposed those parts of the system.   From these different sentiments, and from this combination of interest, I apprehend, Sir, proceeded the fate of what was called the Jersey resolutions, and the report made by the committee of the whole House.

The Jersey propositions being thus rejected, the convention took up those reported by the committee, and proceeded to debate them by paragraphs.   It was now that they, who disapproved the report, found it necessary to make a warm and decided opposition, which took place upon the discussion of the seventh resolution, which related to the inequality of representation in the first branch.   Those who advocated this inequality urged, that, when the articles of confederation were formed, it was only from necessity and expediency that the States were admitted each to have an equal vote ; but that our situation was now altered, and therefore those States who considered it contrary to their interest, would no longer abide by it.   They said, no State ought to wish to have influence in government, except in proportion to what it contributes to it ; that, if it contributes but little, it ought to have but a small vote ; that taxation and representation ought always to go together ; that if one State had sixteen times as many inhabitants as another, or was sixteen times as wealthy, it ought to have sixteen times as many votes ; that an inhabitant of Pennsylvania ought to have as much weight and consequence as an inhabitant of Jersey or Delaware ; that it was contrary to the feelings of the human mind ; what the large States would never submit to; that the large States would have great objects in view, in which they would never permit the smaller States to thwart them; that equality of suffrage was the rotten part of the constitution, and that this was a happy time to get clear of it. In fine, that it was the poison which contaminated our whole system, and the source of all the evils we experienced.

This, Sir, is the substance of the arguments, if arguments they may be called, which were used in favor of inequality of suffrage. Those who advocated the equality of suffrage, took the matter up on the original principles of government; they urged, that all men, considered in a state of nature, before any government is formed, are equally free and independent, no one having any right or authority to exercise power over another, and this without any regard to difference in personal strength, understanding, or wealth. That, when such individuals enter into government, they have each a right to an equal voice in its first formation, and afterwards have each a right to an equal vote in every matter which relates to their government. That, if it could be done conveniently, they have a right to exercise it in person. Where it cannot be done in person, but for convenience representatives are appointed, to act for them, every person has a right to an equal vote in choosing that representative; who is intrusted to do for the whole, that which the whole, if they could assemble, might do in person, and in the transaction of which, each would have an equal voice. That, if we were to admit, because a man was more wise, more strong, or more wealthy, he should be entitled to more votes than another, it would be inconsistent with the freedom and liberty of that other, and

2*

would reduce him to slavery. Suppose, for instance, ten individuals in a state of nature, about to enter into government, nine of whom are equally wise, equally strong, and equally wealthy, the tenth is ten times as wise, ten times as strong, or ten times as rich ; if, for this reason, he is to have ten votes for each vote of either of the others, the nine might as well have no vote at all ; since, though the whole nine might assent to a measure, yet the vote of the tenth would countervail, and set aside all their votes. If this tenth approved of what they wished to adopt, it would be well, but if he disapproved, he could prevent it ; and in the same manner, he could carry into execution any measure he wished, contrary to the opinion of all the others, he having ten votes, and the others altogether but nine. It is evident, that, on these principles, the nine would have no will or discretion of their own, but must be totally dependent on the will and discretion of the tenth ; to him they would be as absolutely slaves, as any negro is to his master. If he did not attempt to carry into execution any measures injurious to the other nine, it could only be said, that they had a good master ; they would not be the less slaves, because they would be totally dependent on the will of another, and not on their own will. They might not feel their chains, but they would, notwithstanding, wear them ; and whenever their master pleased, he might draw them so tight as to gall them to the bone. Hence it was urged, the inequality of representation, or giving to one man more votes than another, on account of his wealth, &c., was altogether inconsistent with the principles of liberty ; and in the same proportion as it should be adopted, in favor of one or more, in that proportion are the others enslaved. It was urged, that though every individual should have an equal voice in the government, yet, even the superior wealth, strength, or understanding, would give great and undue advantages to those who possessed them.   That wealth attracts respect and attention ; superior strength would cause the weaker and more feeble to be cautious how they offended, and to put up with small injuries rather than to engage in an unequal contest ; in like manner, superior understanding would give its possessor many opportunities of profiting at the expense of the more ignorant.

Having thus established these principles, with respect to the rights of individuals in a state of nature, and what is due to each, on entering into government, (principles established by every writer on liberty,) they proceeded to show, that States, when once formed, are considered, with respect to each other, as individuals in a state of nature ; that, like individuals, each State is considered equally free and equally independent, the one having no right to exercise authority over the other, though more strong, more wealthy, or abounding with more inhabitants.   That, when a number of States unite themselves under a federal government, the same principles apply to them, as when a number of individual men unite themselves under a State government.   That every argument which shows one man ought not to have more votes than another, because he is wiser, stronger, or wealthier, proves that one State ought not to have more votes than another, because it is stronger, richer, or more populous.   And, that by giving one State, or one or two States, more votes than the others, the others thereby are enslaved to such State or States, having the greater number of votes, in the same manner as in the case before put, of individuals, when one has more votes than the others. That the reason why each individual man in forming a State government should have an equal vote, is because each individual, before he enters into government, is equally free and independent. So each State, when States enter into a federal government, are entitled to an equal vote; because, before they entered into such federal government, each State was equally free and equally independent. That adequate representation of men formed into a State government, consists in each man having an equal voice, either personally, or, if by representatives, that he should have an equal voice in choosing the representatives. So, adequate representation of States in a federal government, consists in each State having an equal voice, either in person or by its representative, in every thing which relates to the federal government. That this adequacy of representation is more important in a federal, than in a State government, because the members of a State government, the district of which is not very large, have generally such a common interest, that laws can scarcely be made by one part, oppressive to the others, without their suffering in common; but the different States, composing an extensive federal empire, widely distant one from the other, may have interests so totally distinct, that the one part might be greatly benefited by what would be destructive to the other.

They were not satisfied by resting it on principles; they also appealed to history. They showed, that in the amphictyonic confederation of the Grecian cities, each city, however different in wealth, strength, and other circumstances, sent the same number of deputies, and had each an equal voice in every thing that related to the common concerns of Greece. It was shown, that in the seven provinces of the United Netherlands, and the confederated cantons of Switzerland, each canton and each province have an equal vote, although there are as great distinctions of wealth, strength, population, and extent of territory among those provinces and those cantons, as among these States. It was said, that the maxim, that taxation and representation ought to go together, was true so far, that no person ought to be taxed who is not represented, but not in the extent insisted upon, to wit, that the quantum of taxation and representation ought to be the same ; on the contrary, the quantum of representation depends upon the quantum of freedom ; and therefore all, whether individual States, or individual men, who are equally free, have a right to equal representation. That to those who insist, that he who pays the greatest share of taxes ought to have the greatest number of votes, it is a sufficient answer to say, that this rule would be destructive of the liberty of the others, and would render them slaves to the more rich and wealthy. That if one man pays more taxes than another, it is because he has more wealth to be protected by government, and he receives greater benefits from the government. So if one State pays more to the federal government, it is because, as a State, she enjoys greater blessings from it ; she has more wealth protected by it, or a greater number of inhabitants, whose rights are secured, and who share its advantages.

It was urged, that, upon these principles, the Pennsylvanian, or inhabitant of a large State, was of as much consequence as the inhabitant of Jersey, Delaware, Maryland, or any other State. That his conse quence was to be decided by his situation in his own State; that if he was there as free, if he had as great share in the forming of his own government, and in the making and executing its laws, as the inhabitants of those other States, then was he equally important, and of equal consequence. Suppose a confederation of States had never been adopted, but every State had remained absolutely in its independent situation, no person could with propriety say, that the citizen of the large State was not as important as the citizen of the smaller; the confederation of the States cannot alter the case. It was said, that in all transactions between State and State, the freedom, independence, importance, and consequence, even the individuality of each citizen of the different States, might with propriety be said to be swallowed up, or concentrated, in the independence, the freedom, and the individuality of the State of which they are citizens. That the thirteen States are thirteen distinct political individual existences, as to each other; that the federal government is, or ought to be, a government over these thirteen political individual existences, which form the members of that government; and that, as the largest State is only a single individual of this government, it ought to have only one vote; the smallest State, also being one individual member of this government, ought also to have one vote. To those who urged, that for the States to have equal suffrage was contrary to the feelings of the human heart, it was answered, that it was admitted to be contrary to the feelings of pride and ambition, but those were feelings which ought not to be gratified at the expense of freedom.

It was urged, that the position, that great States would have great objects in view, in which they

would not suffer the less States to thwart them, was
one of the strongest reasons why inequality of representation ought not to be admitted. If those great
objects were not inconsistent with the interest of the
less States, they would readily concur in them; but
if they were inconsistent with the interest of a majority of the States composing the government, in that
case two or three States ought not to have it in their
power to aggrandize themselves, at the expense of all
the rest. To those who alleged, that equality of suffrage in our federal government, was the poisonous
source from which all our misfortunes flowed, it was
answered, that the allegation was not founded in fact ;
that equality of suffrage had never been complained
of by the States, as a defect in our federal system ;
that, among the eminent writers, foreigners and others,
who had treated of the defects of our confederation,
and proposed alterations, none had proposed an alteration in this part of the system ; and members of the
convention, both in and out of Congress, who advocated the equality of suffrage, called upon their opponents, both in and out of Congress, and challenged
them to produce one single instance where a bad
measure had been adopted, or a good measure had
failed of adoption, in consequence of the States having
an equal vote ; on the contrary, they urged, that all
our evils flowed from the want of power in the federal
head, and that, let the right of suffrage in the States
be altered in any manner whatever, if no greater powers were given to the government, the same inconveniences would continue.

It was denied that the equality of suffrage was
originally agreed to on principles of necessity or expediency ; on the contrary, that it was adopted on the

principles of the rights of men and the rights of States, which were then well known, and which then influenced our conduct, although now they seem to be forgotten. For this, the Journals of Congress were appealed to; it was from them shown, that when the committee of Congress reported to that body the articles of confederation, the very first article, which became the subject of discussion, was that respecting equality of suffrage. That Virginia proposed divers modes of suffrage, all on the principle of inequality, which were almost unanimously rejected; that on the question for adopting the article, it passed, Virginia being the only State which voted in the negative. That, after the articles of confederation were submitted to the States, by them to be ratified, almost every State proposed certain amendments, which they instructed their delegates to endeavour to obtain before ratification, and that among all the amendments proposed, not one State, not even Virginia, proposed an amendment of that article, securing the equality of suffrage, — the most convincing proof it was agreed to and adopted, not from necessity, but upon a full conviction, that, according to the principles of free government. the States had a right to that equality of suffrage.

But, Sir, it was to no purpose that the futility of their objections were shown, when driven from the pretence, that the equality of suffrage had been originally agreed to on principles of expediency and necessity; the representatives of the large States persisting in a declaration, that they would never agree to admit the smaller States to an equality of suffrage. In answer to this, they were informed, and informed in terms the most strong and energetic that could possibly be used, that we never would agree to a system giving them the undue influence and superiority they proposed. That we would risk every possible consequence. That from anarchy and confusion, order might arise. That slavery was the worst that could ensue, and we considered the system proposed to be the most complete, most abject system of slavery that the wit of man ever devised, under the pretence of forming a government for free States. That we never would submit tamely and servilely, to a present certain evil, in dread of a future, which might be imaginary; that we were sensible the eyes of our country and the world were upon us. That we would not labor under the imputation of being unwilling to form a strong and energetic federal government; but we would publish the system which we approved, and also that which we opposed, and leave it to our country, and the world at large, to judge between us, who best understood the rights of free men and free States, and who best advocated them; and to the same tribunal we would submit, who ought to be answerable for all the consequences, which might arise to the Union from the convention breaking up, without proposing any system to their constituents. During this debate we were threatened, that if we did not agree to the system proposed, we never should have an opportunity of meeting in convention to deliberate on another, and this was frequently urged. In answer, we called upon them to show what was to prevent it, and from what quarter was our danger to proceed; was it from a foreign enemy? Our distance from Europe, and the political situation of that country, left us but little to fear. Was there any ambitious

3

State or States, who, in violation of every sacred obligation, was preparing to enslave the other States, and raise itself to consequence on the ruin of the others ? Or was there any such ambitious individual ? We did not apprehend it to be the case; but suppose it to be true, it rendered it the more necessary, that we should sacredly guard against a system, which might enable all those ambitious views to be carried into effect, even under the sanction of the constitution and government. In fine, Sir, all these threats were treated with contempt, and they were told, that we apprehended but one reason to prevent the States meeting again in convention ; that, when they discovered the part this convention had acted, and how much its members were abusing the trust reposed in them, the States would never trust another convention. At length, Sir, after every argument had been exhausted by the advocates of equality of representation, the question was called, when a majority decided in favor of the inequality ; Massachusetts, Pennsylvania, Virginia, North Carolina, South Carolina, and Georgia voting for it ; Connecticut, New York, New Jersey, and Delaware against it ; Maryland divided. It may be thought surprising, Sir, that Georgia, a State now small and comparatively trifling in the Union, should advocate this system of unequal representation, giving up her present equality in the federal government, and sinking herself almost to total insignificance in the scale ; but, Sir, it must be considered, that Georgia has the most extensive territory in the Union, being larger than the whole island of Great Britain, and thirty times as large as Connecticut. This system being designed to preserve to the States their whole territory unbroken, and to

prevent the erection of new States within the territory
of any of them, Georgia looked forward when, her
population being increased in some measure proportioned to her territory, she should rise in the scale,
and give law to the other States, and hence we found
the delegation of Georgia warmly advocating the
proposition of giving the States unequal representation. Next day the question came on, with respect
to the inequality of representation in the second
branch, but little debate took place ; the subject had
been exhausted on the former question. On the votes
being taken, Massachusetts, Pennsylvania, Virginia,
North Carolina, and South Carolina, voted for the
inequality. Connecticut, New York, New Jersey,
Delaware, and Maryland * were in the negative.
Georgia had only two representatives on the floor,
one of whom (not, I believe, because he was against
the measure, but from a conviction, that we would
go home, and thereby dissolve the convention, before we would give up the question,) voted also in
the negative, by which that State was divided.
Thus, Sir, on this great and important part of the
system, the convention being equally divided, five
States for the measure, five against, and one divided,
there was a total stand, and we did not seem very
likely to proceed any further. At length, it was proposed, that a select committee should be balloted for,
composed of a member from each State, which com-

---

* On this question, Mr. Martin was the only delegate for Maryland present, which circumstance secured the State a negative. Immediately after
the question had been taken, and the President had declared the votes,
Mr. Jenifer came into the convention, when Mr. King, from Massachusetts,
valuing himself on Mr. Jenifer to divide the State of Maryland on this
question, as he had on the former, requested of the President that the
question might be put again ; however, the motion was too extraordinary in
its nature to meet with success.

mittee should endeavour to devise some mode of conciliation or compromise. I had the honor to be on that committee; we met, and discussed the subject of difference; the one side insisted on the inequality of suffrage in both branches, the other insisted on the equality in both; each party was tenacious of their sentiments. When it was found, that nothing could induce us to yield to the inequality in both branches, they at length proposed, by way of compromise, if we would accede to their wishes as to the first branch, they would agree to the equal representation in the second. To this it was answered, that there was no merit in the proposal; it was only consenting, after they had struggled to put ooth their feet on our necks, to take one of them off, provided we would consent to let them keep the other on; when they knew, at the same time, that they could not put one foot on our necks, unless we would consent to it; and that, by being permitted to keep on that one foot, they should afterwards be able to place the other foot on whenever they pleased.

They were also called on, to inform us what security they could give us, should we agree to this compromise, that they would abide by the plan of government formed upon it, any longer that it suited their interests, or they found it expedient. "The States have a right to an equality of representation. This is secured to us by our present articles of confederation; we are in possession of this right; it is now to be torn from us. What security can you give us, that, when you get the power the proposed system will give you, when you have men and money, that you will not force from the States that equality of suffrage in the second branch, which you now deny to be their right, and only give up from absolute necessity? Will you tell us we ought to trust you, because you now enter into a solemn compact with us? This you have done before, and now treat with the utmost contempt. Will you now make an appeal to the Supreme Being, and call on him to guarantee your observance of this compact? The same you have formerly done, for your observance of the articles of confederation, which you are now violating in the most wanton manner.

" The same reasons, which you now urge for destroying our present federal government, may be urged for abolishing the system, which you now propose to adopt ; and, as the method prescribed by the articles of confederation is now totally disregarded by you, as little regard may be shown by you to the rules prescribed for the amendment of the new system, whenever, having obtained power by the government, you shall hereafter be pleased either to discard it entirely, or so to alter it as to give yourselves all that superiority, which you have now contended for, and to obtain which you have shown yourselves disposed to hazard the Union." Such, Sir, was the language used on that occasion, and they were told, that, as we could not possibly have a stronger tie on them, for their observance of the new system, than we had for their observance of the articles of confederation, which had proved totally insufficient, it would be wrong and imprudent to confide in them. It was further observed, that the inequality of the representation would be daily increasing. That many of the States, whose territory was confined, and whose population was at this time large in proportion to their territory, would probably, twenty, thirty, or forty years hence, have no more representatives than at the introduction of the government; whereas, the States having extensive territory, where lands are to be procured cheap, would be daily increasing in the number of their inhabitants, not only from propagation, but from the emigration of the inhabitants of the other States, and would have soon double, or perhaps treble the number of representatives that they are to have at first, and thereby enormously increase their influence in the national councils. However, the majority of the select committee at length agreed to a series of propositions, by way of compromise, part of which related to the representation in the first branch, nearly as the system is now published, and part of them to the second branch, securing, in that, equal representation, — and reported them as a compromise, upon the express terms, that they were wholly to be adopted, or wholly to be rejected. Upon this compromise, a great number of the members so far engaged themselves, that, if the system was progressed upon agreeably to the terms of compromise, they would lend it their names, by signing it, and would not actively oppose it, if their States should appear inclined to adopt it. Some, however, in which number was myself, who joined in the report, and agreed to proceed upon those principles, and see what kind of a system would ultimately be formed upon it, yet reserved to themselves, in the most explicit manner, the right of finally giving a solemn dissent to the system, if it was thought by them inconsistent with the freedom and happiness of their country. This, Sir, will account why the members of the convention so generally signed their names to the system; not because they thought it a proper one; not because they thoroughly approved, or were unanimous for it ; but because they thought it better than the system attempted to be forced upon them.   This report of the select committee was, after long dissension, adopted by a majority of the convention, and the system was proceeded in accordingly. I believe near a fortnight, perhaps more, was spent in the discussion of this business, during which we were on the verge of dissolution, scarce held together by the strength of a hair, though the public papers were announcing our extreme unanimity.

Mr. Speaker, I think it my duty to observe, that, during this struggle to prevent the large States from having all power in their hands, which had nearly terminated in a dissolution of the convention, it did not appear to me, that either of those illustrious characters, the honorable Mr. Washington or the President of the State of Pennsylvania, was disposed to favor the claims of the smaller States, against the undue superiority attempted by the large States ; on the contrary, the honorable President of Pennsylvania was a member of the committee of compromise, and there advocated the right of the large States to an inequality in both branches, and only ultimately conceded it in the second branch on the principle of conciliation, when it was found no other terms would be accepted.   This, Sir, I think it my duty to mention, for the consideration of those, who endeavour to prop up a dangerous and defective system by great names.   Soon after this period, the honorable Mr. Yates and Mr. Lansing, of New York, left us ; they had uniformly opposed the system, and, I believe, despairing of getting a proper one brought forward, or of rendering any real service, they returned no more.   The propositions reported by the committee of the whole House having been fully discussed by the convention, and, with many alterations, having been agreed to by a majority, a committee of five were appointed to detail the system, according to the principles contained in what had been agreed to by that majority; this was likely to require some time, and the convention adjourned for eight or ten days. Before the adjournment, I moved for liberty to be given to the different members to take correct copies of the propositions, to which the convention had then agreed, in order that, during the recess of the convention, we might have an opportunity of considering them, and, if it should be thought that any alterations or amendments were necessary, that we might be prepared, against the convention met, to bring them forward for discussion. But, Sir, the same spirit, which caused our doors to be shut, our proceedings to be kept secret, our journals to be locked up, and every avenue, as far as possible, to be shut to public information, prevailed also in this case; and the proposal, so reasonable and necessary, was rejected by a majority of the convention; thereby precluding even the members themselves from the necessary means of information and deliberation on the important business in which they were engaged.

It has been observed, Mr. Speaker, by my honorable colleagues, that the debate respecting the mode of representation, was productive of considerable warmth. This observation is true. But, Sir, it is equally true, that, if we could have tamely and servilely consented to be bound in chains, and meanly condescended to assist in riveting them fast, we might have avoided all that warmth, and have proceeded with as much calmness and coolness as any Stoic could have wished.

Having thus, Sir, given the honorable members of

this House a short history of some interesting parts of our proceedings, I shall beg leave to take up the system published by the convention, and shall request your indulgence, while I make some observations on different parts of it, and give you such further information as may be in my power. [Here Mr. Martin read the first section of the first article, and then proceeded.] With respect to this part of the system, Mr. Speaker, there was a diversity of sentiment. Those who were for two branches in the legislature, a House of Representatives and a Senate, urged the necessity of a second branch to serve as a check upon the first, and used all those trite and common-place arguments which may be proper and just, when applied to the formation of a State government, over individuals variously distinguished in their habits and manners, fortune and rank; where a body chosen in a select manner, respectable for their wealth and dignity, may be necessary, frequently, to prevent the hasty and rash measures of a representation more popular. But, on the other side, it was urged, that none of those arguments could with propriety be applied to the formation of a federal government over a number of independent States; that it is the State governments which are to watch over and protect the rights of the individual, whether rich or poor, or of moderate circumstances, and in which the democratic and aristocratic influence or principles are to be so blended, modified, and checked, as to prevent oppression and injury; that the federal government is to guard and protect the States and their rights, and to regulate their common concerns; that a federal government is formed by the States, as States, that is, in their sovereign capacities, in the same manner as treaties and alliances are formed; that a sovereignty

considered as such, cannot be said to have jarring interests or principles, the one aristocratic, and the other
democratic ; but that the principles of a sovereignty,
considered as a sovereignty, are the same, whether
that sovereignty is monarchical, aristocratical, demo-
cratical, or mixed ; that the history of mankind doth
not furnish an instance, from its earliest period to the
present time, of a federal government constituted
of two distinct branches ; that the members of the
federal government, if appointed by the States in their
State capacities, that is, by their legislatures, as they
ought, would be select in their choice, and, coming
from different States, having different interests and
views, this difference of interests and views would
always be a sufficient check over the whole.   And it
was shown, that even Adams, who, the reviewers have
justly observed, appears to be as fond of checks and
balances as Lord Chesterfield of the Graces, even he
declares, that a council consisting of one branch has
always been found sufficient in a federal government.

It was urged, that the government we were forming was not in reality a federal, but a national government ; not founded on the principles of the preservation, but the abolition or consolidation of all State
governments ; that we appeared totally to have forgot
the business for which we were sent, and the situation
of the country for which we were preparing our system ; that we had not been sent to form a government
over the inhabitants of America, considered as individuals; that as individuals, they were all subject to
their respective State governments, which governments
would still remain, though the federal government
should be dissolved; that the system of government
we were intrusted to prepare, was a government over

these thirteen States ; but that, in our proceedings, we adopted principles which would be right and proper, only on the supposition that there were no State governments at all, but that all the inhabitants of this extensive continent were, in their individual capacity, without government, and in a state of nature ; that, accordingly, the system proposes the legislature to consist of two branches, the one to be drawn from the people at large, immediately in their individual capacity, the other to be chosen in a more select manner, as a check upon the first. It is, in its very introduction, declared to be a compact between the people of the United States, as individuals ; and it is to be ratified by the people at large, in their capacity as individuals ; all which it was said would be quite right and proper, if there were no State governments, if all the people of this continent were in a state of nature, and we were forming one national government for them as individuals ; and is nearly the same as was done in most of the States when they formed their governments over the people who compose them.

Whereas it was urged, that the principles on which a federal government over States ought to be constructed and ratified, are the reverse ; that instead of the legislature consisting of two branches, one branch was sufficient, whether examined by the dictates of reason, or the experience of ages ; that the representation, instead of being drawn from the people at large, as individuals, ought to be drawn from the States, as States, in their sovereign capacity ; that, in a federal government, the parties to the compact are not the people, as individuals, but the States, as States ; and that it is by the States, as States, in their sovereign capacity, that the system of government ought to be ratified, and not by the people, as individuals.

It was further said, that, in a federal government over States equally free, sovereign, and independent, every State ought to have an equal share in making the federal laws or regulations, in deciding upon them, and in carrying them into execution; neither of which was the case in this system, but the reverse; the States not having an equal voice in the legislature, nor in the appointment of the executive, the judges, and the other officers of government. It was insisted, that, in the whole system, there was but one federal feature, — the appointment of the senators by the States in their sovereign capacity, that is, by their legislatures. and the equality of suffrage in that branch; but it was said, that this feature was only federal in appearance.

To prove this, (and the Senate as constituted could not be a security for the protection and preservation of the State governments,) and that the senators could not be justly considered the representatives of the States, as States, it was observed, that, upon just principles of representation, the representative ought to speak the sentiments of his constituents, and ought to vote in the same manner that his constituents would do, (as far as he can judge,) provided his constituents were acting in person, and had the same knowledge and information with himself; and, therefore, that the representative ought to be dependent on his constituents, and answerable to them; that the connexion between the representative and the represented ought to be as near and as close as possible. According to these principles, Mr. Speaker, in this State it is provided by its constitution, that the representatives in Congress shall be chosen an-

nually, shall be paid by the State, and shall be subject
to recall even within the year ; so cautiously has our
constitution guarded against an abuse of the trust reposed in our representatives in the federal government ;
whereas, by the third and sixth section of the first article of this new system, the senators are to be chosen
for six years, instead of being chosen annually ; instead
of being paid by their States, who send them, they, in
conjunction with the other branch, are to pay themselves, out of the treasury of the United States ; and are
not liable to be recalled during the period for which they
are chosen.   Thus, Sir, for six years the senators are
rendered totally and absolutely independent of their
States, of whom they ought to be the representatives,
without any bond or tie between them.   During that
time, they may join in measures ruinous and destructive to their States, even such as should totally annihilate their State governments, and their States cannot
recall them, nor exercise any control over them.

Another consideration, Mr. Speaker, it was thought
ought to have great weight, to prove that the smaller
States cannot depend on the Senate for the preservation of their rights, either against large and ambitious
States, or against an ambitious and aspiring President.
The Senate, Sir, is so constituted, that they are not
only to compose one branch of the legislature, but, by
the second section of the second article, they are to
compose a privy council for the President ; hence, it
will be necessary, that they should be, in a great
measure, a permanent body, constantly residing at the
seat of government.   Seven years are esteemed for the
life of a man ; it can hardly be supposed, that a senator, especially from the States remote from the seat
of empire, will accept of an appointment which must

estrange him for six years from his State, without giving up, to a great degree, his prospects in his own State. If he has a family, he will take his family with him to the place where the government shall be fixed; that will become his home, and there is every reason to expect, that his future views and prospects will centre in the favors and emoluments of the general government, or of the government of that State where the seat of empire is established. In either case, he is lost to his own State. If he places his future prospects in the favors and emoluments of the general government, he will become the dependent and creature of the President, as the system enables a senator to be appointed to offices, and, without the nomination of the President, no appointment can take place; as such, he will favor the wishes of the President, and concur in his measures; who, if he has no ambitious views of his own to gratify, may be too favorable to the ambitious views of the large States, who will have an undue share in his original appointment, and on whom he will be more dependent afterwards than on the States which are smaller. If the senator places his future prospects in that State where the seat of empire is fixed, from that time he will be, in every question wherein its particular interest may be concerned, the representative of that State, not of his own.

But even this provision, apparently for the security of the State governments, inadequate as it is, is entirely left at the mercy of the general government; for, by the fourth section of the first article, it is expressly provided, that the Congress shall have a power to make and alter all regulations concerning the time and manner of holding elections for senators; a provision expressly

looking forward to, and, I have no doubt, designed for,
the utter extinction and abolition of all State governments.   Nor will this, I believe, be doubted by any
person, when I inform you, that some of the warm
advocates and patrons of the system, in convention,
strenuously opposed the choice of the senators by the
State legislatures; insisting, that the State governments ought not to be introduced in any manner, so
as to be component parts of, or instruments for carrying into execution, the general government.   Nay, so
far were the friends of the system from pretending that
they meant it, or considered it as a federal system, that
on the question being proposed, "that a union of the
States, merely federal, ought to be the sole object of
the exercise of the powers vested in the convention,"
it was negatived by a majority of the members, and it
was resolved "that a national government ought to be
formed."   Afterwards the word "national" was struck
out by them, because they thought the word might
tend to alarm; and although, now, they who advocate
the system pretend to call themselves federalists, in
convention the distinction was quite the reverse; those
who opposed the system were there considered and
styled the federal party, those who advocated it, the
antifederal.

Viewing it as a national, not a federal government,
as calculated and designed not to protect and preserve,
but to abolish and annihilate the State governments,
it was opposed for the following reasons.   It was said,
that this continent was much too extensive for one
national government, which should have sufficient
power and energy to pervade and hold in obedience
and subjection all its parts, consistent with the enjoy-
ment and preservation of liberty; that the genius and

habits of the people of America were opposed to such a government. That, during their connexion with Great Britain, they had been accustomed to have all their concerns transacted within a narrow circle, their colonial district; they had been accustomed to have their seats of government near them, to which they might have access, without much inconvenience, when their business should require it. That, at this time, we find, if a county is rather large, the people complain of the inconvenience, and clamor for a division of their county, or for a removal of the place where their courts are held, so as to render it more central and convenient. That, in those States, the territory of which is extensive, as soon as the population increases remote from the seat of government, the inhabitants are urgent for the removal of the seat of their government, or to be erected into a new State. As a proof of this, the inhabitants of the western parts of Virginia and North Carolina, of Vermont and the province of Maine, were instances; even the inhabitants of the western parts of Pennsylvania, who, it is said, already seriously look forward to the time when they shall either be erected into a new State, or have their seat of government removed to the Susquehanna. If the inhabitants of the different States consider it as a grievance to attend a county court, or the seat of their own government, when a little inconvenient, can it be supposed they would ever submit to have a national government established, the seat of which would be more than a thousand miles removed from some of them?

It was insisted, that governments of a republican nature are those best calculated to preserve the freedom and happiness of the citizen; that governments of this kind are only calculated for a territory but small in its extent; that the only method by which an extensive continent like America could be connected and united together, consistent with the principles of freedom, must be by having a number of strong and energetic State governments for securing and protecting the rights of individuals forming those governments, and for regulating all their concerns; and a strong, energetic federal government over those States, for the protection and preservation, and for regulating the common concerns of the State. It was further insisted, that, even if it was possible to effect a total abolition of the State governments at this time, and to establish one general government over the people of America, it could not long subsist, but in a little time would again be broken into a variety of governments of a smaller extent, similar, in some manner, to the present situation of this continent; the principal difference, in all probability, would be, that the governments so established, being affected by some violent convulsion, might not be formed on principles so favorable to liberty as those of our present State governments. That this ought to be an important consideration to such of the States as had excellent governments, which was the case with Maryland and most others, whatever it might be to persons, who, disapproving of their particular State government, would be willing to hazard every thing to overturn and destroy it. These reasons, Sir, influenced me to vote against two branches in the legislature, and against every part of the system which was repugnant to the principles of a federal government. Nor was there a single argument urged, or reason assigned, which to my mind was satisfactory, to prove, that a good government on federal principles was unattainable; the whole of their arguments only proving,

4*

what none of us controverted, that our federal government, as originally formed, was defective, and wanted amendment. However, a majority of the convention hastily and inconsiderately, without condescending to make a fair trial, in their great wisdom decided, that a kind of government, which a Montesquieu and a Price have declared the best calculated of any to preserve internal liberty, and to enjoy external strength and security, and the only one by which a large continent can be connected and united, consistently with the principles of liberty, was totally impracticable ; and they acted accordingly.

With respect to that part of the second section of the first article, which relates to the apportionment of representation and direct taxation, there were considerable objections made to it, besides the great objection of inequality. It was urged, that no principle could justify taking slaves into computation in apportioning the number of representatives a State should have in the government. That it involved the absurdity of increasing the power of a State in making laws for freemen in proportion as that State violated the rights of freedom. That it might be proper to take slaves into consideration, when taxes were to be apportioned, because it had a tendency to discourage slavery ; but to take them into account in giving representation tended to encourage the slave-trade, and to make it the interest of the States to continue that infamous traffic. That slaves could not be taken into account as men or citizens, because they were not admitted to the rights of citizens, in the States which adopted or continued slavery. If they were to be taken into account as property, it was asked, what peculiar circumstance should render this property, (of all others the most odious in its nature,) entitled to the high privilege of conferring consequence and power in the government to its possessors, rather than any other property? and why slaves should, as property, be taken into account, rather than horses, cattle, mules, or any other species? and it was observed by an honorable member from Massachusetts, that he considered it as dishonorable and humiliating to enter into compact with the slaves of the Southern States, as it would with the horses and mules of the Eastern. It was also objected, that the numbers of representatives appointed by this section, to be sent by the particular States to compose the first legislature, were not precisely agreeable to the rule of representation adopted by this system, and that the numbers in this section are artfully lessened for the large States, while the smaller States have their full proportion, in order to prevent the undue influence which the large States will have in the government from being too apparent; and I think, Mr. Speaker, that this objection is well founded. I have taken some pains to obtain information of the number of freemen and slaves in the different States, and I have reason to believe, that, if the estimate was now taken, which is directed, and one delegate to be sent for every thirty thousand inhabitants, Virginia would have at least twelve delegates, Massachusetts eleven, and Pennsylvania ten, instead of the number stated in this section; whereas the other States, I believe, would not have more than the number there allowed them, nor would Georgia, most probably, at present, send more than two. If I am right, Mr. Speaker, upon the enumeration being made, and the representation being apportioned according to the rule prescribed, the whole number of dele-

gates would be seventy-one, thirty-six of which would
be a quorum to do business; the delegates of Virginia,
Massachusetts, and Pennsylvania, would amount to
thirty-three of that quorum. Those three States
will, therefore, have much more than equal power and
influence in making the laws and regulations, which
are to affect this continent, and will have a moral cer-
tainty of preventing any laws or regulations which
they disapprove, although they might be thought ever
so necessary by a great majority of the States. It was
further objected, that even if the States who had most
inhabitants ought to have a greater number of delegates, yet the number of delegates ought not to be in
exact proportion to the number of inhabitants, because
the influence and power of those States whose delegates are numerous, will be greater, when compared
to the influence and power of the other States, than
the proportion which the numbers of their delegates
bear to each other; as, for instance, though Delaware
has one delegate, and Virginia but ten, yet Virginia
has more than ten times as much power and influence
in the government as Delaware; to prove this, it was
observed, that Virginia would have a much greater
chance to carry any measure, than any number of
States whose delegates were altogether ten, (suppose
the States of Delaware, Connecticut, Rhode Island,
and New Hampshire,) since the ten delegates from
Virginia, in every thing that related to the interest of
that State, would act in union, and move in one solid
and compact body; whereas, the delegates of these
four States, though collectively equal in number to
those from Virginia, coming from different States,
having different interests, will be less likely to harmonize and move in concert. As a further proof, it

was said, that Virginia, as the system is now reported, by uniting with her the delegates of four other States, can carry a question against the sense and interest of eight States, by sixty-four different combinations; the four States voting with Virginia being every time so far different, as not to be composed of the same four; whereas, the State of Delaware can only, by uniting four other States with her, carry a measure against the sense of eight States, by two different combinations, — a mathematical proof, that the State of Virginia has thirty-two times greater chance of carrying a measure, against the sense of eight States, than Delaware, although Virginia has only ten times as many delegates.

It was also shown, that the idea was totally fallacious, which was attempted to be maintained, that, if a State had one thirteenth part of the numbers composing the delegation in this system, such State would have as much influence as under the articles of confederation. To prove the fallacy of this idea, it was shown, that, under the articles of confederation, the State of Maryland had but one vote in thirteen, yet no measure could be carried against her interests without seven States, a majority of the whole, concurring in it; whereas, in this system, though Maryland has six votes, which is more than the proportion of one in thirteen, yet five States may, in a variety of combinations, carry a question against her interest, though seven other States concur with her; and six States, by a much greater number of combinations, may carry a measure against Maryland, united with six other States. I shall here, Sir, just observe, that, as the committee of detail reported the system, the delegates from the different States were to be one for every forty thousand inhabitants; it was afterwards altered to one for every thirty thousand. This alteration was made after I left the convention, at the instance of whom I know not ; but it is evident, that the alteration is in favor of the States which have large and extensive territory, to increase their power and influence in the government, and to the injury of the smaller States, — since it is the States of extensive territory, who will most speedily increase the number of their inhabitants, as before has been observed, and will, therefore, most speedily procure an increase to the number of their delegates. By this alteration, Virginia, North Carolina, or Georgia, by obtaining one hundred and twenty thousand additional inhabitants, will be entitled to four additional delegates; whereas, such State would only have been entitled to three, if forty thousand had remained the number by which to apportion the delegation. As to that part of this section that relates to direct taxation, there was also an objection, for the following reasons. It was said, that a large sum of money was to be brought into the national treasury by the duties on commerce, which would be almost wholly paid by the commercial States; it would be unequal and unjust, that the sum which was necessary to be raised by direct taxation, should be apportioned equally upon all the States, obliging the commercial States to pay as large a share of the revenue arising therefrom, as the States from whom no revenue had been drawn by imposts; since the wealth and industry of the inhabitants of the commercial States will, in the first place, be severely taxed through their commerce, and afterwards be equally taxed with the industry and wealth of the inhabitants of the other States, who have paid no part of that revenue; so that, by this provision, the inhabitants of the commercial States are, in this system, obliged to bear an unreasonable and disproportionate share in the expenses of the Union, and the payment of that foreign and domestic debt, which was incurred not more for the benefit of the commercial than of the other States.

In the sixth section of the first article, it is provided, that senators and representatives may be appointed to any civil office under the authority of the United States, except such as shall have been created, or the emoluments of which have been increased, during the time for which they were elected. Upon this subject, Sir, there was a great diversity of sentiment among the members of the convention. As the propositions were reported by the committee of the whole House, a senator or representative could not be appointed to any office under a particular State, or under the United States, during the time for which they were chosen, nor to any office under the United States, until one year after the expiration of that time. It was said, and, in my opinion, justly, that no good reason could be assigned, why a senator or representative should be incapacitated to hold an office in his own government, since it can only bind him more closely to his State, and attach him the more to its interests, which, as its representative, he is bound to consult and sacredly guard, as far as is consistent with the welfare of the Union ; and therefore, at most, would only add the additional motive of gratitude for discharging his duty ; and, according to this idea, the clause which prevented senators or delegates from holding offices in their own States, was rejected by a considerable majority. But, Sir, we sacredly endeavoured to preserve all that part of the resolution which prevented them from being eligible to offices under the United States ; as we considered it essentially necessary to preserve the integrity, independence, and dignity of the legislature, and to secure its members from corruption.

I was in the number of those who were extremely solicitous to preserve this part of the report ; but there was a powerful opposition made by such as wished the members of the legislature to be eligible to offices under the United States.   Three different times did they attempt to procure an alteration, and as often failed ; a majority firmly adhering to the resolution as reported by the committee ; however, an alteration was at length, by dint of perseverance, obtained, even within the last twelve days of the convention ; for it happened after I left Philadelphia.   As to the exception, that they cannot be appointed to offices created by themselves, or the emoluments of which are by themselves increased, it is certainly of little consequence, since they may easily evade it by creating new offices, to which may be appointed the persons who fill the offices before created, and thereby vacancies will be made, which may be filled by the members who, for that purpose, have created the new offices.

It is true, the acceptance of an office vacates their seat, nor can they be reëlected during their continuance in office.   But it was said, that the evil would first take place ; that the price for the office would be paid before it was obtained ; that vacating the seat of the person who was appointed to office, made way for the admission of a new member, who would come there as desirous to obtain an office as he whom he succeeded, and as ready to pay the price necessary to obtain it ; in fine, that it would be only driving away the flies who were filled, to make room for those that were hungry; and as the system is now reported, the President having the power to nominate to all offices, it must be evident, that there is no possible security for the integrity and independence of the legislature, but that they are most unduly placed under the influence of the President, and exposed to bribery and corruption.

The seventh section of this article was also the subject of contest. It was thought by many members of the convention, that it was very wrong to confine the origination of all revenue bills to the House of Representatives, since the members of the Senate will be chosen by the people, as well as the members of the House of Delegates, if not immediately, yet mediately, being chosen by the members of the State legislature, which members are elected by the people; and that it makes no real difference, whether we do a thing in person, or by a deputy or agent appointed by us for that purpose.

That no argument can be drawn from the House of Lords in the British constitution, since they are neither mediately nor immediately the representatives of the people, but are one of the three estates composing that kingdom, having hereditary rights and privileges, distinct from, and independent of, the people.

That it may, and probably will, be a future source of dispute and controversy between the two branches, what are or are not revenue bills, and the more so as they are not defined in the constitution; which controversies may be difficult to settle, and may become serious in their consequences, there being no power in the constitution to decide upon, or authorized, in cases of absolute necessity, to terminate them by a prorogation or dissolution of either of the branches; a remedy

provided in the British constitution, where the King
has that power, which has been found necessary at
times to be exercised, in case of violent dissensions
between the Lords and Commons on the subject of
money bills.

That every regulation of commerce, every law relative to excises, stamps, the post-office, the imposing of
taxes and their collection, the creation of courts and
offices, in fine, every law for the Union, if enforced
by any pecuniary sanctions, as they would tend to
bring money into the continental treasury, might, and
no doubt would, be considered a revenue act; that,
consequently, the Senate, the members of which will,
it may be presumed, be the most select in their choice,
and consist of men the most enlightened, and of the
greatest abilities, who, from the duration of their appointment and the permanency of their body, will
probably be best acquainted with the common concerns
of the States, and with the means of providing for
them, will be rendered almost useless as a part of the
legislature; and that they will have but little to do in
that capacity, except patiently to wait the proceedings
of the House of Representatives, and afterwards examine and approve, or propose amendments.

There were also objections to that part of this section which relates to the negative of the President.
There were some who thought no good reason could
be assigned for giving the President a negative of any
kind. Upon the principle of a check to the proceedings of the legislature, it was said to be unnecessary;
that the two branches having a control over each
other's proceedings, and the Senate being chosen by
the State legislatures, and being composed of members
from the different States, there would always be a

sufficient guard against measures being hastily or
rashly adopted; that the President was not likely to
have more wisdom or integrity than the senators, or
any of them, or to better know or consult the interest
of the States, than any member of the Senate, so as to
be entitled to a negative on that principle; and as to
the precedent from the British constitution, (for we
were eternally troubled with arguments and prece-
dents from the British government,) it was said it
would not apply. The King of Great Britain there
composed one of the three estates of the kingdom; he
was possessed of rights and privileges as such, distinct
from the Lords and Commons; rights and privileges
which descended to his heirs, and were inheritable by
them; that, for the preservation of these, it was necessary he should have a negative, but that this was not
the case with the President of the United States, who
was no more than an officer of government, the sovereignty was not in him, but in the legislature. And
it was further urged, even if he was allowed a negative,
it ought not to be of so great extent as that given by
the system, since his single voice is to countervail the
whole of either branch, and any number less than
two thirds of the other; however, a majority of the
convention was of a different opinion, and adopted it
as it now makes a part of the system.

By the eighth section of this article, Congress is to
have power to lay and collect taxes, duties, imposts,
and excises. When we met in convention after our
adjournment, to receive the report of the committee of
detail, the members of that committee were requested
to inform us, what powers were meant to be vested in
Congress by the word *duties* in this section, since the
word *imposts* extended to duties on goods imported,

and by another part of the system no duties on exports were to be laid.   In answer to this inquiry, we were informed, that it was meant to give the general government the power of laying stamp duties on paper, parchment, and vellum.   We then proposed to have the power inserted in express words, lest disputes hereafter might arise on the subject, and that the meaning might be understood by all who were to be affected by it; but to this it was objected, because it was said, that the word stamp would probably sound odiously in the ears of many of the inhabitants, and be a cause of objection.   By the power of imposing stamp duties, the Congress will have a right to declare, that no wills, deeds, or other instruments of writing shall be good and valid, without being stamped ; that, without being reduced to writing and being stamped, no bargain, sale, transfer of property, or contract of any kind or nature whatsoever, shall be binding ; and also that no exemplifications of records, depositions, or probates of any kind, shall be received in evidence, unless they have the same solemnity.   They may likewise oblige all proceedings of a judicial nature to be stamped, to give them effect.   Those stamp duties may be imposed to any amount they please ; and, under the pretence of securing the collection of these duties, and to prevent the laws which imposed them from being evaded, the Congress may bring the decision of all questions relating to the conveyance, disposition, and rights of property, and every question relating to contracts between man and man, into the courts of the general government,—their inferior courts in the first instance, and the superior court by appeal.   By the power to lay and collect imposts, they may impose duties on any or every article of commerce imported into these

States, to what amount they please.   By the power to
lay excises, (a power very odious in its nature, since
it authorizes officers to go into your houses, your kitch-
ens, your cellars, and to examine into your private
concerns,) the Congress may impose duties on every
article of use or consumption, — on the food that we
eat, on the liquors we drink, on the clothes that we
wear, the glass which enlightens our houses, or the
hearths necessary for our warmth and comfort.   By
the power to lay and collect taxes, they may proceed
to direct taxation on every individual, either by a capitation tax on their heads, or an assessment on their
property.   By this part of the section, therefore, the
government has power to lay what duties they please
on goods imported; to lay what duties they please,
afterwards, on whatever we use or consume; to impose stamp duties to what amount they please, and in
whatever case they please; afterwards to impose on
the people direct taxes, by capitation tax, or by assessment, to what amount they choose; and thus to sluice
them at every vein, as long as they have a drop of
blood, without any control, limitation, or restraint;
while all the officers for collecting these taxes, stamp
duties, imposts, and excises, are to be appointed by the
general government, under its directions, not account-
able to the States; nor is there even a security, that
they shall be citizens of the respective States in which
they are to exercise their offices.   At the same time,
the construction of every law imposing any and all
these taxes and duties, and directing the collection of
them, and every question arising thereon, and on the
conduct of the officers appointed to execute these laws
and to collect these taxes and duties, so various in
their kinds, is taken away from the courts of justice

of the different States, and confined to the courts of
the general government, there to be heard and determined by judges holding their offices under the appointment not of the States, but of the general government.

Many of the members, and myself among the number, thought, that the States were much better judges
of the circumstances of their citizens, and what sum
of money could be collected from them by direct taxation, and of the manner in which it could be raised,
with the greatest ease and convenience to their citizens, than the general government could be ; and that
the general government ought not to have the power
of laying direct taxes in any case but in that of the
delinquency of a State.   Agreeably to this sentiment,
I brought in a proposition, on which a vote of the convention was taken.   The proposition was as follows ;
" And whenever the legislature of the United States
shall find it necessary that revenue should be raised
by direct taxation, having apportioned the same by the
above rule, requisitions shall be made of the respective
States to pay into the continental treasury their respective quotas, within a time in the said requisition to be
specified ; and in case of any of the States failing to
comply with such requisition, then, and then only, to
have power to devise and pass acts directing the mode
and authorizing the collection of the same." Had
this proposition been acceded to, the dangerous and
oppressive power in the general government, of imposing direct taxes on the inhabitants, which it now
enjoys in all cases, would have been only vested in it
in case of the non-compliance of a State, as a punishment for its delinquency, and would have ceased the
moment that the State complied with the requisition.

But the proposition was rejected by a majority, consistently with their aim and desire of increasing the power of the general government, as far as possible, and destroying the powers and influence of the States. And, though there is a provision, that all duties, imposts, and excises shall be uniform, that is, to be laid to the same amount on the same articles in each State, yet this will not prevent Congress from having it in their power to cause them to fall very unequal, and much heavier on some States than on others, because these duties may be laid on articles but little or not at all used in some States, and of absolute necessity for the use and consumption of others; in which case, the first would pay little or no part of the revenue arising therefrom, while the whole, or nearly the whole of it, would be paid by the last, to wit, the States which use and consume the articles on which the imposts and excises are laid.

By our original articles of confederation, the Congress have a power to borrow money and emit bills of credit, on the credit of the United States; agreeably to which, was the report on this system as made by the committee of detail. When we came to this part of the report, a motion was made to strike out the words "to emit bills of credit." Against the motion we urged, that it would be improper to deprive the Congress of that power; that it would be a novelty unprecedented to establish a government which should not have such authority; that it was impossible to look forward into futurity so far as to decide, that events might not happen, that should render the exercise of such a power absolutely necessary; and that we doubted, whether, if a war should take place, it would be possible for this country to defend itself, without having recourse to paper credit; in which case, there would be a necessity of becoming a prey to our enemies, or violating the constitution of our government; and that, considering the administration of the government would be principally in the hands of the wealthy, there could be little reason to fear an abuse of the power, by an unnecessary or injurious exercise of it.   But, Sir, a majority of the convention, being wise beyond every event, and being willing to risk any political evil, rather than admit the idea of a paper emission, in any possible case, refused to trust this authority to a government, to which they were lavishing the most unlimited powers of taxation, and to the mercy of which they were willing blindly to trust the liberty and property of the citizens of every State in the Union; and they erased that clause from the system. Among other powers given to this government in the eighth section, it has that of appointing tribunals inferior to the Supreme Court.   To this power there was an opposition.   It was urged, that there was no occasion for inferior courts of the general government to be appointed in the different States, and that such ought not to be admitted; that the different State judiciaries in the respective States would be competent to, and sufficient for, the cognizance, in the first instance, of all cases that should arise under the laws of the general government, which, being by this system made the supreme law of the States, would be binding on the different State judiciaries; that, by giving an appeal to the Supreme Court of the United States, the general government would have a sufficient check over their decisions, and security for the enforcing of their laws; that to have inferior courts appointed under the authority of Congress in the different States.

would eventually absorb and swallow up the State judiciaries, by drawing all business from them to the courts of the general government, which the extensive and undefined powers, legislative and judicial, of which it is possessed, would easily enable it to do ; that it would unduly and dangerously increase the weight and influence of Congress in the several States, be productive of a prodigious number of officers, and be attended with an enormous additional and unnecessary expense ; that the judiciaries of the respective States, not having power to decide upon the laws of the general government, but the determination of those laws being confined to the judiciaries appointed under the authority of Congress, in the first instance, as well as on appeal, there would be a necessity for judges or magistrates of the general government, and those to a considerable number, in each county of every State ; that there would be a necessity for courts to be holden by them in each county, and that these courts would stand in need of all the proper officers, such as sheriffs, clerks, and others, commissioned under the authority of the general government ; in fine, that the administration of justice, as it will relate to the laws of the general government, would require in each State all the magistrates, courts, officers, and expense, which is now found necessary in the respective States, for the administration of justice as it relates to the laws of the State governments. But here, again, we were overruled by a majority, who, assuming it as a principle, that the general government and the State governments (as long as they should exist) would be at perpetual variance and enmity, and that their interests would constantly be opposed to each other, insisted, for that reason, that the State judges, being citizens of their respective States, and holding their commissions under them, ought not, though acting on oath, to be intrusted with the administration of the laws of the general government.

By the eighth section of the first article, the Congress have also the power given them to raise and support armies, without any limitation as to numbers, and without any restriction in time of peace. Thus, Sir, this plan of government, instead of guarding against a standing army, that engine of arbitrary power, which has so often and so successfully been used for the subversion of freedom, has in its formation given it an express and constitutional sanction, and hath provided for its introduction ; nor could this be prevented. I took the sense of the convention on a proposition, by which the Congress should not have power, in time of peace, to keep embodied more than a certain number of regular troops, — that number to be ascertained by what should be considered a respectable peace establishment. This proposition was rejected by a majority ; it being their determination, that the power of Congress to keep up a standing army, even in peace, should only be restrained by their will and pleasure.

This section proceeds, further, to give a power to the Congress to provide for the calling forth the militia, to execute the laws of the Union, suppress insurrections, and repel invasions. As to giving such a power, there was no objection ; but it was thought by some, hat this power ought to be given with certain restrictions. It was thought, that not more than a certain part of the militia of any one State ought to be obliged to march out of the same, or be employed out of the same, at any one time, without the consent of the legislature of such State. This amendment I endeavoured

to obtain ; but it met with the same fate which attended almost every attempt to limit the powers given to
the general government, and constitutionally to guard
against their abuse ; it was not adopted. As it now
stands, the Congress will have the power, if they
please, to march the whole militia of Maryland to the
remotest part of the Union, and keep them in service as
long as they think proper, without being in any respect
dependent upon the government of Maryland for this
unlimited exercise of power over its citizens; all of
whom, from the lowest to the greatest, may, during
such service, be subjected to military law, and tied up
and whipped at the halbert, like the meanest of slaves.

By the next paragraph, Congress is to have the
power to provide for organizing, arming, and disciplining the militia, and for governing such part of them
as may be employed in the service of the United
States.

For this extraordinary provision, by which the militia, the only defence and protection which the State
can have for the security of their rights against arbitrary encroachments of the general government, is taken
entirely out of the power of their respective States, and
placed under the power of Congress, it was speciously
assigned as a reason, that the general government would
cause the militia to be better regulated and better disciplined than the State governments, and that it would
be proper for the whole militia of the Union to have a
uniformity in their arms and exercise.   To this it was
answered, that the reason, however specious, was not
just ; that it would be absurd, the militia of the western settlements, who were exposed to an Indian
enemy, should either be confined to the same arms or
exercise as the militia of the eastern or middle States ;

that the same penalties which would be sufficient to enforce an obedience to militia laws in some States, would be totally disregarded in others; that, leaving the power to the several States, they would respectively best know the situation and circumstances of their citizens, and the regulations that would be necessary and sufficient to effect a well-regulated militia in each; that we were satisfied the militia had heretofore been as well disciplined as if they had been under the regulations of Congress, and that the States would now have an additional motive to keep their militia in proper order, and fit for service, as it would be the only chance to preserve their existence against a general government armed with powers sufficient to destroy them.

These observations, Sir, procured from some of the members an open avowal of those reasons, by which we believed before that they were actuated. They said, that, as the States would be opposed to the general government, and at enmity with it, (which, as I have already observed, they assumed as a principle,) if the militia was under the control and the authority of the respective States, it would enable them to thwart and oppose the general government. They said, the States ought to be at the mercy of the general government, and, therefore, that the militia ought to be put under its power, and not suffered to remain under the power of the respective States. In answer to these declarations, it was urged, that, if after having retained to the general government the great powers already granted, and among those, that of raising and keeping up regular troops without limitations, the power over the militia should be taken away from the States, and also given to the general government, it ought to be considered as the last *coup de grace* to the State governments; that it must be the most convincing proof, the advocates of this system design the destruction of the State governments, and that no professions to the contrary ought to be trusted; and that every State in the Union ought to reject such a system with indignation, since, if the general government should attempt to oppress and enslave them, they could not have any possible means of self-defence; because, the proposed system taking away from the States the right of organizing, arming, and disciplining the militia, the first attempt made by a State to put the militia in a situation to counteract the arbitrary measures of the general government would be construed into an act of rebellion or treason; and Congress would instantly march their troops into the State. It was further observed, that, when a government wishes to deprive its citizens of freedom, and reduce them to slavery, it generally makes use of a standing army for that purpose, and leaves the militia in a situation as contemptible as possible, lest they might oppose its arbitrary designs; that, in this system, we give the general government every provision it could wish for, and even invite it to subvert the liberties of the States and their citizens; since we give it the right to increase and keep up a standing army as numerous as it would wish, and, by placing the militia under its power, enable it to leave the militia totally unorganized, undisciplined, and even to disarm them; while the citizens, so far from complaining of this neglect, might even esteem it a favor in the general government, as thereby they would be freed from the burden of militia duties, and left to their own private occupations or pleasures. However, all arguments, and every reason that could be urged on this subject, as well as on many others, were obliged to yield to one that was unanswerable, — a majority upon the division.

By the ninth section of this article, the importation of such persons as any of the States now existing shall think proper to admit, shall not be prohibited prior to the year one thousand eight hundred and eight; but a duty may be imposed on such importation, not exceeding ten dollars for each person.

The design of this clause is to prevent the general government from prohibiting the importation of slaves; but the same reasons which caused them to strike out the word *national*, and not admit the word *stamps*, influenced them here to guard against the word *slaves*. They anxiously sought to avoid the admission of expressions which might be odious in the ears of Americans, although they were willing to admit into their system those things which the expressions signified. And hence it is, that the clause is so worded, as really to authorize the general government to impose a duty of ten dollars on every foreigner who comes into a State to become a citizen, whether he comes absolutely free, or qualifiedly so, as a servant; although this is contrary to the design of the framers, and the duty was only meant to extend to the importation of slaves.

This clause was the subject of a great diversity of sentiment in the convention. As the system was reported by the committee of detail, the provision was general, that such importation should not be prohibited, without confining it to any particular period. This was rejected by eight States, — Georgia, South Carolina, and, I think, North Carolina, voting for it.

We were then told by the delegates of the two first

of those States, that their States would never agree to a system, which put it in the power of the general government to prevent the importation of slaves, and that they, as delegates from those States, must withhold their assent from such a system.

A committee of one member from each State was chosen by ballot, to take this part of the system under their consideration, and to endeavour to agree upon some report, which should reconcile those States. To this committee also was referred the following proposition, which had been reported by the committee of detail, to wit; "No navigation act shall be passed without the assent of two thirds of the members present in each House "; a proposition which the staple and commercial States were solicitous to retain, lest their commerce should be placed too much under the power of the eastern States; but which these last States were as anxious to reject. This committee, of which also I had the honor to be a member, met and took under their consideration the subjects committed to them. I found the eastern States, notwithstanding their aversion to slavery, were very willing to indulge the southern States, at least with a temporary liberty to prosecute the slave-trade, provided the southern States would, in their turn, gratify them, by laying no restriction on navigation acts; and after a very little time the committee, by a great majority, agreed on a report, by which the general government was to be prohibited from preventing the importation of slaves for a limited time, and the restrictive clause relative to navigation acts was to be omitted.

This report was adopted by a majority of the convention, but not without considerable opposition. It was said, that we had just assumed a place among independent nations, in consequence of our opposition to the attempts of Great Britain to enslave us; that this opposition was grounded upon the preservation of those rights to which God and nature had entitled us, not in particular, but in common with all the rest of mankind; that we had appealed to the Supreme Being for his assistance, as the God of freedom, who could not but approve our efforts to preserve the rights which he had thus imparted to his creatures; that now, when we scarcely had risen from our knees, from supplicating his aid and protection, in forming our government over a free people, a government formed pretendedly on the principles of liberty, and for its preservation, — in that government, to have a provision not only putting it out of its power to restrain and prevent the slave-trade, even encouraging that most infamous traffic, by giving the States power and influence in the Union, in proportion as they cruelly and wantonly sport with the rights of their fellow creatures, ought to be considered as a solemn mockery of, and insult to that God whose protection we had then implored, and could not fail to hold us up in detestation, and render us contemptible to every true friend of liberty in the world. It was said, it ought to be considered that national crimes can only be, and frequently are punished in this world, by national punishments; and that the continuance of the slave-trade, and thus giving it a national sanction and encouragement, ought to be considered as justly exposing us to the displeasure and vengeance of Him, who is equally Lord of all, and who views with equal eye the poor African slave and his American master.

It was urged, that, by this system, we were giving the general government full and absolute power to regulate commerce, under which general power it would have a right to restrain, or totally prohibit, the slave-trade; it must, therefore, appear to the world absurd and disgraceful to the last degree, that we should except from the exercise of that power, the only branch of commerce which is unjustifiable in its nature, and contrary to the rights of mankind; that, on the contrary, we ought rather to prohibit expressly in our constitution, the further importation of slaves; and to authorize the general government, from time to time, to make such regulations as should be thought most advantageous for the gradual abolition of slavery, and the emancipation of the slaves which are already in the States. That slavery is inconsistent with the genius of republicanism, and has a tendency to destroy those principles on which it is supported, as it lessens the sense of the equal rights of mankind, and habituates us to tyranny and oppression.

It was further urged, that, by this system of government, every State is to be protected both from foreign invasion and from domestic insurrections; that, from this consideration, it was of the utmost importance it should have a power to restrain the importation of slaves; since, in proportion as the number of slaves are increased in any State, in the same proportion the State is weakened, and exposed to foreign invasion or domestic insurrection, and by so much less will it be able to protect itself against either; and, therefore, will by so much the more want aid from, and be a burden to the Union. It was further said, that as, in this system, we were giving the general government a power, under the idea of national character, or national interest, to regulate even our weights and measures, and have prohibited all

possibility of emitting paper money, and passing in-
solvent laws, &c., it must appear still more extraordinary, that we should prohibit the government from
interfering with the slave-trade, than which, nothing
could so materially affect both our national honor and
interest. These reasons influenced me, both on the
committee and in convention, most decidedly to oppose
and vote against the clause as it now makes a part of
the system.

You will perceive, Sir, not only that the general
government is prohibited from interfering in the slave-
trade before the year eighteen hundred and eight, but
that there is no provision in the constitution that it
shall afterwards be prohibited, nor any security that
such prohibition will ever take place; and I think
there is great reason to believe, that, if the importation
of slaves is permitted until the year eighteen hundred
and eight, it will not be prohibited afterwards. At
this time, we do not generally hold this commerce in
so great abhorrence as we have done. When our liberties were at stake, we warmly felt for the common
rights of men. The danger being thought to be past,
which threatened ourselves, we are daily growing
more insensible to those rights. In those States which
have restrained or prohibited the importation of slaves,
it is only done by legislative acts, which may be repealed. When those States find, that they must, in
their national character and connexion, suffer in the
disgrace, and share in the inconveniences attendant
upon that detestable and iniquitous traffic, they may
be desirous also to share in the benefits arising from
it; and the odium attending it will be greatly effaced
by the sanction which is given to it in the general
government.

By the next paragraph, the general government is to have a power of suspending the *habeas corpus* act, in cases of rebellion or invasion.

As the State governments have a power of suspending the *habeas corpus* act in those cases, it was said, there could be no reason for giving such a power to the general government; since, whenever the State which is invaded, or in which an insurrection takes place, finds its safety requires it, it will make use of that power. And it was urged, that, if we gave this power to the general government, it would be an engine of oppression in its hands; since, whenever a State should oppose its views, however arbitrary and unconstitutional, and refuse submission to them, the general government may declare it to be an act of rebellion, and, suspending the *habeas corpus* act, may seize upon the persons of those advocates of freedom, who have had virtue and resolution enough to excite the opposition, and may imprison them during its pleasure, in the remotest part of the Union; so that a citizen of Georgia might be *bastiled* in the furthest part of New Hampshire, or a citizen of New Hampshire in the furthest extreme to the south, cut off from their family, their friends, and their every connexion. These considerations induced me, Sir, to give my negative also to this clause.

In this same section, there is a provision, that no preference should be given to the ports of one State over another, and that vessels bound to or from one State shall not be obliged to enter, clear, or pay duties in another. This provision, as well as that which relates to the uniformity of impost duties and excises, was introduced, Sir, by the delegation of this State. Without such a provision, it would have been in the

power of the general government to have compelled
all ships sailing into or out of the Chesapeake, to clear
and enter at Norfolk, or some port in Virginia; a regulation which would be extremely injurious to our
commerce, but which would, if considered merely as
to the interest of the Union, perhaps not be thought
unreasonable; since it would render the collection of
the revenue arising from commerce more certain and
less expensive.

But, Sir, as the system is now reported, the general
government have a power to establish what ports they
please in each State, and to ascertain at what ports in
every State ships shall clear and enter in such State;
a power which may be so used as to destroy the effect
of that provision; since by it may be established a
port in such a place, as shall be so inconvenient to the
States, as to render it more eligible for their shipping
to clear and enter in another than in their own States.
Suppose, for instance, the general government should
determine, that all ships which cleared or entered in
Maryland, should clear and enter at Georgetown, on the
Potomac; it would oblige all the ships which sailed
from or were bound to any other port of Maryland, to
clear or enter in some port in Virginia. To prevent
such a use of the power which the general government now has, of limiting the number of ports in a
State, and fixing the place or places where they shall
be, we endeavoured to obtain a provision, that the
general government should only, in the first instance,
have authority to ascertain the number of ports proper
to be established in each State, and transmit information thereof to the several States, the legislatures of
which, respectively, should have the power to fix the
places where those ports should be, according to their

idea of what would be most advantageous to the commerce of their State, and most for the ease and convenience of their citizens ; and that the general government should not interfere in the establishment of the places, unless the legislature of the State should neglect or refuse so to do; but we could not obtain this alteration.

By the tenth section every State is prohibited from emitting bills of credit. As it was reported by the committee of detail, the States were only prohibited from emitting them without the consent of Congress; but the convention was so smitten with the paper money dread, that they insisted the prohibition should be absolute. It was my opinion, Sir, that the States ought not to be totally deprived of the right to emit bills of credit, and that, as we had not given an authority to the general government for that purpose, it was the more necessary to retain it in the States. I considered that this State, and some others, had formerly received great benefit from paper emissions, and that, if public and private credit should once more be restored, such emissions might hereafter be equally advantageous; and, further, that it is impossible to foresee, that events may not take place, which shall render paper money of absolute necessity ; and it was my opinion, if this power was not to be exercised by a State, without the permission of the general government, it ought to be satisfactory even to those who were the most haunted by the apprehensions of paper money. I therefore thought it my duty to vote against this part of the system.

The same section also puts it out of the power of the States to make any thing but gold and silver coin a tender in payment of debts, or to pass any law impairing the obligation of contracts.

I considered, Sir, that there might be times of such great public calamities and distress, and of such extreme scarcity of specie, as should render it the duty of a government, for the preservation of even the most valuable part of its citizens, in some measure to interfere in their favor, by passing laws totally or partially stopping the courts of justice, or authorizing the debtor to pay by instalments, or by delivering up his property to his creditors at a reasonable and honest valuation. The times have been such as to render regulations of this kind necessary in most or all of the States, to prevent the wealthy creditor and the moneyed man from totally destroying the poor, though even industrious debtor. Such times may again arrive. I therefore voted against depriving the States of this power, — a power which I am decided they ought to possess, but which, I admit, ought only to be exercised on very important and urgent occasions. I apprehend, Sir, the principal cause of complaint among the people at large is, the public and private debt with which they are oppressed, and which, in the present scarcity of cash, threatens them with destruction, unless they can obtain so much indulgence in point of time, that by industry and frugality they may extricate themselves.

This government proposal, I apprehend, so far from removing, will greatly increase those complaints, since, grasping in its all-powerful hand the citizens of the respective States, it will, by the imposition of the variety of taxes, imposts, stamps, excises, and other duties, squeeze from them the little money they may acquire, the hard earnings of their industry, as you would squeeze the juice from an orange, till not a drop more can be extracted, and then let loose upon them their private creditors, to whose mercy it consigns them, by whom their property is to be seized upon and sold, in this scarcity of specie, at a sheriff's sale, where nothing but ready cash can be received, for a tenth part of its value, and themselves and their families to be consigned to indigence and distress, without their governments having a power to give them a moment's indulgence, however necessary it might be, and however desirous to grant them aid.

By this same section, every State is also prohibited from laying any imposts or duties on imports or exports, without the permission of the general government. It was urged, that, as almost all sources of taxation were given to Congress, it would be but reasonable to leave the States the power of bringing revenue into their treasuries, by laying a duty on exports if they should think proper, which might be so light as not to injure or discourage industry, and yet might be productive of considerable revenue. Also, that there might be cases in which it would be proper, for the purpose of encouraging manufactures, to lay duties to prohibit the exportation of raw materials; and, even in addition to the duties laid by Congress on imports for the sake of revenue, to lay a duty to discourage the importation of particular articles into a State, or to enable the manufacturer here to supply us on as good terms as they could be obtained from a foreign market. However, the most we could obtain was, that this power might be exercised by the States with, and only with the consent of Congress, and subject to its control. And so anxious were they to seize on every shilling of our money, for the general government, that they insisted even the little revenue that might thus arise, should not be appropriated to the use of the respective States where it was collected, but should be paid into the treasury of the United States; and accordingly it is so determined.

The second article relates to the executive,—his mode of election, his powers, and the length of time he shall continue in office.

On these subjects there was a great diversity of sentiment. Many of the members were desirous, that the President should be elected for seven years, and not to be eligible a second time ; others proposed, that he should not be absolutely ineligible, but that he should not be capable of being chosen a second time, until the expiration of a certain number of years. The supporters of the above propositions went upon the idea, that the best security for liberty was a limited duration and a rotation of office in the chief executive department.

There was a party who attempted to have the President appointed during good behaviour, without any limitation as to time ; and, not being able to succeed in that attempt, they then endeavoured to have him reëligible without any restraint. It was objected, that the choice of a President to continue in office during good behaviour, would be at once rendering our system an elective monarchy ; and that, if the President was to be reëligible without any interval of disqualification, it would amount nearly to the same thing ; since, with the powers that the President is to enjoy, and the interests and influence with which they will be attended, he will be almost absolutely certain of being reëlected, from time to time, as long as he lives. As the propositions were reported by the committee of the whole House, the President was to be chosen for seven years, and not to be eligible at any time after. In the same manner the proposition was agreed to in convention, and so it was reported by the committee of detail, although a variety of attempts were made to alter that part of the system, by those who were of a contrary opinion, in which they repeatedly failed ; but, Sir, by never losing sight of their object, and choosing a proper time for their purpose, they succeeded at length in obtaining the alteration, which was not made until within the last twelve days before the convention adjourned.

As the propositions were agreed to by the committee of the whole House, the President was to be appointed by the national legislature ; and as it was reported by the committee of detail, the choice was to be made by ballot, in such a manner that the States should have an equal voice in the appointment of this officer, as they, of right, ought to have ; but those who wished as far as possible to establish a national instead of a federal government, made repeated attempts to have the President chosen by the people at large. On this the sense of the convention was taken, I think, not less than three times while I was there, and as often rejected ; but, within the last fortnight of their session, they obtained the alteration in the manner it now stands, by which the large States have a very undue influence in the appointment of the President. There is no case where the States will have an equal voice in the appointment of the President, except where two persons shall have an equal number of votes, and those a majority of the whole number of electors, (a case very unlikely to happen,) or where no person has a majority of the votes. In these instances the House of Representatives are to choose by ballot, each State having an equal voice ; but they are confined, in the last instance, to the five who have the greatest number of votes, which gives the largest States a very unequal chance of having the President chosen under their nomination.

As to the Vice-President, that great officer of government, who is, in case of death, resignation, removal, or inability of the President, to supply his place, and be vested with his powers, and who is officially to be the President of the Senate, there is no provision by which a majority of the voices of the electors are necessary for his appointment; but, after it is decided who is chosen President, that person who has the next greatest number of votes of the electors, is declared to be legally elected to the Vice-Presidency; so that by this system it is very possible, and not improbable, that he may be appointed by the electors of a single large State; and a very undue influence in the Senate is given to that State of which the Vice-President is a citizen, since, in every question where the Senate is divided, that State will have two votes, the President having on those occasions a casting voice. Every part of the system which relates to the Vice-President, as well as the present mode of electing the President, was introduced and agreed upon after I left Philadelphia.

Objections were made to that part of this article, by which the President is appointed Commander-in-chief of the army and navy of the United States, and of the militia of the several States, and it was wished to be so far restrained, that he should not command in person; but this could not be obtained. The power given to the President, of granting reprieves and pardons, was also thought extremely dangerous, and as such opposed. The President thereby has the power of pardoning those who are guilty of treason, as well as of other offences; it was said, that no treason was so likely to take place as that in which the President himself might be engaged, — the attempt to assume to himself powers not given by the constitution, and establish himself in regal authority; in which attempt a provision is made for him to secure from punishment the creatures of his ambition, the associates and abettors of his treasonable practices, by granting them pardons, should they be defeated in their attempts to subvert the Constitution.

To that part of this article also, which gives the President a right to nominate, and, with the consent of the Senate, to appoint all the officers, civil and military, of the United States, there was considerable opposition. It was said, that the person who nominates will always in reality appoint, and that this was giving the President a power and influence, which, together with the other powers bestowed upon him, would place him above all restraint or control. In fine, it was urged, that the President, as here constituted, was a king, in every thing but the name; that, though he was to be chosen for a limited time, yet at the expiration of that time, if he is not re-elected, it will depend entirely upon his own moderation whether he will resign that authority with which he has once been invested; that, from his having the appointment of all the variety of officers, in every part of the civil department for the Union, who will be very numerous, in them and their connexions, relations, friends, and dependents, he will have a formidable host, devoted to his interest, and ready to support his ambitious views. That the army and navy, which may be increased without restraint as to numbers, the officers of which, from the highest to the lowest, are all to be appointed by him, and dependent on his will and pleasure, and commanded by him in person, will, of course, be subservient to his wishes, and ready to execute his commands; in addition to which, the militia also are entirely subjected to his orders. That these circumstances, combined together, will enable him, when he pleases, to become a king in name, as well as in substance, and establish himself in office not only for his own life, but even, if he chooses, to have that authority perpetuated to his family.

It was further observed, that the only appearance of responsibility in the President, which the system holds up to our view, is the provision for impeachment; but that when we reflect that he cannot be impeached but by the House of Delegates, and that the members of this House are rendered dependent upon, and unduly under the influence of the President, by being appointable to offices of which he has the sole nomination, so that without his favor and approbation they cannot obtain them, there is little reason to believe, that a majority will ever concur in impeaching the President, let his conduct be ever so reprehensible; especially, too, as the final event of that impeachment will depend upon a different body, and the members of the House of Delegates will be certain, should the decision be ultimately in favor of the President, to become thereby the objects of his displeasure, and to bar to themselves every avenue to the emoluments of government.

Should he, contrary to probability, be impeached, he is afterwards to be tried and adjudged by the

Senate, and, without the concurrence of two thirds of the members who shall be present, he cannot be convicted. This Senate being constituted a privy council to the President, it is probable many of its leading and influential members may have advised or concurred in the very measures for which he may be impeached; the members of the Senate also are by the system, placed as unduly under the influence of, and dependent upon the President, as the members of the other branch, since they also are appointable to offices, and cannot obtain them but through the favor of the President. There will be great, important, and valuable offices under this government, should it take place, more than sufficient to enable him to hold out the expectation of one of them to each of the senators. Under these circumstances, will any person conceive it to be difficult for the President always to secure to himself more than one third of that body? Or, can it reasonably be believed, that a criminal will be convicted, who is constitutionally empowered to bribe his judges, at the head of whom is to preside on those occasions the Chief Justice, which officer, in his original appointment, must be nominated by the President, and will, therefore, probably, be appointed not so much for his eminence in legal knowledge and for his integrity, as from favoritism and influence; since the President, knowing that in case of impeachment the Chief Justice is to preside at his trial, will naturally wish to fill that office with a person of whose voice and influence he shall consider himself secure? These are reasons to induce a belief, that there will be but little probability of the President ever being either impeached or convicted; but it was also urged, that, vested with the powers which the system gives him, and with the influence attendant upon those powers, to him it would be of little consequence whether he was impeached or convicted, since he will be able to set both at defiance. These considerations occasioned a part of the convention to give a negative to this part of the system establishing the executive, as it is now offered for our acceptance.

By the third article, the judicial power of the United States is vested in one supreme court, and in such inferior courts, as the Congress may from time to time ordain and establish. These courts, and these only, will have a right to decide upon the laws of the United States, and all questions arising upon their construction, and in a judicial manner to carry those laws into execution; to which the courts, both superior and inferior, of the respective States, and their judges and other magistrates, are rendered incompetent. To the courts of the general government are also confined all cases in law or equity, arising under the proposed constitution, and treaties made under the authority of the United States; all cases affecting ambassadors, other public ministers, and consuls; all cases of admiralty and maritime jurisdiction; all controversies to which the United States are a party; all controversies between two or more States; between a State and citizens of another State; between citizens of the same State, claiming lands under grants of different States; and between a State, or the citizens thereof, and foreign States, citizens, or subjects. Whether, therefore, any laws or regulations of the Congress, or any acts of its President or other officers, are contrary to, or not warranted by the constitution, rests only with the judges who are appointed by Congress to determine; by whose determinations every State must be bound. Should any question arise between a foreign consul and any of the citizens of the United States, however remote from the seat of empire, it is to be heard before the judiciary of the general government, and in the first instance to be heard in the Supreme Court, however inconvenient to the parties, and however trifling the subject of dispute.

Should the mariners of an American or foreign vessel, while in any American port, have occasion to sue for their wages, or in any other instance a controversy belonging to the admiralty jurisdiction should take place between them and their masters or owners, it is in the courts of the general government the suit must be instituted; and either party may carry it by appeal to its Supreme Court. The injury to commerce, and the oppression to individuals, which may thence arise, need not be enlarged upon. Should a citizen of Virginia, Pennsylvania, or any other of the United States, be indebted to, or have debts due from a citizen of this State, or any other claim be subsisting on one side or the other, in consequence of commercial or other transactions, it is only in the courts of Congress that either can apply for redress. The case is the same should any claim subsist between citizens of this State and foreigners, merchants, mariners, and others, whether of a commercial or of any other nature; they must be prosecuted in the same courts; and though in the first instance they may be brought in the inferior, yet an appeal may be made to the supreme judiciary, even from the remotest State in the Union.

The inquiry concerning, and trial of, every offence against, and breach of, the laws of Congress, are also

confined to its courts; the same courts also have the
sole right to inquire concerning and try every offence,
from the lowest to the highest, committed by the ci-
izens of any other State, or of a foreign nation, against
the laws of this State, within its territory; and in all
these cases, the decision may be ultimately brought
before the supreme tribunal, since the appellate jurisdiction extends to criminal as well as to civil cases.
And in all those cases where the general government
has jurisdiction in civil questions, the proposed constitution not only makes no provision for trial by jury in
the first instance, but, by its appellate jurisdiction, absolutely takes away that inestimable privilege; since
it expressly declares the Supreme Court shall have
appellate jurisdiction both as to law and fact.   Should,
therefore, a jury be adopted in the inferior court, it
would only be a needless expense, since, on an appeal,
the determination of that jury, even on questions of
fact, however honest and upright, is to be of no possible effect.   The Supreme Court is to take up all
questions of fact, to examine the evidence relative
thereto, to decide upon them in the same manner as
if they had never been tried by a jury; nor is trial by
jury secured in criminal cases.   It is true, that, in the
first instance, in the inferior court, the trial is to be by
jury.   In this, and in this only, is the difference between criminal and civil cases.   But, Sir, the appellate
jurisdiction extends, as I have observed, to cases criminal as well as to civil; and, on the appeal, the court
is to decide not only on the law, but on the fact.   If,
therefore, even in criminal cases, the general government is not satisfied with the verdict of the jury, its
officer may remove the prosecution to the Supreme
Court, and there the verdict of the jury is to be of no

effect, but the judges of this court are to decide upon the fact as well as the law, the same as in civil cases.

Thus, Sir, jury trials, which have ever been the boast of the English constitution, which have been by our several State constitutions so cautiously secured to us, — jury trials, which have so long been considered the surest barrier against arbitrary power, and the palladium of liberty, with the loss of which the loss of our freedom may be dated, are taken away, by the proposed form of government, not only in a great variety of questions between individual and individual, but in every case, whether civil or criminal, arising under the laws of the United States, or the execution of those laws. It is taken away in those very cases, where, of all others, it is most essential for our liberty to have it sacredly guarded and preserved; in every case, whether civil or criminal, between government and its officers on the one part, and the subject or citizen on the other. Nor was this the effect of inattention, nor did it arise from any real difficulty in establishing and securing jury trials by the proposed constitution, if the convention had wished so to do; but the same reason influenced here as in the case of the establishment of inferior courts; as they could not trust State judges, so would they not confide in State juries. They alleged, that the general government and the State governments would always be at variance; that the citizens of the different States would enter into the views and interests of their respective States, and therefore ought not to be trusted in determining causes in which the general government was any way interested, without giving the general government an opportunity, if it disapproved the verdict of the jury, to appeal, and to have the facts examined

into again, and decided upon by its own judges, on
whom it was thought a reliance might be had by the
general government, they being appointed under its
authority.

Thus, Sir, in consequence of this appellate jurisdiction, and its extension to facts as well as to law, every
arbitrary act of the general government, and every
oppression of all that variety of officers appointed
under its authority, for the collection of taxes, duties,
impost, excise, and other purposes, must be submitted
to by the individual, or must be opposed with little
prospect of success, and almost a certain prospect of
ruin, at least in those cases where the middle and
common class of citizens are interested ; since, to avoid
that oppression, or to obtain redress, the application
must be made to one of the courts of the United States.
By good fortune should this application be in the first
instance attended with success, and should damages
be recovered equivalent to the injury sustained, an
appeal lies to the Supreme Court; in which case, the
citizen must at once give up his cause, or he must attend to it at the distance of perhaps more than a thousand miles from the place of his residence, and must
take measures to procure before that court, on the appeal, all the evidence necessary to support his action,
which, even if ultimately prosperous, must be attended
with a loss of time, a neglect of business, and an expense which will be greater than the original grievance,
and to which men in moderate circumstances would
be utterly unequal.

By the third section of this article, it is declared,
that treason against the United States shall consist in
levying war against them, or in adhering to their enemies, giving them aid or comfort.

By the principles of the American revolution, arbitrary power may and ought to be resisted, even by arms if necessary. The time may come, when it shall be the duty of a State, in order to preserve itself from the oppression of the general government, to have recourse to the sword; in which case, the proposed form of government declares, that the State and every of its citizens who act under its authority are guilty of a direct act of treason;—reducing, by this provision, the different States to this alternative, that they must tamely and passively yield to despotism, or their citizens must oppose it at the hazard of the halter if unsuccessful: and reducing the citizens of the State which shall take arms, to a situation in which they must be exposed to punishment, let them act as they will; since, if they obey the authority of their State government, they will be guilty of treason against the United States; if they join the general government, they will be guilty of treason against their own State.

To save the citizens of the respective States from this disagreeable dilemma, and to secure them from being punishable as traitors to the United States, when acting expressly in obedience to the authority of their own State, I wished to have obtained, as an amendment to the third section of this article, the following clause : " Provided, that no act or acts done by one or more of the States against the United States, or by any citizen of any one of the United States, under the authority of one or more of the said States, shall be deemed treason, or punished as such; but, in case of war being levied by one or more of the States against the United States, the conduct of each party towards the other, and their adherents respectively, shall be regulated by the laws of war and of nations."

But this provision was not adopted, being too much opposed to the great object of many of the leading members of the convention, which was, by all means to leave the States at the mercy of the general government, since they could not succeed in their immediate and entire abolition.

By the third section of the fourth article, no new State shall be formed or erected within the jurisdiction of any other State, without the consent of the legislature of such State.

There are a number of States which are so circumstanced, with respect to themselves and to the other States, that every principle of justice and sound policy require their dismemberment or division into smaller States. Massachusetts is divided into two districts, totally separated from each other by the State of New Hampshire, on the northeast side of which lie the Provinces of Maine and Sagadahoc, more extensive in point of territory, but less populous than old Massachusetts, which lies on the other side of New Hampshire. No person can cast his eye on the map of that State but he must in a moment admit, that every argument drawn from convenience, interest, and justice, require, that the Provinces of Maine and Sagadahoc should be erected into a new State, and that they should not be compelled to remain connected with old Massachusetts under all the inconveniences of their situation.

The State of Georgia is larger in extent than the whole island of Great Britain, extending from its seacoast to the Mississippi, a distance of eight hundred miles or more; its breadth, for the most part, about three hundred miles. The States of North Carolina and Virginia, in the same manner, reach from the seacoast unto the Mississippi.

The hardship, the inconvenience, and the injustice of compelling the inhabitants of those States who may dwell on the western side of the mountains, and along the Ohio and Mississippi rivers, to remain connected with the inhabitants of those States respectively, on the Atlantic side of the mountains, and subject to the same State governments, would be such, as would, in my opinion, justify even recourse to arms, to free themselves from, and to shake off, so ignominious a yoke.

This representation was made in convention, and it was further urged, that the territory of these States was too large, and that the inhabitants thereof would be too much disconnected for a republican government to extend to them its benefits, which is only suited to a small and compact territory. That a regard, also, for the peace and safety of the Union ought to excite a desire, that those States should become in time divided into separate States, since, when their population should become proportioned in any degree to their territory, they would, from their strength and power, become dangerous members of a federal government. It was further said, that, if the general government was not by its constitution to interfere, the inconvenience would soon remedy itself, for that, as the population increased in those States, their legislatures would be obliged to consent to the erection of new States to avoid the evils of a civil war; but as, by the proposed constitution, the general government is obliged to protect each State against domestic violence, and, consequently, will be obliged to assist in suppressing such commotions and insurrections, as may take place from the struggle to have new States erected, the general government ought to have a pow-

er to decide upon the propriety and necessity of establishing or erecting a new State, even without the
approbation of the legislature of such States, within
whose jurisdiction the new State should be erected;
and for this purpose I submitted to the convention
the following proposition: "That, on the application
of the inhabitants of any district of territory, within
the limits of any of the States, it shall be lawful for
the legislature of the United States, if they shall
under all circumstances think it reasonable, to erect
the same into a new State, and admit it into the
Union, without the consent of the State of which
the said district may be a part." And it was said,
that we surely might trust the general government
with this power with more propriety than with many
others, with which they were proposed to be intrusted; and that, as the general government was bound
to suppress all insurrections and commotions, which
might arise on this subject, it ought to be in the
power of the general government to decide upon it,
and not in the power of the legislature of a single
State, by obstinately and unreasonably opposing the
erection of a new State, to prevent its taking effect,
and thereby extremely to oppress that part of its citizens which live remote from, and inconvenient to,
the seat of its government, and even to involve the
Union in war to support its injustice and oppression.
But, upon the vote being taken, Georgia, South Carolina, North Carolina, Virginia, Pennsylvania, and Massachusetts were in the negative. New Hampshire,
Connecticut, Jersey, Delaware, and Maryland, were
in the affirmative. New York was absent.

That it was inconsistent with the rights of free and
independent States, to have their territory dismem-

bered without their consent, was the principal argument used by the opponents of this proposition. The truth of the objection we readily admitted, but at the same time insisted, that it was not more inconsistent with the rights of free and independent States, than that inequality of suffrage and power which the large States had extorted from the others; and that, if the smaller States yielded up their rights in that instance, they were entitled to demand from the States of extensive territory a surrender of their rights in this instance; and in a particular manner, as it was equally necessary for the true interest and happiness of the citizens of their own States, as of the Union. But, Sir, although, when the large States demanded undue and improper sacrifices to be made to their pride and ambition, they treated the rights of free States with more contempt, than ever a British Parliament treated the rights of her colonial establishments; yet, when a reasonable and necessary sacrifice was asked from them, they spurned the idea with ineffable disdain. They then perfectly understood the full value and the sacred obligation of State rights, and at the least attempt to infringe them, where they were concerned, they were tremblingly alive, and agonized at every pore.

When we reflect how obstinately those States contended for that unjust superiority of power in the government, which they have in part obtained, and for the establishment of this superiority by the constitution; when we reflect that they appeared willing to hazard the existence of the Union, rather than not to succeed in their unjust attempt; that, should their legislatures consent to the erection of new States within their jurisdiction, it would be an immediate

sacrifice of that power, to obtain which they appeared
disposed to sacrifice every other consideration ; when
we further reflect, that they now have a motive for
desiring to preserve their territory entire and unbroken, which they never had before, — the gratification of their ambition, in possessing and exercising
superior power over their sister States, — and that this
constitution is to give them the means to effect this
desire, of which they were formerly destitute ; the
whole force of the United States pledged to them for
restraining intestine commotions, and preserving to
them the obedience and subjection of their citizens,
even in the extremest part of their territory ; — I say,
Sir, when we consider these things, it would be too
absurd and improbable to deserve a serious answer,
should any person suggest, that these States mean
ever to give their consent to the erection of new
States within their territory.   Some of them, it is
true, have been for some time past amusing their inhabitants, in those districts that wished to be erected
into new States ; but, should this constitution be adopted, armed with a sword and halter to compel their
obedience and subjection, they will no longer act
with indecision ; and the State of Maryland may,
and probably will, be called upon to assist, with her
wealth and her blood, in subduing the inhabitants of
Franklin, Kentucky, Vermont, and the provinces of
Maine and Sagadahoc, and in compelling them to
continue in subjection to the States which respectively claim jurisdiction over them.

     Let it not be forgotten at the same time, that a
great part of the territory of these large and extensive
States, which they now hold in possession, and over
which they now claim and exercise jurisdiction, were

crown lands, unlocated and unsettled when the American revolution took place,—lands which were acquired by the common blood and treasure, and which ought to have been the common stock, and for the common benefit of the Union. Let it be remembered, that the State of Maryland was so deeply sensible of the injustice that these lands should be held by particular States for their own emolument, even at a time when no superiority of authority or power was annexed to extensive territory, that, in the midst of the late war and all the dangers which threatened us, it withheld, for a long time, its assent to the articles of confederation for that reason ; and, when it ratified those articles, it entered a solemn protest against what it considered so flagrant injustice. But, Sir, the question is not now, whether those States shall hold that territory unjustly to themselves, but whether, by that act of injustice, they shall have superiority of power and influence over the other States, and have a constitutional right to domineer and lord it over them. Nay, more, whether we will agree to a form of government, by which we pledge to those States the whole force of the Union, to preserve to them their extensive territory entire and unbroken ; and, with our blood and wealth, to assist them, whenever they please to demand it, to preserve the inhabitants thereof under their subjection, for the purpose of increasing their superiority over us, — of gratifying their unjust ambition, — in a word, for the purpose of giving ourselves masters, and of riveting our chains !

The part of the system which provides, that no religious test shall ever be required as a qualification to any office or public trust under the United States, was adopted by a great majority of the convention,

8 *

and without much debate ; however, there were some members so unfashionable as to think, that a belief of the existence of a Deity, and of a state of future rewards and punishments would be some security for the good conduct of our rulers, and that, in a Christian country, it would be at least decent to hold out some distinction between the professors of Christianity and downright infidelity or paganism.

The seventh article declares, that the ratification of nine States shall be sufficient for the establishment of this constitution, between the States ratifying the same.

It was attempted to obtain a resolve, that, if seven States, whose votes in the first branch should amount to a majority of the representation in that branch, concurred in the adoption of the system, it should be sufficient; and this attempt was supported on the principle, that a majority ought to govern the minority ; but to this it was objected, that, although it was true, after a constitution and form of government is agreed on, in every act done under and consistent with that constitution and form of government, the act of the majority, unless otherwise agreed in the constitution, should bind the minority, yet it was directly the reverse in originally forming a constitution, or dissolving it; that, in originally forming a constitution, it was necessary that every individual should agree to it, to become bound thereby ; and that, when once adopted, it could not be dissolved by consent, unless with the consent of every individual who was party to the original agreement ; that in forming our original federal government, every member of that government, that is, each State, expressly consented to it ; that it is a part of the compact made and entered into,

in the most solemn manner, that there should be no
dissolution or alteration of that federal government,
without the consent of every State, the members of,
and parties to, the original compact ; that, therefore,
no alteration could be made by a consent of a part of
these States, or by the consent of the inhabitants of a
part of the States, which could either release the States
so consenting from the obligation they are under to
the other States, or which could in any manner become obligatory upon those States that should not
ratify such alterations. Satisfied of the truth of these
positions, and not holding ourselves at liberty to violate
the compact, which this State had solemnly entered
into with the others, by altering it in a different manner from that which by the same compact is provided
and stipulated, a number of the members, and among
those the delegation of this State, opposed the ratification of this system in any other manner, than by the
unanimous consent and agreement of all the States.

By our original articles of confederation, any alterations proposed are, in the first place, to be approved by
Congress. Accordingly, as the resolutions were originally adopted by the convention, and as they were
reported by the committee of detail, it was proposed
that this system should be laid before Congress for its
approbation. But, Sir, the warm advocates of this
system, fearing it would not meet with the approbation of Congress, and determined, even though Congress and the respective State legislatures should disapprove the same, to force it upon them, if possible,
through the intervention of the people at large, moved
to strike out the words "for their approbation," and
succeeded in their motion ; to which, it being directly
in violation of the mode prescribed by the articles of

confederation for the alteration of our federal government, a part of the convention, and myself in the
number, thought it a duty to give a decided negative.

Agreeably to the articles of confederation, entered
into in the most solemn manner, and for the observance of which the States pledged themselves to each
other, and called upon the Supreme Being as a witness
and avenger between them, no alterations are to be
made in those articles, unless, after they are approved
by Congress, they are agreed to and ratified by the
legislature of every State ; but, by the resolve of the
convention, this constitution is not to be ratified by
the legislatures of the respective States, but is to be
submitted to conventions chosen by the people, and,
if ratified by them, is to be binding.

This resolve was opposed, among others, by the
delegation of Maryland. Your delegates were of
opinion, that, as the form of government proposed
was, if adopted, most essentially to alter the constitution of this State ; and as our constitution had pointed
out a mode by which, and by which only, alterations
were to be made therein, a convention of the people
could not be called to agree to and ratify the said form
of government, without a direct violation of our constitution, which it is the duty of every individual in
this State to protect and support. In this opinion, all
your delegates who were attending were unanimous.
I, Sir, opposed it also upon a more extensive ground,
as being directly contrary to the mode of altering our
federal government, established in our original compact ; and, as such, being a direct violation of the mutual faith plighted by the States to each other, I gave
it my negative.

I was also of opinion, that the States, considered as

States, in their political capacity, are the members of a federal government; that the States, in their political capacity, or as sovereignties, are entitled, and only entitled originally to agree upon the form of, and submit themselves to, a federal government, and afterwards, by mutual consent, to dissolve or alter it; that every thing which relates to the formation, the dissolution, or the alteration of a federal government over States equally free, sovereign, and independent, is the peculiar province of the States, in their sovereign or political capacity, in the same manner as what relates to forming alliances or treaties of peace, amity, or commerce; and that the people at large, in their individual capacity, have no more right to interfere in the one case than in the other. That according to these principles we originally acted, in forming our confederation; it was the States, as States, by their representatives in Congress, that formed the articles of confederation; it was the States, as States, by their legislatures, who ratified those articles; and it was there established and provided, that the States, as States, that is, by their legislatures, should agree to any alterations that should hereafter be proposed in the federal government, before they should be binding; and any alterations agreed to in any other manner, cannot release the States from the obligation they are under to each other, by virtue of the original articles of confederation. The people of the different States never made any objection to the manner the articles of confederation were formed or ratified, or to the mode by which alterations were to be made in that government; with the rights of their respective States they wished not to interfere. Nor do I believe the people, in their individual capacity, would ever have expected or desired to have been appealed to, on the present occasion, in violation of the rights of their respective States, if the favorers of the proposed constitution, imagining they had a better chance of forcing it to be adopted by a hasty appeal to the people at large, who could not be so good judges of the dangerous consequence, had not insisted upon this mode. Nor do these positions in the least interfere with the principle, that all power originates from the people; because, when once the people have exercised their power in establishing and forming themselves into a State government, it never devolves back to them, nor have they a right to resume or again to exercise that power, until such events take place as will amount to a dissolution of their State government. And it is an established principle, that a dissolution or alteration of a federal government doth not dissolve the State governments which compose it. It was also my opinion, that, upon principles of sound policy, the agreement or disagreement to the proposed system ought to have been by the State legislatures; in which case, let the event have been what it would, there would have been but little prospect of the public peace being disturbed thereby. Whereas, the attempt to force down this system, although Congress and the respective State legislatures should disapprove, by appealing to the people, and to procure its establishment in a manner totally unconstitutional, has a tendency to set the State governments and their subjects at variance with each other, to lessen the obligations of government, to weaken the bands of society, to introduce anarchy and confusion, and to light the torch of discord and civil war throughout this continent. All these considerations weighed with me most forcibly against giving my assent to the mode by which it is resolved this system is to be ratified, and were urged by me in opposition to the measure.

I have now, Sir, in discharge of the duty I owe to this House, given such information as hath occurred to me, which I consider most material for them to know ; and you will easily perceive, from this detail, that a great portion of that time, which ought to have been devoted calmly and impartially to consider what alterations in our federal government would be most likely to procure and preserve the happiness of the Union, was employed in a violent struggle on the one side to obtain all power and dominion in their own hands, and on the other to prevent it; and that the aggrandizement of particular States and particular individuals, appears to have been much more the object sought after, than the welfare of our country.

The interest of this State, not confined merely to itself, abstracted from all others, but considered relatively, as far as was consistent with the common interest of the other States, I thought it my duty to pursue, according to the best opinion I could form of it.

When I took my seat in the convention, I found it attempting to bring forward a system, which I was sure never had entered into the contemplation of those I had the honor to represent, and which, upon the fullest consideration, I considered not only injurious to the interest and the rights of this State, but also incompatible with the political happiness and freedom of the States in general. From that time until my business compelled me to leave the convention, I gave it every possible opposition, in every stage of its progression. I opposed the system there with the same

explicit frankness with which I have here given you
a history of our proceedings; an account of my own
conduct, which in a particular manner I consider you
as having a right to know. While there, I endeavoured to act as became a free man, and the delegate
of a free State. Should my conduct obtain the approbation of those who appointed me, I will not deny it
would afford me satisfaction; but to me that approbation was at most no more than a secondary consideration; my first was to deserve it. Left to myself, to
act according to the best of my discretion, my conduct
should have been the same, had I been even sure your
censure would have been my only reward; since I
hold it sacredly my duty to dash the cup of poison, if
possible, from the hand of a State, or an individual,
however anxious the one or the other might be to
swallow it.

Indulge me, Sir, in a single observation further.
There are persons who endeavour to hold up the idea,
that this system is only opposed by the officers of government. I, Sir, am in that predicament. I have the
honor to hold an appointment in this State. Had it
been considered any objection, I presume I should not
have been appointed to the convention. If it could
have had any effect on my mind, it would only be
that of warming my heart with gratitude, and rendering me more anxious to promote the true interest of
that State which has conferred on me the obligation,
and to heighten my guilt had I joined in sacrificing its
essential rights. But, Sir, it would be well to remember, that this system is not calculated to diminish the
number or the value of offices; on the contrary, if
adopted, it will be productive of an enormous increase
in their number; many of them will be also of great

honor and emoluments. Whether, Sir, in this variety of appointments, and in the scramble for them, I might not have as good a prospect to advantage myself as many others, is not for me to say; but this, Sir, I can say with truth, that, so far was I from being influenced in my conduct by interest, or the consideration of office, that I would cheerfully resign the appointment I now hold; I would bind myself never to accept another, either under the general government or that of my own State. I would do more, Sir; — so destructive do I consider the present system to the happiness of my country, I would cheerfully sacrifice that share of property with which Heaven has blessed a life of industry; I would reduce myself to indigence and poverty, and those who are dearer to me than my own existence I would intrust to the care and protection of that Providence, which hath so kindly protected myself, if on those terms only I could procure my country to reject those chains which are forged for it.

SECRET DEBATES

OF THE

FEDERAL CONVENTION.

Notes of the Secret Debates of the Federal Convention of 1787, taken by the late Hon. ROBERT YATES, Chief Justice of the State of New York, and one of the Delegates from that State to the said Convention.

FRIDAY, MAY 25th, 1787.

Attended the convention of the States, at the State House in Philadelphia, when the following States were represented:

New York,	Alexander Hamilton,
	Robert Yates.
New Jersey,	David Brearley,
	William Churchill Houston,
	William Patterson.
Pennsylvania,	Robert Morris,
	Thomas Fitzsimons,
	James Wilson,
	Gouverneur Morris.
Delaware,	George Read,
	Richard Bassett,
	Jacob Broom.
Virginia,	George Washington,
	Edmund Randolph,
	George Wythe,

George Mason,
James Madison,
John Blair,
James M'Clurg.

NORTH CAROLINA,   Alexander Martin,
William Richardson Davie,
Richard Dobbs Spaight,
Hugh Williamson.

SOUTH CAROLINA,   John Rutledge,
Charles Cotesworth Pinckney,
Charles Pinckney,
Pierce Butler.

A motion by *R. Morris*, and seconded, that General Washington take the chair, unanimously agreed to.

When seated, he (General Washington) declared, that, as he had never been in such a situation, he felt himself embarrassed; that he hoped his errors, as they would be unintentional, would be excused.

Mr. Hamilton, in behalf of the State of New York, moved, that Major Jackson be appointed secretary; the delegates for Pennsylvania moved for Temple Franklin; by a majority Mr. Jackson carried it. — Called in and took his seat.

After which, the respective credentials of the seven States were read. N. B. That of Delaware restrained its delegates from assenting to an abolition of the fifth article of the confederation, by which it is declared, that each State shall have one vote.

Door-keeper and messengers being appointed, the House adjourned to Monday, the 28th day of May, at ten o'clock.

MONDAY, MAY 28TH, 1787.

Met pursuant to adjournment.

A committee of three members (whose appointment I omitted in the entry of the proceedings of Friday last) reported a set of rules for the order of the convention, which, being considered by articles, were agreed to, and additional ones proposed and referred to the same committee. The representation was this day increased to nine States, Massachusetts and Connecticut becoming represented.

Adjourned to next day.

TUESDAY, MAY 29TH, 1787.

The additional rules agreed to.

His excellency Governor *Randolph*, a member from Virginia, got up, and, in a long and elaborate speech, showed the defects in the system of the present federal government, as totally inadequate to the peace, safety, and security of the confederation, and the absolute necessity of a more energetic government.

He closed these remarks with a set of resolutions, fifteen in number, which he proposed to the convention for their adoption, and as leading principles whereon to form a new government. He candidly confessed, that they were not intended for a federal government; he meant a strong, consolidated union, in which the idea of States should be nearly annihilated. [I have taken a copy of these resolutions, which are hereunto annexed.]

He then moved, that they should be taken up in committee of the whole House.

Mr. C. Pinckney, a member from South Carolina, then added, that he had reduced his ideas of a new government to a system, which he read, and confessed that it was grounded on the same principle as that of the above resolutions.

The House then resolved, that they would the next day form themselves into a committee of the whole, to take into consideration the state of the Union.

Adjourned to next day.

WEDNESDAY, MAY 30th, 1787.

Convention met pursuant to adjournment.

The convention, pursuant to order, resolved itself into a committee of the whole, — Mr. Gorham, a member from Massachusetts, appointed chairman.

Mr. Randolph then moved his first resolve, to wit: " Resolved, that the articles of the confederation ought to be so corrected and enlarged, as to accomplish the objects proposed by their institution, namely, common defence, security of liberty, and general welfare."

Mr. G. Morris observed, that it was an unnecessary resolution, as the subsequent resolutions would not agree with it. It was then withdrawn by the proposer, and in lieu thereof the following were proposed, to wit:

" 1. *Resolved,* That a union of the States, merely federal, will not accomplish the objects proposed by the articles of the confederation, namely, common defence, security of liberty, and general welfare.

" 2. *Resolved,* That no treaty or treaties among any of the States, as sovereign, will accomplish or secure their common defence, liberty, or welfare.

" 3. *Resolved,* That a national government ought to be established, consisting of a supreme judicial, legislative, and executive."

In considering the question on the first resolve, various modifications were proposed, when *Mr. Pinckney* observed, at last, that, if the convention agreed to it, it appeared to him that their business was at an end; for, as the powers of the House in general were to revise the present confederation, and to alter or amend it, as the case might require, to determine its insufciency or incapability of amendment or improvement, must end in the dissolution of the powers.

This remark had its weight, and, in consequence of it, the first and second resolves were dropped, and the question agitated on the third.

This last resolve had also its difficulties. The term *supreme* required explanation. It was asked, whether it was intended to annihilate State governments? It was answered, only so far as the powers intended to be granted to the new government should clash with the States, when the latter was to yield.

For the resolution, — Massachusetts, Pennsylvania, Delaware, Virginia, North Carolina, South Carolina.

Against it, — Connecticut, New York divided, New Jersey, and the other States unrepresented.

The next question was on the following resolve:

In substance, that the mode of the present representation was unjust, — the suffrage ought to be in proportion to number or property.

To this Delaware objected, in consequence of the restrictions in their credentials, and moved to have the consideration thereof postponed, to which the House agreed.

Adjourned to to-morrow.

THURSDAY, MAY 31st, 1787.

Met pursuant to adjournment.

This day the State of Jersey was represented, so that there were now ten States in convention.

The House went again into committee of the whole, Mr. Gorham in the chair.

The third resolve, to wit, "That the national legislature ought to consist of two branches," was taken into consideration, and without any debate agreed to. [N. B. As a previous resolution had already been agreed to, to have a supreme legislature, I could not see any objection to its being in two branches.]

The fourth resolve, "That the members of the first branch of the national legislature ought to be elected by the people of the several States," was opposed; and, strange to tell, by Massachusetts and Connecticut, who supposed they ought to be chosen by the legislatures; and Virginia supported the resolve, alleging, that this ought to be the democratic branch of government, and, as such, immediately vested in the people.

This question was carried, but the remaining part of the resolve, detailing the powers, was postponed.

The fifth resolve, That the members of the second branch of the national legislature ought to be elected by those of the first, out of a proper number of persons nominated by the individual legislatures, and the detail of the mode of election, and duration of office, was postponed.

The sixth resolve is taken in detail: "That each branch ought to possess the right of originating acts." Agreed to.

"That the national legislature ought to be empowered to enjoy the legislative rights vested in Congress by the confederation." Agreed to.

"And, moreover, to legislate in all cases to which the separate States are incompetent." Agreed to.

FRIDAY, JUNE 1st, 1787.

Met pursuant to adjournment.

The seventh resolve, that a national executive be instituted.   Agreed to.

To continue in office for seven years.   Agreed to.

A general authority to execute the laws.   Agreed to.

To appoint all officers not otherwise provided for. Agreed to.

Adjourned to the next day.

SATURDAY, JUNE 2D, 1787.

Met pursuant to adjournment.   Present, eleven States.

Mr. Pinckney called for the order of the day.

The convention went into committee of the whole.

Mr. Wilson moved, that the States should be divided into districts, consisting of one or more States, and each district to elect a number of senators, to form the second branch of the national legislature.   The senators to be elected, and a certain proportion to be annually dismissed, — avowedly on the plan of the New York Senate. Question put.   Rejected.

In the seventh resolve, the words "to be chosen by the national legislature," were agreed to.

President Franklin moved, that the consideration of that part of the seventh resolve, which had in object the making provision for a compensation for the service of the executive, be postponed for the purpose of considering a motion, " That the executive should receive no salary, stipend, or emolument for the devotion of his time to the public services, but that his expenses should be paid." Postponed.

Mr. Dickinson moved, that, in the seventh resolution, the words "and removable on impeachment and conviction for mal-conduct or neglect in the execution of his office," should be inserted after the words "ineligible a second time." Agreed to. The remainder postponed.

Mr. Butler moved to fill the number of which the executive should consist.

Mr. Randolph. The sentiments of the people ought to be consulted. They will not hear of the semblance of monarchy. He preferred three divisions of the States, and an executive to be taken from each. If a single executive, those remote from him would be neglected; local views would be attributed to him, — frequently well-founded, often without reason. This would excite disaffection. He was, therefore, for an executive of three.

Mr. Butler. Delays, divisions, and dissensions arise from an executive consisting of many. Instance Holland's distracted state, occasioned by her many counsellors. Further consideration postponed.

Mr. C. Pinckney gave notice for the reconsideration of the mode of election of the first branch.

Adjourned till Monday next.

MONDAY, JUNE 4th, 1787.

Met pursuant to adjournment.

Mr. Pinckney moved, that the blank in the seventh resolve, "consisting of   ," be filled up with an individual.

Mr. Wilson, in support of the motion, asserted, that it would not be obnoxious to the minds of the people, as they, in their State governments, were accustomed and reconciled to a single executive. Three executives might divide so that two could not agree in one proposition; the consequence would be anarchy and confusion.

Mr. Sherman thought there ought to be one executive, but that he ought to have a council. Even the king of Great Britain has his privy council.

Mr. Gerry was for one executive; if otherwise, it would be absurd to have it consist of three. Numbers equally in rank would oddly apply to a general or admiral.

Question put. Seven States for, and three against. New York against it.

The eighth resolve, That the executive and a number of the judicial officers ought to compose a council of revision.

Mr. Gerry objects to the clause. Moves its postponement, in order to let in a motion, " That the right of revision should be in the executive only."

Mr. Wilson contends, that the executive and judicial ought to have a joint and full negative; they cannot otherwise preserve their importance against the legislature.

Mr. King was against the interference of the judicial. They may be biassed in the interpretation. He is, therefore, to give the executive a complete negative.

Carried to be postponed, six States against four. New York for it.

The next question, that the executive have a complete negative; and it was therefore moved to expunge the remaining part of the clause.

Dr. Franklin against the motion. The power dangerous, and would be abused so as to get money for passing bills.

Mr. Madison against it, because of the difficulty

of an executive venturing on the exercise of this negative; and is therefore of opinion, that the revisional
authority is better.

Mr. Bedford is against the whole, either negative
or revisional; the two branches are sufficient checks
on each other; no danger of subverting the executive,
because his powers may by the convention be so well
defined, that the legislature cannot overleap the
bounds.

Mr. Mason against the negative power in the executive, because it will not accord with the genius of
the people.

On this the question was put and carried, *nem. con.*,
against expunging part of the clause, so as to establish
a complete negative.

Mr. Butler then moved, that all acts passed by the
legislature be suspended for the space of   days by
the executive.

Unanimously in the negative.

It was resolved and agreed, that the blank be filled
up with the words "two thirds of the legislature."
Agreed to.

The question was then put on the whole of the resolve as amended and filled up. Carried; eight States
for, two against. New York for it.

Mr. Wilson then moved for the addition of a convenient number of the national judicial to the executive, as a council of revision. Ordered to be taken
into consideration to-morrow.

Adjourned until to-morrow.

TUESDAY, JUNE 5TH, 1787.

Met pursuant to adjournment.

The ninth resolve, "That a national judicial be
established, to consist of one supreme tribunal, and of

inferior tribunals, to hold their offices during good behaviour, and no augmentation or diminution in the
stipends during the time of holding their offices.
Agreed to.

Mr. Wilson moved, that the judicial be appointed
by the executive, instead of the national legislature.

Mr. Madison opposed the motion, and inclined to
think, that the executive ought by no means to make
the appointments, but rather that branch of the legislature called the senatorial ; and moves, that the words
" of the appointment of the legislature," be expunged.

Carried by eight States ; against it, two.

The remaining part of the resolve postponed.

The tenth resolve read and agreed to.

The eleventh resolve agreed to be postponed.

The twelfth resolve agreed to without debate.

The thirteenth and fourteenth resolves postponed.

The fifteenth or last resolve, " That the amendment
which shall be offered to the confederation, ought, at
a proper time or times, after the approbation of Congress, to be submitted to an assembly or assemblies of
representatives, recommended by the several legislatures, to be expressly chosen by the people, to consider
and decide thereon," was taken into consideration.

Mr. Madison endeavoured to enforce the necessity
of this resolve, because the new national constitution
ought to have the highest source of authority, at least
paramount to the powers of the respective constitutions
of the States ; points out the mischiefs that have
arisen in the old confederation, which depends upon
no higher authority than the confirmation of an ordinary act of a legislature ; instances the law operation
of treaties, when contravened by any antecedent acts
of a particular State.

Mr. King supposes, that, as the people have tacitly agreed to a federal government, therefore the legislature in every State have a right to confirm any alterations or amendments in it; a convention in each State to approve of a new government, he supposes, however, the most eligible.

Mr. Wilson is of opinion, that the people, by a convention, are the only power that can ratify the proposed system of the new government.

It is possible, that not all the States, nay, that not even a majority, will immediately come into the measure; but such as do ratify it will be immediately bound by it, and others as they may from time to time accede to it.

Question put for postponement of this resolve. Seven States for postponement, three against it.

Question on the ninth resolve, to strike out the words "and of inferior tribunals."

Carried by five States against four; two States divided, of which last number New York was one.

Mr. Wilson then moved, "that the national legislature shall have the authority to appoint inferior tribunals," be added to this resolve.

Carried by seven States against three. New York divided. [N. B. Mr. Lansing, from New York, was prevented by sickness from attending this day.]

Adjourned to to-morrow morning.

WEDNESDAY, JUNE 6th, 1787

Met pursuant to adjournment.

Mr. Pinckney moved, (pursuant to a standing order for reconsideration,) that, in the fourth resolve, the words "by the people," be expunged, and the words "by the legislature," be inserted.

Mr. Gerry. If the national legislature are appointed by the State legislatures, demagogues and corrupt members will creep in.

Mr. Wilson is of opinion, that the national legislative powers ought to flow immediately from the people, so as to contain all their understanding, and to be an exact transcript of their minds.   He observed, that the people had already parted with as much of their power as was necessary, to form on its basis a perfect government; and the particular States must part with such a portion of it, as to make the present national government adequate to their peace and the security of their liberties.   He admitted, that the State governments would probably be rivals and opposers of the national government.

Mr. Mason observed, that the national legislature, as to one branch, ought to be elected by the people; because the objects of their legislation will not be on States, but on individual persons.

Mr. Dickinson is for combining the State and national legislatures in the same views and measures, and that this object can only be effected by the national legislature flowing from the State legislatures.

Mr. Read is of opinion, that the State governments must sooner or later be at an end, and that therefore we must make the present national government as perfect as possible.

Mr. Madison is of opinion, that, when we agreed to the first resolve of having a national government, consisting of a supreme executive, judicial, and legislative power, it was then intended to operate to the exclusion of a federal government, and the more extensive we made the basis, the greater probability of duration, happiness, and good order.

The question for the amendment was negatived, by eight States against three. New York in the majority.

On the eighth resolve, *Mr. Wilson* moved, (in consequence of a vote to reconsider the question on the revisional powers vested in the executive,) that there be added these words, " with a convenient number of the national judicial."

Upon debate, carried in the negative; three States for, and eight against. New York for the addition.

Adjourned to to-morrow morning.

THURSDAY, JUNE 7th, 1787.

Met pursuant to adjournment.

Mr. Rutledge moved to take into consideration the mode of electing the second branch of the national legislature.

Mr. Dickinson thereupon moved, "that the second branch of the national legislature be chosen by the legislatures of the individual States. He observed, that this mode will more intimately connect the State governments with the national legislature; it will also draw forth the first characters, either as to family or talent, and that it ought to consist of a considerable number.

Mr. Wilson against the motion, because the two branches thus constituted, cannot agree, they having different views and different sentiments.

Mr. Dickinson is of opinion, that the mode by him proposed, like the British House of Lords and Commons, whose powers flow from different sources, are mutual checks on each other, and will thus promote the real happiness and security of the country. A government thus established, would harmonize the whole ;

and, like the planetary system, the national council, like the sun, would illuminate the whole,—the planets revolving round it in perfect order; or, like the union of several small streams, would at last form a respectable river, gently flowing to the sea.

Mr. Wilson. The State governments ought to be preserved. The freedom of the people, and their internal good police, depends on their existence in full vigor; but such a government can only answer local purposes. That it is not possible a general government, as despotic as even that of the Roman emperors, could be adequate to the government of the whole, without this distinction. He hoped that the national government would be independent of State governments, in order to make it vigorous, and therefore moved, that the above resolution be postponed, and that the convention, in its room, adopt the following resolve; "That the second branch of the national legislature be chosen by districts, to be formed for that purpose."

Mr. Sherman supposes the election of the national legislature will be better vested in the State legislatures than in the people; for, by pursuing different objects, persons may be returned who have not one tenth of the votes.

Mr. Gerry observed, that the great mercantile interest, and of stockholders, is not provided for in any mode of election; they will, however, be better represented, if the State legislatures choose the second branch.

Question carried against the postponement; ten States against one.

Mr. Mason then spoke to the general question; observing on the propriety, that the second branch of the national legislature should flow from the legislature of each State, to prevent the encroachments on each other, and to harmonize the whole.

The question put on the first motion, and carried unanimously.

Adjourned to to-morrow morning.

FRIDAY, JUNE 8th, 1787.

Met pursuant to adjournment.   Eleven States.

Mr. Pinckney moved, "That the national legislature shall have the power of negativing all laws to be passed by the State legislatures which they may judge improper," in the room of the clause as it stood reported.

He grounds his motion on the necessity of one supreme, controlling power, and he considers this as the corner-stone of the present system; and hence the necessity of retrenching the State authorities, in order to preserve the good government of the national council.

Mr. Williamson against the motion.   The national legislature ought to possess the power of negativing such laws only as will encroach on the national government.

Mr. Madison wished, that the line of jurisprudence could be drawn; he would be for it; but upon reflection, he finds it impossible, and therefore he is for the amendment.   If the clause remains without the amendment, it is inefficient.   The judges of the State must give the State laws their operation, although the law abridges the rights of the national government.   How is it to be repealed? — by the power which made it? How shall you compel them? — by force?   To prevent this disagreeable expedient, the power of negativing is absolutely necessary. This is the only attractive principle which will retain its centrifugal force ; and without this, the planets will fly from their orbits.

Mr. Gerry supposes, that this power ought to extend to all laws already made ; but the preferable mode would be, to designate the powers of the national legislature, to which the negative ought to apply. He has no objection to restrain the laws which may be made for issuing paper money. Upon the whole he does not choose, on this important trust, to " take a leap in the dark."

Mr. Pinckney supposes, that the proposed amendment had no retrospect to the State laws already made. The adoption of the new government must operate as a complete repeal of all the constitutions and State laws, as far as they are inconsistent with the new government.

Mr. Wilson supposes the surrender of the rights of a federal government to be a surrender of sovereignty. True, we may define some of the rights, but when we come near the line, it cannot be found. One general excepting clause must, therefore, apply to the whole. In the beginning of our troubles, Congress themselves were as one State ; dissensions or State interests were not known ; they gradually crept in after the formation of the constitution, and each took to himself a slice. The original draft of confederation was drawn on the first ideas, and the draft concluded on how different !

Mr. Bedford was against the motion, and states the proportion of the intended representation of the number ninety. Delaware one, Pennsylvania and Virginia one third. On this computation, where is the weight of the small States, when the interest of the one is in competition with the other on trade, manufactures, and agriculture? When he sees this mode of government so strongly advocated by the members of the great States, he must suppose it a question of interest.

Mr. Madison confesses it is not without its difficulties on many accounts; some may be removed, others modified, and some are unavoidable. May not this power be vested in the senatorial branch? They will probably be always sitting. Take the question on the other ground, who is to determine the line when drawn in doubtful cases. The State legislatures cannot, for they will be partial in support of their own powers; no tribunal can be found. It is impossible that the articles of confederation can be amended; they are too tottering to be invigorated; nothing but the present system, or something like it, can restore the peace and harmony of the country.

The question put on Mr. Pinckney's motion; seven States against it. Delaware divided. Virginia, Pennsylvania, and Massachusetts for it.

Adjourned to to-morrow morning.

SATURDAY, JUNE 9TH, 1787.

Met pursuant to adjournment.

Motion by *Mr. Gerry* to reconsider the appointment of the national executive.

"That the national executive be appointed by the State executives."

He supposed, that in the national legislature there will be a great number of bad men of various descriptions; these will make a wrong appointment. Besides, an executive thus appointed, will have his partiality in favor of those who appointed him. That this will not be the case by the effect of his motion, and the executive will by this means be independent of the national legislature ; but the appointment by the State executives ought to be made by votes in proportion to their weight in the scale of the representation.

Mr. Randolph opposes the motion. The power vested by it is dangerous ; confidence will be wanting ; the large States will be masters of the election ; an executive ought to have great experience, integrity, and activity. The executives of the States cannot know the persons properly qualified as possessing these. An executive thus appointed will court the officers of his appointment; and will relax him in the duties of commander of the militia. Your single executive is already invested with negativing laws of the State. Will he duly exercise the power? Is there no danger in the combinations of States to appoint such an executive as may be too favorable to local State governments? Add to this the expense and difficulty of bringing the executives to one place to exercise their powers. Can you suppose they will ever cordially raise the great oak, when they must sit as shrubs under its shade?

Carried against the motion, ten noes, and Delaware divided.

On motion of *Mr. Patterson*, the consideration of the 2d resolve was taken up, which is as follows : " Resolved, therefore, that the rights of suffrage in the national legislature ought to be apportioned to the quotas of contribution, or to the number of inhabitants, as the one or other rule may seem best in different cases."

Judge Brearley. The present question is an important one. On the principle that each State in the Union was sovereign, Congress, in the articles of confederation, determined that each State in the public councils had *one* vote. If the States still remain sovereign, the form of the present resolve is founded on principles of injustice. He then stated the comparative weight of each State ; the number of votes ninety. Georgia would be one, Virginia sixteen, and so of the rest. This vote must defeat itself, or end in despotism. If we must have a national government, what is the remedy ? Lay the map of the confederation on the table, and extinguish the present boundary lines of the respective State jurisdictions, and make a new division, so that each State is equal, then a government on the present system will be just.

Mr. Patterson opposed the resolve. Let us consider, with what powers are we sent here ? (Moved to have the credentials of Massachusetts read, which was done.) By this and the other credentials we see, that the basis of our present authority is founded on a revision of the articles of the present confederation, and to alter or amend them in such parts where they may appear defective. Can we on this ground form a national government ? I fancy not. Our commissions give a complexion to the business ; and can we suppose, that, when we exceed the bounds of our duty, the people will approve our proceedings ?

We are met here as the deputies of thirteen independent, sovereign States, for federal purposes. Can we consolidate their sovereignty and form one nation, and annihilate the sovereignties of our States, who have sent us here for other purposes ?

What, pray, is intended by a proportional representation ? Is property to be considered as part of it ? Is a man, for example, possessing a property of £ 4000 to have forty votes to one possessing only £ 100 ?

This has been asserted on a former occasion. If State distinctions are still to be held up, shall I submit the welfare of the State of New Jersey, with five votes in the national council, opposed to Virginia who has sixteen votes? Suppose, as it was in agitation before the war, that America had been represented in the British Parliament, and had sent two hundred members; what would this number avail against six hundred? We would have been as much enslaved in that case as when unrepresented; and, what is worse, without the prospect of redress. But it is said, that this national government is to act on individuals and not on States; and cannot a federal government be so framed as to operate in the same way? It surely may. I therefore declare, that I will never consent to the present system, and I shall make all the interest against it in the State which I represent that I can. Myself or my State will never submit to tyranny or despotism.

Upon the whole, every sovereign State according to a confederation must have an equal vote, or there is an end to liberty. As long, therefore, as State distinctions are held up, this rule must invariably apply; and if a consolidated national government must take place, then State distinctions must cease, or the States must be equalized.

Mr. Wilson was in favor of the resolve. He observed, that a majority, nay, even a minority of the States have a right to confederate with each other, and the rest may do as they please. He considered numbers as the best criterion to determine representation. Every citizen of one State possesses the same rights with the citizen of another. Let us see how this rule will apply to the present question. Pennsylvania, from its numbers, has a right to twelve votes, when, on the same principle, New Jersey is entitled to five votes. Shall New Jersey have the same right or influence in the councils of the nation with Pennsylvania? I say no. It is unjust; I never will confederate on this plan. The gentleman from New Jersey is candid in declaring his opinion; I commend him for it; I am equally so. I say again I never will confederate on his principles. If no State will part with any of its sovereignty, it is in vain to talk of a national government. The State who has five times the number of inhabitants ought, nay, must have the same proportion of weight in the representation. If there was a probability of equalizing the States, he would be for it. But we have no such power. If, however, we depart from the principle of representation in proportion to numbers, we will lose the object of our meeting.

The question postponed for farther consideration.

Adjourned to to-morrow morning.

MONDAY, JUNE 11th, 1787.

Met pursuant to adjournment. Present, eleven States.

Mr. Sherman moved, " That the first branch of the national legislature be chosen in proportion to the number of the whole inhabitants in each State." He observed, that as the people ought to have the election of one of the branches of the legislature, the legislature of each State ought to have the election of the second branch, in order to preserve the State sovereignty ; and that each State ought in this branch to have one vote.

Governor Rutledge moved, as an amendment of the

first proposition, " That the proportion of representation ought to be according to and in proportion to the contribution of each State."

Mr. Butler supported the motion, by observing, that money is strength ; and every State ought to have its weight in the national council in proportion to the quantity it possesses. He further observed, that when a boy, he read this as one of the remarks of Julius Cæsar, who declared, if he had but money, he would find soldiers and every thing necessary to carry on a war.

Mr. King observed, that it would be better first to establish a principle ; that is to say, whether we will depart from federal grounds in forming a national government ; and therefore, to bring this point to view, he moved, as a previous question, that the sense of the committee be taken on the following question :

" That the right of suffrage, in the first branch of the national legislature, ought not to be according to the rule in the articles of confederation, but according to some equitable ratio of representation."

Governor Franklin's written remarks on this point were read by Mr. Wilson. In these Governor Franklin observes, that representation ought to be in proportion to the importance of numbers or wealth in each State ; that there can be no danger of undue influence of the greater against the lesser States. This was the apprehension of Scotland, when the union with England was proposed, when in Parliament they were allowed only sixteen peers and forty-five commons ; yet experience has proved, that their liberties and influence were in no danger.

The question on Mr. King's motion was carried in the affirmative ; seven ayes, three noes, and Maryland

11

divided. New York, New Jersey, and Delaware in the negative.

Mr. Dickinson moved, as an amendment, to add the words, "according to the taxes and contributions of each State actually collected and paid into the national treasury."

Mr. Butler was of opinion, that the national government will only have the right of making and collecting the taxes, but that the States individually must lay their own taxes.

Mr. Wilson was of opinion, and therefore moved, " that the mode of representation of each of the States ought to be from the number of its free inhabitants, and of every other description three fifths to one free inhabitant." He supposed, that the impost will not be the only revenue ; the post-office, he supposes, will be another substantial source of revenue. He observed, further, that this mode had already received the approbation of eleven States, in their acquiescence to the quota made by Congress. He admitted, that this resolve would require further restrictions; for, where numbers determined the representation, a census, at different periods of five, seven, or ten years, ought to be taken.

Mr. Gerry. The idea of property ought not to be the rule of representation. Blacks are property, and are used at the southward as horses and cattle at the northward ; and why should their representation be increased at the southward on account of the number of slaves, any more than horses and oxen at the north ?

Mr. Madison was of opinion, at present, to fix the standard of representation, and let the detail be the business of a sub-committee.

Mr. Rutledge's motion was postponed.

Mr. Wilson's motion was then put, and carried by nine States against two.   New York in the majority.

Mr. Wilson then moved, as an amendment to Mr. Sherman's motion, " that the same proportion be observed in the election of the second branch as the first."

The question, however, was first put on Mr. Sherman's motion, and lost.   Six States against, and five for it.

Then Mr. Wilson's motion was put and carried. Six ayes, five noes.

The eleventh resolve was then taken into consideration.   *Mr. Madison* moved to add after the word "junctions," the words " or separation."

Mr. Read against the resolve *in toto*.   We must put away State governments, and we will then remove all cause of jealousy.   The guarantee will confirm the assumed rights of several States to lands which do belong to the confederation.

Mr. Madison moved an amendment, to add to or alter the resolution as follows: " The republican constitutions and the existing laws of each State to be guarantied by the United States."

Mr. Randolph was for the present amendment, because a republican government must be the basis of our national union ; and no State in it ought to have it in its power to change its government into a monarchy.   Agreed to.

Thirteenth resolve, — the first part agreed to.

Fourteenth resolve, — taken into consideration.

Mr. Williamson.   This resolve will be unnecessary, as the union will become the law of the land.

Governor Randolph.   He supposes it to be absolutely necessary.   Not a State government, but its officers will infringe on the rights of the national government. If the State judges are not sworn to the observance of the new government, will they not judicially determine in favor of their State laws? We are erecting a supreme, national government; ought it not to be supported? and can we give it too many sinews?

Mr. Gerry rather supposes, that the national legislators ought to be sworn to preserve the State constitutions, as they will run the greatest risk to be annihilated, and therefore moved it.

For Mr. Gerry's amendment, seven ayes, four noes. Main question then put on the clause or resolve. Six ayes, five noes. New York in the negative.

Adjourned to to-morrow morning.

TUESDAY, JUNE 12th, 1787.

Met pursuant to adjournment. Present, eleven States.

The fifteenth or last resolve was taken into consideration. No debate arose on it, and the question was put and carried. Five States for it, three against, and two divided. New York in the negative.

Having thus gone through with the resolves, it was found necessary to take up such parts of the preceding resolves as had been postponed or not agreed to. The remaining part of the fourth resolve was taken into consideration.

Mr. Sherman moved, that the blank of the duration of the first branch of the national legislature, be filled with "one year," *Mr. Rutledge* with "two years," and *Mr. Jenifer* with "three years."

Mr. Madison was for the last amendment; observing, that it will give it stability, and induce gentlemen of the first weight to engage in it.

Mr. Gerry is afraid the people will be alarmed, as savoring of despotism.

Mr. Madison. The people's opinions cannot be known, as to the particular modifications which may be necessary in the new government. In general, they believe there is something wrong in the present system, that requires amendment ; and he could wish to make the republican system the basis of the change, because, if our amendments should fail of securing their happiness, they will despair it can be done in this way, and incline to monarchy.

Mr. Gerry could not be governed by the prejudices of the people. Their good sense will ever have its weight. Perhaps a limited monarchy would be the best government, if we could organize it by creating a house of peers ; but that cannot be done.

The question was put on the three years' amendment, and carried. Seven ayes, four noes. New York in the affirmative.

On motion to expunge the clause of the qualification as to age, it was carried. Ten States against one.

On the question for fixed stipends, without augmentation or diminution, to this branch of the legislature, it was moved, that the words "to be paid by the national treasury," be added. Carried. Eight States for, and three against. New York in the negative.

The question was then put on the clause as amended, and carried. Eight ayes, three noes. New York in the negative.

On the clause respecting the ineligibility to any other office, it was moved, that the words "by any particular State," be expunged. Four States for, five against, and two divided. New York affirmative.

The question was then put on the whole clause, and carried. Ten ayes, one no.

The last blank was filled up with "one year," and carried. Eight ayes, two noes, and one divided.

Mr. Pinckney moved to expunge the clause. Agreed to, *nem. con.*

The question to fill up the blank with "thirty years." Agreed to. Seven States for, four against.

It was moved to fill the blank, as to the duration, with "seven years."

Mr. Pierce moved to have it for three years. Instanced the danger of too long a continuance, from the evils arising in the British parliaments from their septennial duration, and the clamors against it in that country, by its real friends.

Mr. Sherman was against the seven years, because, if they are bad men, it is too long; and if good, they may be again elected.

Mr. Madison was for seven years. Considers this branch as a check on the democracy. It cannot, therefore, be made too strong.

For the motion, eight ayes; one no; two States divided. New York one of the last.

Mr. Butler moved to expunge the clause of the stipends. Lost. Seven against, three for, one divided.

Agreed, that the second branch of the national legislature be paid in the same way as the first branch.

Upon the subject of ineligibility, it was agreed, that the same rule should apply as to the first branch.

Sixth resolve agreed to be postponed, *sine die.*

Ninth resolve taken into consideration, but postponed to to-morrow.

Adjourned to to-morrow morning.

WEDNESDAY, JUNE 13TH, 1787.

Met pursuant to adjournment. Present, eleven States.

Governor Randolph observed the difficulty in establishing the powers of the judiciary; the object, however, at present, is, to establish this principle, to wit, the security of foreigners where treaties are in their favor, and to preserve the harmony of States. and that of the citizens thereof. This being once established, it will be the business of a sub-committee to detail it; and, therefore, moved to obliterate such parts of the resolve so as only to establish the principle, to wit, " that the jurisdiction of the national judiciary shall extend to all cases of national revenue, impeachment of national officers, and questions which involve the national peace or harmony. Agreed to, unanimously.

It was further agreed, that the judiciary be paid out of the national treasury.

Mr. Pinckney moved, that the judiciary be appointed by the national legislature.

Mr. Madison is of opinion, that the second branch of the legislature ought to appoint the judiciary, which the convention agreed to.

Mr. Gerry moved, that the first branch shall have the only right of originating bills to supply the treasury.

Mr. Butler against the motion. We are constantly running away with the idea of the excellence of the British Parliament, and with or without reason copying from them; when, in fact, there is no similitude in our situations. With us, both Houses are appointed by the people, and both ought to be equally trusted.

Mr. Gerry. If we dislike the British government for the oppressive measures by them carried on against us, yet he hoped we would not be so far prejudiced as to make ours in every thing opposite to theirs.

Mr. Madison's question carried.

The committee having now gone through the whole of the propositions from Virginia, — *Resolved,* That the committee do report to the convention their proceedings. This was accordingly done. [See a copy of it hereunto annexed.]

The House resolved, on the report being read, that the consideration thereof be postponed to to-morrow, and that members have leave to take copies thereof.

Adjourned to to-morrow morning.

THURSDAY, JUNE 14th, 1787.

Met pursuant to adjournment. Present, eleven States.

Mr. Patterson moved, that the further consideration of the report be postponed until to-morrow, as he intended to give in principles to form a federal system of government, materially different from the system now under consideration. Postponement agreed to.

Adjourned until to-morrow morning.

FRIDAY, JUNE 15th, 1787.

Met pursuant to adjournment. Present, eleven States.

Mr. Patterson, pursuant to his intentions as mentioned yesterday, read a set of resolves, as the basis of amendment to the confederation. [See those resolves annexed.]

He observed, that no government could be energetic on paper only, which was no more than straw; that the remark applied to the one as well as to the other system ; and is therefore of opinion, that there must be a small standing force, to give every government weight.

Mr. Madison moved for the report of the committee, and the question may then come on whether the convention will postpone it, in order to take into consideration the system now offered.

Mr. Lansing is of opinion, that the two systems are fairly contrasted. The one now offered, is on the basis of amending the federal government, and the other to be reported as a national government, on propositions which exclude the propriety of amendment. Considering, therefore, its importance, and that justice may be done to its weighty consideration, he is for postponing it a day.

Colonel Hamilton cannot say he is in sentiment with either plan ; supposes both might again be considered as federal plans, and by this means they will be fairly in committee, and be contrasted so as to make a comparative estimate of the two.

Thereupon it was agreed, that the report be postponed, and that the House will resolve itself into a committee of the whole, to take into consideration both propositions to-morrow.

Adjourned to to-morrow morning.

SATURDAY, JUNE 16th, 1787.

Met pursuant to adjournment. Present, eleven States.

Mr. Lansing moved to have the first article of the last plan of government read ; which being done, he observed, that this system is fairly contrasted with the one ready to be reported, — the one federal, and the

other national.   In the first, the powers are exercised as
flowing from the respective State governments.   The
second, deriving its authority from the people of the
respective States ; which latter must ultimately destroy or annihilate the State governments.   To determine the powers on these grand objects with which
we are invested, let us recur to the credentials of the
respective States, and see what the views were of
those who sent us.   The language is there expressive ;
it is, upon the revision of the present confederation, to
alter and amend such parts as may appear defective, so
as to give additional strength to the Union.   And he
would venture to assert, that, had the legislature of
the State of New York apprehended, that their powers
would have been construed to extend to the formation
of a national government, to the extinguishment of
their independency, no delegates would have here
appeared on the part of that State.   This sentiment
must have had its weight on a former occasion, even
in this House ; for when the second resolution of Virginia, which declared, in substance, that a federal government could not be amended for the good of the
whole, the remark of an honorable member of South
Carolina, that, by determining this question in the
affirmative, their deliberative powers were at an end,
induced this House to waive the resolution.   It is in
vain to adopt a mode of government, which we have
reason to believe the people gave us no power to recommend ; as they will consider themselves, on this
ground, authorized to reject it.   See the danger of
exceeding your powers, by the example which the
requisition of Congress of 1783 afforded.   They required an impost on all imported articles ; to which,
on federal grounds, they had no right, unless volunta-

rily granted. What was the consequence? Some, who had least to give, granted it; and others, under various restrictions and modifications, so that it could not be systematized. If we form a government, let us do it on principles which are likely to meet the approbation of the States. Great changes can only be gradually introduced. The States will never sacrifice their essential rights to a national government. New plans, annihilating the rights of States, (unless upon evident necessity,) can never be approved. I may venture to assert, that the prevalent opinion of America is, that granting additional powers to Congress would answer their views; and every power recommended for their approbation, exceeding this idea, will be fruitless.

Mr. Patterson. As I had the honor of proposing a new system of government for the Union, it will be expected that I should explain its principles.

1st. The plan accords with our own powers.

2d. It accords with the sentiments of the people.

But if the subsisting confederation is so radically defective as not to admit of amendment, let us say so, and report its insufficiency, and wait for enlarged powers. We must, in the present case, pursue our powers, if we expect the approbation of the people. I am not here to pursue my own sentiments of government, but of those who have sent me; and I believe, that a little practical virtue is to be preferred to the finest theoretical principles, which cannot be carried into effect. Can we, as representatives of independent States, annihilate the essential powers of independency? Are not the votes of this convention taken on every question under the idea of independency? Let us turn to the fifth article of confederation. In this it is mutually agreed, that each State should have one vote.   It is a fundamental principle arising from confederated governments.   The thirteenth article provides for amendments ; but they must be agreed to by every State ; the dissent of one renders every proposal null.   The confederation is in the nature of a compact ; and can any State, unless by the consent of the whole, either in politics or law, withdraw their powers?   Let it be said by Pennsylvania and the other large States, that they, for the sake of peace, assented to the confederation ; can she now resume her original right without the consent of the donee ?

And although it is now asserted, that the larger States reluctantly agreed to that part of the confederation which secures an equal suffrage to each, yet let it be remembered, that the smaller States were the last who approved the confederation.

On this ground, representation must be drawn from the States, to maintain their independency, and not from the people composing those States.

The doctrine advanced by a learned gentleman from Pennsylvania, that all power is derived from the people, and that in proportion to their numbers they ought to participate equally in the benefits and rights of government, is right in principle, but, unfortunately for him, wrong in the application to the question now in debate.

When independent societies confederate for mutual defence, they do so in their collective capacity ; and then each State, for those purposes, must be considered as one of the contracting parties.   Destroy this balance of equality, and you endanger the rights of the lesser societies by the danger of usurpation in the greater.

Let us test the government intended to be made by

the Virginia plan, on these principles. The representatives in the national legislature are to be in proportion
to the number of inhabitants in each State. So far it
is right, upon the principles of equality, when State
distinctions are done away; but those, to certain purposes, still exist. Will the government of Pennsylvania admit a participation of their common stock of land
to the citizens of New Jersey? I fancy not. It therefore follows, that a national government, upon the
present plan, is unjust, and destructive of the common
principles of reciprocity. Much has been said, that
this government is to operate on persons, not on States.
This, upon examination will be found equally fallacious; for the fact is, it will, in the quotas of revenue,
be proportioned among the States, as States; and in
this business, Georgia will have one vote, and Virginia
sixteen. The truth is, both plans may be considered
to compel individuals to a compliance with their requisitions, although the requisition is made on the States.

Much has been said in commendation of two branches in a legislature, and of the advantages resulting from
their being checks to each other. This may be true
when applied to State governments, but will not
equally apply to a national legislature whose legislative objects are few and simple.

Whatever may be said of Congress, or their conduct
on particular occasions, the people in general, are
pleased with such a body, and, in general, wish an increase of their powers, for the good government of the
Union. Let us now see the plan of the national government on the score of expense. The least the second branch of the legislature can consist of, is ninety
members; the first branch, of at least two hundred
and seventy. How are they to be paid, in our present

impoverished situation? Let us, therefore, fairly try whether the confederation cannot be mended; and, if it can, we shall do our duty, and, I believe, the people will be satisfied.

Mr. Wilson first stated the difference between the two plans.

Virginia plan proposes two branches in the legislature.

Jersey, a single legislative body.

Virginia, the legislative powers derived from the people.

Jersey, from the States.

Virginia, a single executive.

Jersey, more than one.

Virginia, a majority of the legislature can act.

Jersey, a small minority can control.

Virginia, the legislature can legislate on all national concerns.

Jersey, only on limited objects.

Virginia, legislature to negative all State laws.

Jersey, giving power to the executive to compel obedience by force.

Virginia, to remove the executive by impeachment.

Jersey, on application of a majority of the States.

Virginia, for the establishment of inferior judiciary tribunals.

Jersey, no provision.

It is said, and insisted on, that the Jersey plan accords with our powers. As for himself, he considers his powers to extend to every thing or nothing; and therefore, that he has a right, and is at liberty to agree to either plan or none. The people expect relief from their present embarrassed situation, and look up for it to this national convention; and it follows, that they expect a national government, and therefore the plan from Virginia has the preference to the other.   I would, said he, with a reluctant hand, add any powers to Congress, because they are not a body chosen by the people, and consist only of one branch, and each State in it has one vote.   Inequality in representation poisons every government.   The English courts are hitherto pure, just, and incorrupt, while their legislature are base and venal.   The one arises from unjust representation ; the other, from their independency of the legislature.   Lord Chesterfield remarks, that one of the States of the United Netherlands withheld its assent to a proposition, until a major of their State was provided for.   He needed not to have added, (for the conclusion was self-evident,) that it was one of the lesser States.   I mean no reflection. but I leave it to gentlemen to consider, whether this has not also been the case in Congress ?   The argument in favor of the Jersey plan goes too far, as it cannot be completed unless Rhode Island assents.   A single legislature is very dangerous.   Despotism may present itself in various shapes.   May there not be legislative despotism, if, in the exercise of their power, they are unchecked and unrestrained by another branch ?   On the contrary, an executive, to be restrained, must be an individual. The first triumvirate of Rome, combined without law, was fatal to its liberties ; and the second, by the usurpation of Augustus, ended in despotism.   The two kings of Sparta, and the consuls of Rome, by sharing the executive, distracted their governments.

Mr. C. C. Pinckney supposes, that, if New Jersey was indulged with one vote out of thirteen, she would have no objection to a national government.   He supposes, that the convention have already determined, virtually, that the federal government cannot be made efficient. A national government being, therefore, the object, this plan must be pursued; as our business is not to conclude, but to recommend.

Judge Ellsworth is of opinion, that the first question on the new plan will decide nothing materially on principle, and therefore moved the postponemen thereof, in order to bring on the second.

Governor Randolph. The question now is, which of the two plans is to be preferred. If the vote on the first resolve will determine it, and it is so generally understood, he has no objection that it be put. The resolutions from Virginia must have been adopted on the supposition that a federal government was impracticable. And it is said, that power is wanting to institute such a government. But when our all is at stake, I will consent to any mode that will preserve us. View our present deplorable situation; France, to whom we are indebted in every motive of gratitude and honor, is left unpaid the large sums she has supplied us with in the day of our necessity. Our officers and soldiers, who have successfully fought our battles, and the loaners of money to the public, look up to you for relief. The bravery of our troops is degraded by the weakness of our government.

It has been contended, that the fifth article of the confederation cannot be repealed under the powers to new modify the confederation by the thirteenth article. This surely is false reasoning, since the whole of the confederation, upon revision, is subject to amendment and alteration; besides, our business consists in recommending a system of government, not to make it. There are great seasons, when persons with limited powers are justified in exceeding them, and a person would be contemptible not to risk it.   Originally, our confederation was founded on the weakness of each State to repel a foreign enemy; and we have found, that the powers granted to Congress are insufficient. The body of Congress is ineffectual to carry the great objects of safety and protection into execution.   What would their powers be over the commander of the military, but for the virtue of the commander?   As the State assemblies are constantly encroaching on the powers of Congress, the Jersey plan would rather encourage such encroachment than be a check to it; and, from the nature of the institution, Congress would ever be governed by cabal and intrigue.   They are, besides, too numerous for an executive; nor can any additional powers be sufficient to enable them to protect us against foreign invasion.   Amongst other things, Congress was intended to be a body to preserve peace among the States; and, in the rebellion of Massachusetts, it was found they were not authorized to use the troops of the confederation to quell it. Every one is impressed with the idea of a general regulation of trade and commerce.   Can Congress do this, when, from the nature of their institution, they are so subject to cabal and intrigue?   And would it not be dangerous to intrust such a body with the power, when they are dreaded on these grounds?   I am certain, that a national government must be established, and this is the only moment when it can be done.   And let me conclude by observing, that the best exercise of power is, to exert it for the public good.

Adjourned to Monday morning.

MONDAY, JUNE 19th, 1787.

Met pursuant to adjournment. Present, eleven States.

Mr. Hamilton. To deliver my sentiments on so important a subject, when the first characters in the Union have gone before me, inspires me with the greatest diffidence, especially when my own ideas are so materially dissimilar to the plans now before the committee. My situation is disagreeable, but it would be criminal not to come forward on a question of such magnitude. I have well considered the subject, and am convinced, that no amendment of the confederation can answer the purpose of a good government, so long as State sovereignties do, in any shape, exist ; and I have great doubts whether a national government, on the Virginia plan, can be made effectual. What is federal ? An association of several independent states into one. How or in what manner this association is formed, is not so clearly distinguishable. We find the diet of Germany has, in some instances, the power of legislation on individuals. We find the United States of America have it, in an extensive degree, in the cases of piracies.

Let us now review the powers with which we are invested. We are appointed for the sole and express purpose of revising the confederation, and to alter or amend it, so as to render it effectual for the purposes of a good government. Those who suppose it must be federal, lay great stress on the terms *sole* and *express*, as if these words intended a confinement to a federal government ; when the manifest import is no more, than that the institution of a good government must be the sole and express object of your deliberations. Nor can we suppose an annihilation of our powers by forming a national government, as many of the States have made, in their constitutions, no provision for any alteration; and thus much I can say for the State I have the honor to represent, that, when our credentials were under consideration in the Senate, some members were for inserting a restriction in the powers, to prevent an encroachment on the constitution. It was answered by others; and thereupon the resolve carried on the credentials, that it might abridge some of the constitutional powers of the State, and that, possibly, in the formation of a new Union, it would be found necessary. This appears reasonable, and therefore leaves us at liberty to form such a national government as we think best adapted for the good of the whole. I have, therefore, no difficulty as to the extent of our powers, nor do I feel myself restrained in the exercise of my judgment under them. We can only propose and recommend; the power of ratifying or rejecting is still in the States. But on this great question I am still greatly embarrassed. I have before observed my apprehension of the inefficacy of either plan; and I have great doubts, whether a more energetic government can pervade this wide and extensive country. I shall now show, that both plans are materially defective.

1. A good government ought to be constant, and ought to contain an active principle.

2. Utility and necessity.

3. An habitual sense of obligation.

4. Force.

5. Influence.

I hold it, that different societies have all different views and interests to pursue, and always prefer local

to general concerns. For example: New York legislature made an external compliance lately to a requisition of Congress ; but do they not, at the same time,
counteract their compliance by gratifying the local objects of the State, so as to defeat their concession ? And
this will ever be the case. Men always love power, and
States will prefer their particular concerns to the general welfare ; and as the States become large and important, will they not be less attentive to the general
government ? What, in process of time, will Virginia
be ? She contains now half a million of inhabitants ;
in twenty-five years she will double the number
Feeling her own weight and importance, must she
not become indifferent to the concerns of the Union ?
And where, in such a situation, will be found national
attachment to the general government ?

By "force," I mean the coercion of law and the coercion of arms. Will this remark apply to the power intended to be vested in the government to be instituted
by either plan ? A delinquent must be compelled to
obedience by force of arms.   How is this to be done ?
If you are unsuccessful, a dissolution of your government must be the consequence ; and in that case the
individual legislatures will reassume their powers ;
nay, will not the interest of the States be thrown into
the State governments?

By influence, I mean the regular weight and support it will receive from those who will find it their
interest to support a government intended to preserve
the peace and happiness of the community of the
whole. The State governments, by either plan, will
exert the means to counteract it. They have their
State judges and militia all combined to support their
State interests : and these will be influenced to oppose

a national government.   Either plan is therefore pre-
carious.   The national government cannot long exist
when opposed by such a weighty rival.   The experience of ancient and modern confederacies evince this
point, and throw considerable light on the subject.
The amphictyonic council of Greece had a right to
require of its members troops, money, and the force of
the country.   Were they obeyed in the exercise of
those powers?   Could they preserve the peace of the
greater states and republics?   Or where were they
obeyed *   History shows that their decrees were disregarded, and that the stronger states, regardless of
their power, gave law to the lesser.

Let us examine the federal institution of Germany.
It was instituted upon the laudable principle of securing the independency of the several States of which
it was composed, and to protect them against foreign
invasion.   Has it answered these good intentions?
Do we not see, that their councils are weak and distracted, and that it cannot prevent the wars and con-
fusions which the respective electors carry on against
each other?   The Swiss cantous, or the Helvetic
union, are equally inefficient.

Such are the lessons which the experience of others
afford us, and from whence results the evident conclusion, that all federal governments are weak and
distracted.   To avoid the evils deducible from these
observations, we must establish a general and national
government, completely sovereign, and annihilate the
State distinctions and State operations ; and, unless
we do this, no good purpose can be answered.   What
does the Jersey plan propose ?   It surely has not this
for its object.   By this we grant the regulation of trade
and a more effectual collection of the revenue, and

some partial duties. These, at five or ten per cent. would only perhaps amount to a fund to discharge the debt of the corporation.

Let us take a review of the variety of important objects, which must necessarily engage the attention of a national government. You have to protect your rights against Canada on the north, Spain on the south, and your western frontier against the savages. You have to adopt necessary plans for the settlement of your frontiers, and to institute the mode in which settlements and good government are to be made.

How is the expense of supporting and regulating these important matters to be defrayed? By requisition on the States, according to the Jersey plan? Will this do it? We have already found it ineffectual? Let one State prove delinquent, and it will encourage others to follow the example; and thus the whole will fail. And what is the standard to quota among the States their respective proportions? Can lands be the standard? How would that apply between Russia and Holland? Compare Pennsylvania with North Carolina, or Connecticut with New York. Does not commerce or industry in the one or other make a great disparity between these different countries, and may not the comparative value of the States from these circumstances, make an unequal disproportion when the data is numbers? I therefore conclude, that either system would ultimately destroy the confederation, or any other government which is established on such fallacious principles. Perhaps imposts, taxes on specific articles, would produce a more equal system of drawing a revenue.

Another objection against the Jersey plan is, the unequal representation. Can the great States consent to this ? If they did, it would eventually work its own destruction. How are forces to be raised by the Jersey plan ? By quotas ? Will the States comply with the requisition ?. As much as they will with the taxes.

Examine the present confederation, and it is evident, they can raise no troops, nor equip vessels, before war is actually declared. They cannot, therefore, take any preparatory measure before an enemy is at your door. How unwise and inadequate their powers ! And this must ever be the case when you attempt to define powers. Something will always be wanting. Congress, by being annually elected, and subject to recall, will ever come with the prejudices of their States rather than the good of the Union. Add, therefore, additional powers to a body thus organized, and you establish a sovereignty of the worst kind, consisting of a single body. Where are the checks ? None. They must either prevail over the State governments, or the prevalence of the State governments must end in their dissolution. This is a conclusive objection to the Jersey plan.

Such are the insuperable objections to both plans ; and what is to be done on this occasion ? I confess, I am at a loss. I foresee the difficulty, on a consolidated plan, of drawing a representation from so extensive a continent to one place. What can be the inducements for gentlemen to come six hundred miles to a national legislature ? The expense would at least amount to £100,000. This, however, can be no conclusive objection, if it eventuates in an extinction of State governments. The burden of the latter would be saved, and the expense then would not be great. State distinctions would be found unnecessary ; and yet, I confess, to carry government to the extremities, the State governments, reduced to corporations, and with very limited powers, might be necessary, and the expense of the national government become less burdensome.

Yet, I confess, I see great difficulty of drawing forth a good representation. What, for example, will be the inducements for gentlemen of fortune and abilities to leave their houses and business to attend annually and long ? It cannot be the wages ; for these, I presume, must be small. Will not the power, therefore, be thrown into the hands of the demagogue or middling politician, who, for the sake of a small stipend and the hopes of advancement, will offer himself as a candidate, and the real men of weight and influence, by remaining at home, add strength to the State governments ? I am at a loss to know what must be done ; I despair, that a republican form of government can remove the difficulties. Whatever may be my opinion, I would hold it, however, unwise to change that form of government. I believe the British government forms the best model the world ever produced, and such has been its progress in the minds of the many, that this truth gradually gains ground. This government has for its object public strength and individual security. It is said with us to be unattainable. If it was once formed it would maintain itself. All communities divide themselves into the few and the many. The first are the rich and well born, the other the mass of the people. The voice of the people has been said to be the voice of God ; and, however generally this maxim has been quoted and believed, it is not true in fact. The people are turbulent and changing ; they seldom judge or determine right.

Give, therefore, to the first class a distinct, permanent share in the government. They will check the unsteadiness of the second, and, as they cannot receive any advantage by a change, they therefore will ever maintain good government. Can a democratic assembly, who annually revolve in the mass of the people, be supposed steadily to pursue the public good? Nothing but a permanent body can check the imprudence of democracy. Their turbulent and uncontrolling disposition requires checks. The Senate of New York, although chosen for four years, we have found to be inefficient. Will, on the Virginia plan, a continuance of seven years do it? It is admitted, that you cannot have a good executive upon a democratic plan. See the excellency of the British executive. He is placed above temptation. He can have no distinct interests from the public welfare. Nothing short of such an executive can be efficient. The weak side of a republican government is the danger of foreign influence. This is unavoidable, unless it is so constructed as to bring forward its first characters in its support. I am, therefore, for a general government, yet would wish to go the full length of republican principles.

Let one body of the legislature be constituted during good behaviour or life.

Let one executive be appointed who dares execute his powers.

It may be asked, is this a republican system? It is strictly so, as long as they remain elective.

And let me observe, that an executive is less dangerous to the liberties of the people when in office during life, than for seven years.

It may be said, this constitutes an elective monarchy? Pray, what is a monarchy? May not the gov-

13

ernors of the respective States be considered in that light? But, by making the executive subject to impeachment, the term monarchy cannot apply. These elective monarchs have produced tumults in Rome, and are equally dangerous to peace in Poland; but this cannot apply to the mode in which I would propose the election. Let electors be appointed in each of the States to elect the executive, [Here Mr. H. produced his plan, a copy whereof is hereunto annexed,] to consist of two branches; and I would give them the unlimited power of passing all laws, without exception. The Assembly to be elected for three years, by the people, in districts. The Senate to be elected by electors, to be chosen for that purpose by the people, and to remain in office during life. The executive to have the power of negativing all laws; to make war or peace, with the advice of the Senate; to make treaties with their advice, but to have the sole direction of all military operations, and to send ambassadors, and appoint all military officers; and to pardon all offenders, treason excepted, unless by advice of the Senate. On his death or removal, the President of the Senate to officiate, with the same powers, until another is elected. Supreme judicial officers to be appointed by the executive and the Senate. The legislature to appoint courts in each State, so as to make the State governments unnecessary to it.

All State laws to be absolutely void, which contravene the general laws. An officer to be appointed in each State, to have a negative on all State laws. All the militia, and the appointment of officers, to be under the national government.

I confess, that this plan, and that from Virginia, are very remote from the idea of the people. Perhaps the

Jersey plan is nearest their expectation. But the people are gradually ripening in their opinions of government; they begin to be tired of an excess of democracy; and what even is the Virginia plan, but "pork still, with a little change of the sauce."

Adjourned to to-morrow.

TUESDAY, JUNE 19th, 1787.

Met pursuant to adjournment. Present, eleven States.

On the consideration of the first resolve of the Jersey plan.

Mr. Madison. This is an important question. Many persons scruple the powers of the convention. If this remark has any weight, it is equally applicable to the adoption of either plan. The difference of drawing the powers, in the one from the people, and in the other from the States, does not affect the powers. There are two States in the Union, where the members of Congress are chosen by the people. A new government must be made. Our all is depending on it; and if we have but a clause that the people will adopt, there is then a chance for our preservation. Although all the States have assented to the confederation, an infraction of any one article by one of the States, is a dissolution of the whole. This is the doctrine of the civil law on treaties.

Jersey pointedly refused complying with a requisition of Congress, and was guilty of this infraction, although she afterwards rescinded her non-complying resolve. What is the object of a confederation? It is twofold; first, to maintain the Union; secondly, good government. Will the Jersey plan secure these points? No; it is still in the power of the confeder-

ated States to violate treaties. Has not Georgia, in
direct violation of the confederation, made war with
the Indians, and concluded treaties?   Have not Virginia and Maryland entered into a partial compact?
Have not Pennsylvania and Jersey regulated the
bounds of the Delaware? Has not the State of Massachusetts, at this time, a considerable body of troops in
pay?   Has not Congress been obliged to pass a conciliatory act, in support of a decision of their federal
court, between Connecticut and Pennsylvania, instead
of having the power of carrying into effect the judgment of its own court? Nor does the Jersey plan
provide for a ratification, by the respective States, of
the powers intended to be vested.   It is also defective
in the establishment of the judiciary, granting only an
appellate jurisdiction, without providing for a second
trial; and in case the executive of a State should pardon an offender, how will it effect the definitive judgment on appeal?   It is evident, if we do not radically
depart from a federal plan, we shall share the fate of
ancient and modern confederacies.   The amphictyonic
council, like the American Congress, had the power
of judging in the *last resort* in war and peace, calling
out forces, and sending ambassadors.   What was its
fate or continuance?   Philip of Macedon, with little
difficulty, destroyed every appearance of it.   The
Athenian had nearly the same fate.   The Helvetic
confederacy is rather a league.   In the German confederacy, the parts are too strong for the whole.   The
Dutch are in a most wretched situation ; weak in all
its parts, and only supported by surrounding contending powers.

The rights of individuals are infringed by many of
the State laws ; such as issuing paper money, and in-

stituting a mode to discharge debts, differing from the form of the contract. Has the Jersey plan any checks to prevent the mischief? Does it, in any instance, secure internal tranquillity? Right and force, in a system like this, are synonymous terms. When force is employed to support the system, and men obtain military habits, is there no danger they may turn their arms against their employers? Will the Jersey plan prevent foreign influence? Did not Persia and Macedon distract the councils of Greece by acts of corruption? And are not Jersey and Holland, at this day, subject to the same distractions? Will not the plan be burdensome to the smaller States, if they have an equal representation? But how is military coercion to enforce government? True, a smaller State may be brought to obedience, or crushed; but what if one of the larger States should prove disobedient; are you sure you can by force effect a submission? Suppose we cannot agree on any plan, what will be the condition of the smaller States? Will Delaware and Jersey be safe against Pennsylvania, or Rhode Island against Massachusetts? And how will the smaller States be situated in case of partial confederacies? Will they not be obliged to make larger concessions to the greater States? The point of representation is the great point of difference, and which the greater States cannot give up; and although there was an equalization of States, State distinctions would still exist. But this is totally impracticable; and what would be the effect of the Jersey plan, if ten or twelve new States were added?

Mr. King moved, that the committee rise, and report, that the Jersey plan is not admissible, and report the first plan.

Mr. Dickinson supposed, that there were good regulations in both. Let us, therefore, contrast the one with the other, and consolidate such parts of them as the committee approve.

Mr. King's motion was then put. For it, seven States ; three against it ; one divided. New York in the minority.

The committee rose and reported again the first plan, and the inadmissibility of the Jersey plan.

The convention then proceeded to take the first plan into consideration.

The first resolve was read.

Mr. Wilson. I am, to borrow a sea phrase, for taking a new departure, and I wish to consider in what direction we sail, and what may be the end of our voyage. I am for a national government, though the idea of federal is, in my view, the same. With me, it is not a desirable object to annihilate the State governments, and here I differ from the honorable gentleman from New York. In all extensive empires, a subdivision of power is necessary. Persia, Turkey, and Rome, under its emperors, are examples in point. These, although despots, found it necessary. A general government over a great extent of territory, must, in a few years, make subordinate jurisdictions. Alfred the Great, that wise legislator, made this gradation ; and the last division, on his plan, amounted only to ten territories. With this explanation, I shall be for the first resolve.

Mr. Hamilton. I agree to the proposition. I did not intend, yesterday, a total extinguishment of State governments; but my meaning was, that a national government ought to be able to support itself without the aid or interference of the State governments, and that therefore it was necessary to have full sovereignty. Even with corporate rights, the States will be dangerous to the national government, and ought to be extinguished, new modified, or reduced to a smaller scale.

Mr. King. None of the States are now sovereign or independent. Many of these essential rights are vested in Congress. Congress, by the confederation, possesses the rights of the United States. This is a union of the men of those States. None of the States, individually or collectively, but in Congress, have the rights of peace or war. The magistracy in Congress possesses the sovereignty. To certain points we are now a united people. Consolidation is already established. The confederation contains an article to make alterations; Congress has the right to propose such alterations. The eighth article, respecting the quotas of the States, has been altered, and eleven States have agreed to it. Can it not be altered in other instances? It can, excepting the guarantee of the States.

Mr. Martin. When the States threw off their allegiance to Great Britain, they became independent of her and each other. They united and confederated for mutual defence; and this was done on principles of perfect reciprocity. They will now again meet on the same ground. But when a dissolution takes place, our original rights and sovereignties are resumed. Our accession to the Union has been by States. If any other principle is adopted by this convention, he will give it every opposition.

Mr. Wilson. The declaration of independence preceded the State constitutions. What does this declare? In the name of the people of these States, we are declared to be free and independent. The power of war, peace, alliances, and trade, are declared to be vested in Congress.

Mr. Hamilton. I agree to Mr. Wilson's remark. Establish a weak government and you must at times overleap the bounds. Rome was obliged to create dictators. Cannot you make propositions to the people because we before confederated on other principles? The people can yield to them, if they will. The three great objects of government, agriculture, commerce, and revenue, can only be secured by a general government.

Adjourned to to-morrow morning.

WEDNESDAY, JUNE 20TH, 1787.

Met pursuant to adjournment. Present, eleven States.

Judge Ellsworth. I propose, and therefore move, to expunge the word *national,* in the first resolve, and to place in the room of it, *government of the United States;* which was agreed to, *nem. con.*

Mr. Lansing then moved, that the first resolve be postponed, in order to take into consideration the following: "That the powers of legislation ought to be vested in the United States in Congress."

I am clearly of opinion, that I am not authorized to accede to a system which will annihilate the State governments, and the Virginia plan is declarative of such extinction. It has been asserted, that the public mind is not known. To some points it may be true, but we may collect from the fate of the requisition of the impost, what it may be on the principles of a national government. When many of the States were so tenacious of their rights on this point, can we expect that thirteen States will surrender their governments up to a national plan? Rhode Island pointedly refused granting it. Certainly she had a federal right so to do; and I hold it as an undoubted truth, as long as State distinctions remain, let the national government be modified as you please, both branches of your legislature will be impressed with local and State attachments. The Virginia plan proposes a negative on the State laws, where, in the opinion of the national legislature, they contravene the national government; and no State laws can pass unless approved by them. They will have more than a law in a day to revise; and are they competent to judge of the wants and necessities of remote States?

This national government will, from their power, have great influence in the State governments; and the existence of the latter are only saved in appearance. And has it not been asserted, that they expect their extinction? If this be the object, let us say so, and extinguish them at once. But remember, if we devise a system of government which will not meet the approbation of our constituents, we are dissolving the Union; but if we act within the limits of our power, it will be approved of; and should it upon experiment prove defective, the people will intrust a future convention again to amend it. Fond as many are of a general government, do any of you believe it can pervade the whole continent so effectually as to secure the peace, harmony, and happiness of the whole? The excellence of the British model of government has been much insisted on; but we are endeavouring to complicate it with State governments, on principles which will gradually destroy the one or the other. You are sowing the seeds of rivalship, which must at last end in ruin.

Mr. Mason. The material difference between the
two plans has already been clearly pointed out. The
objection to that of Virginia arises from the want of
power to institute it, and the want of practicability to
carry it into effect. Will the first objection apply to
a power merely recommendatory? In certain seasons
of public danger it is commendable to exceed power.
The treaty of peace, under which we now enjoy the
blessings of freedom, was made by persons who exceeded their powers. It met the approbation of the
public, and thus deserved the praises of those who
sent them. The impracticability of the plan is still
more groundless. These measures are supported by
one, who, at his time of life, has little to hope or expect from any government. Let me ask, will the
people intrust their dearest rights and liberties to the
determination of one body of men, and those not chosen by them, and who are invested both with the
sword and purse? They never will; they never can;
to a conclave, transacting their business secret from
the eye of the public. Do we not discover by their
public journals of the years 1778, 1779, and 1780,
that factions and party spirit had guided many of their
acts? The people of America, like all other people,
are unsettled in their minds, and their principles fixed
to no object, except that a republican government is
the best, and that the legislature ought to consist of
two branches. The constitutions of the respective
States, made and approved of by them, evince this
principle. Congress, however, from other causes, received a different organization. What, would you
use military force to compel the observance of a social
compact? It is destructive to the rights of the people.
Do you expect the militia will do it, or do you mean

a standing army? The first will never, on such an occasion, exert any power; and the latter may turn its arms against the government which employs them. I never will consent to destroy State governments, and will ever be as careful to preserve the one as the other. If we should, in the formation of the latter, have omitted some necessary regulation, I will trust my posterity to amend it. That the one government will be productive of disputes and jealousies against the other, I believe; but it will produce mutual safety. I shall close with observing, that, though some gentlemen have expressed much warmth on this and former occasions, I can excuse it, as the result of sudden passion; and hope, that, although we may differ in some particular points, if we mean the good of the whole, that our good sonse, upon reflection, will prevent us from spreading our discontent further.

Mr. Martin. I know that government must be supported; and, if the one was incompatible with the other, I would support the State government at the expense of the Union; for I consider the present system as a system of slavery. Impressed with this idea, I made use, on a former occasion, of expressions perhaps rather harsh. If gentlemen conceive, that the legislative branch is dangerous, divide them into two. They are as much the representatives of the States, as the State assemblies are the representatives of the people. Are not the powers which we here exercise given by the legislatures? [After giving a detail of the Revolution and of State governments, Mr. Martin continued.] I confess, when the confederation was made, Congress ought to have been invested with more extensive powers; but when the States saw that Congress indirectly aimed at sovereignty, they were jealous, and therefore refused any further concessions. The time is now come, that we can constitutionally grant them not only new powers, but to modify their government, so that the State governments are not endangered. But, whatever we have now in our power to grant, the grant is a State grant, and therefore it must be so organized, that the State governments are interested in supporting the Union. Thus systematized, there can be no danger if a small force is maintained.

Mr. Sherman. We have found during the war, that, though Congress consisted of but one branch, it was that body which carried us through the whole war, and we were crowned with success. We closed the war, performing all the functions of a good government, by making a beneficial peace. But the great difficulty now is, how we shall pay the public debt incurred during that war. The unwillingness of the States to comply with the requisitions of Congress, has embarrassed us greatly. But to amend these defects in government I am not fond of speculation. I would rather proceed on experimental ground. We can so modify the powers of Congress, that we will all be mutual supporters of one another. The disparity of the States can be no difficulty. We know this by experience. Virginia and Massachusetts were the first who unanimously ratified the old confederation. They then had no claim to more votes in Congress than one. Foreign states have made treaties with us as confederated States, not as a national government. Suppose we put an end to that government under which those treaties were made, will not these treaties be void?

Mr. Wilson. The question before us may admit of the three following considerations :

1. Whether the legislature shall consist of one or two branches.

2. Whether they are to be elected by the State governments or by the people.

3. Whether in proportion to State importance, or States individually.

Confederations are usually of a short date. The amphictyonic council was instituted in the infancy of the Grecian republics; as those grew in strength, the council lost its weight and power. The Achæan league met the same fate; Switzerland and Holland are supported in their confederation, not by its intrinsic merit, but the incumbent pressure of arrounding bodies. Germany is kept together by the house of Austria. True, Congress carried us through the war, even against its own weakness. That powers were wanting, you, Mr. President, must have felt. To other causes, not to Congress, must the success be ascribed. That the great States acceded to the confederation, and that they, in the hour of danger, made a sacrifice of their interest to the lesser States is true. Like the wisdom of Solomon in adjudging the child to its true mother, from tenderness to it, the greater States well knew, that the loss of a limb was fatal to the confederation; they too, through tenderness, sacrificed their dearest rights to preserve the whole. But the time is come, when justice will be done to their claims. Situations are altered.

Congress have frequently made their appeal to the people. I wish they had always done it; the national government would have been sooner extricated.

Question then put on Mr. Lansing's motion and

lost. Six States against four; one divided. New York in the minority.

Adjourned till to-morrow morning.

THURSDAY, JUNE 21st, 1787.

Met pursuant to adjournment. Present, eleven States.

Dr. Johnson. It appears to me, that the Jersey plan has for its principal object the preservation of the State governments. So far, it is a departure from the plan of Virginia; which, although it concentres in a distinct national government, is not totally independent of that of the States. A gentleman from New York, with boldness and decision, proposed a system totally different from both; and though he has been praised by everybody, he has been supported by none. How can the State governments be secured on the Virginia plan? I could have wished, that the supporters of the Jersey system could have satisfied themselves with the principles of the Virginia plan, and that the individuality of the States could be supported. It is agreed on all hands, that a portion of government is to be left to the States. How can this be done? It can be done by joining the States in their legislative capacity with the right of appointing the second branch of the national legislature, to represent the States individually.

Mr. Wilson. If security is necessary to preserve the one, it is equally so to preserve the other. How can the national government be secured against the States? Some regulation is necessary. Suppose the national government had a component number in the State legislature? But where the one government clashed with the other, the State government ought to yield, as the preservation of the general interest must be preferred to a particular.   But let us try to designate the powers of each, and then no danger can be apprehended, nor can the general government be possessed of any ambitious views to encroach on the State rights.

Mr. Madison.   I could have wished, that the gentleman from Connecticut had more accurately marked his objections to the Virginia plan.   I apprehend the greatest danger is from the encroachment of the States on the national government.   This apprehension is justly founded on the experience of ancient confederacies, and our own is a proof of it.

The right of negativing, in certain instances, the State laws, affords one security to the national government.   But is the danger well founded?   Have any State governments ever encroached on the corporate rights of cities?   And if it was the case, that the national government usurped the State government, if such usurpation was for the good of the whole, no mischief could arise.   To draw the line between the two, is a difficult task.   I believe it cannot be done, and therefore I am inclined for a general government. If we cannot form a general government, and the States become totally independent of each other, it would afford a melancholy prospect.

The second resolve was then put and carried. Seven States for, three against, and one divided. New York in the minority.

The third resolve was then taken into consideration by the convention.

Mr. Pinckney.   I move, "that the members of the first branch be appointed in such manner as the several State legislatures shall direct." instead of the mode reported.   If this motion is not agreed to, the other will operate with great difficulty, if not injustice.   If you make district elections, and join, as I presume you must, many counties in one district, the largest county will carry the election, as its united influence will give a decided majority in its favor.

Mr. Madison.   I oppose the motion.   There are difficulties, but they may be obviated in the details connected with the subject.

Mr. Hamilton.   It is essential to the democratic rights of the community, that this branch be directly elected by the people.   Let us look forward to probable events.   There may be a time when State legislatures may cease, and such an event ought not to embarrass the national government.

Mr. Mason.   I am for preserving inviolably the democratic branch of the government.   True, we have found inconveniences from pure democracies; but, if we mean to preserve peace and real freedom, they must necessarily become a component part of a national government.   Change this necessary principle, and, if the government proceeds to taxation, the States will oppose your powers.

Mr. Sherman thought, that an amendment to the proposed amendment is necessary.

Governor Rutledge.   It is said, that an election by representatives is not an election by the people.   This proposition is not correct.   What is done by my order, is done by myself.   I am convinced, that the mode of election by legislatures will be more refined, and better men will be sent.

Mr. Wilson.   The legislatures of the States, by the proposed motion, will have an uncontrollable sway over the general government.   Election is the exercise of original sovereignty in the people ; but if by represent-atives, it is only relative sovereignty.

Mr. King. The magistrates of the States will ever pursue schemes of their own, and this, on the proposed motion, will pervade the national government; and we know the State governments will be ever hostile to the general government.

Mr. Pinckney. All the reasoning of the gentlemen opposed to my motion has not convinced me of its impropriety.   There is an *esprit de corps* which has made, heretofore, every unfederal member of Congress, after his election, become strictly federal ; and this, I presume, will ever be the case, in whatever manner they may be elected.

Question put on Mr. Pinckney's motion, and carried by six States against four ; one divided.

Question then put on the resolve.   Nine States for, one against, and one divided.

Governor Randolph.   I move, that, in the resolve for the duration of the first branch of the general legis-lature, the word " three " be expunged, and the words " two years " be inserted.

Mr. Dickinson.   I am against the amendment.   I propose, that the word " three " shall remain, but that they shall be removable annually in classes.

Mr. Sherman.   I am for one year.   Our people are accustomed to annual elections.   Should the members have a longer duration of service, and remain at the seat of government, they may forget their constituents, and perhaps imbibe the interest of the State in which they reside, or there may be danger of catching the *esprit de corps.*

Mr. Mason.   I am for two years.   One year is too short.   In extensive States, four months may elapse

14*

before the returns can be known.   Hence the danger of their remaining too long unrepresented.

Mr. Hamilton.   There is a medium in every thing. I confess, three years is not too long.   A representative ought to have full freedom of deliberation, and ought to exert an opinion of his own.   I am convinced, that the public mind will adopt a solid plan.   The government of New York, although higher toned than that of any other State, still we find great listlessness and indifference in the electors; nor do they, in general, bring forward the first characters to the legislature. The public mind is perhaps not now ready to receive the best plan of government, but certain circumstances are now progressing, which will give a different complexion to it.

Two years' duration agreed to.

Adjourned to to-morrow morning.

FRIDAY, JUNE 22d, 1787.

Met pursuant to adjournment.

The clause of the third resolve, respecting the stipends, taken into consideration.

Judge Ellsworth.   I object to this clause.   I think the State legislatures ought to provide for the members of the general legislature ; and as each State will have a proportionate number, it will not be burdensome to the smaller States.   I therefore move to strike out the clause.

Mr. Gorham.   If we intend to fix the stipend, it may be an objection against the system, as the States would never adopt it.   I join in sentiment to strike out the whole.

Governor Randolph.   I am against the motion. Are the members to be paid ?   Certainly.   We have no sufficient fortunes to induce gentlemen to attend for nothing. If the State legislatures pay the members of the national council, they will control the members, and compel them to pursue State measures. I confess, the payment will not operate impartially, but the members must be paid, and be made easy in their circumstances. Will they attend the service of the public, without being paid?

Mr. Sherman. The States ought to pay their members; and I judge of the approbation of the people, on matters of government, by what I suppose they will approve.

Mr. Wilson. I am against going as far as the resolve. If, however, it is intended to throw the national legislature into the hand of the States, I shall be against it. It is possible, the States may become unfederal, and they may then shake the national government. The members ought to be paid out of the national treasury.

Mr. Madison. Our attention is too much confined to the present moment, when our regulations are intended to be perpetual. Our national government must operate for the good of the whole, and the people must have a general interest in its support; but if you make its legislators subject to, and at the mercy of, the State governments, you ruin the fabric; and whatever new States may be added to the general government, the expense will be equally borne.

Mr. Hamilton. I do not think the States ought to pay the members, nor am I for a fixed sum. It is a general remark, that he who pays is the master. If each State pays its own members, the burden would be disproportionate, according to the distance of the States from the seat of government. If a national government can exist, members will make it a desirable object to attend, without accepting any stipend ; and it ought to be so organized as to be efficient.

Mr. Wilson. I move, "that the stipend be ascertained by the legislature, and paid out of the national treasury."

Mr. Madison. I oppose this motion. Members are too much interested in the question. Besides, it is indecent, that the legislature should put their hands in the public purse, to convey it into their own.

Question put on Mr. Wilson's motion, and negatived. Seven States against, two for, and two divided.

Mr. Mason moved to change the phraseology of the resolve, that is to say, "to receive an adequate compensation for their services," and to be paid out of the treasury. This motion was agreed to.

Mr. Rutledge. I move, that the question be taken on these words, "to be paid out of the national treasury."

Mr. Hamilton. It has been often asserted, that the interests of the general and of the State legislatures are precisely the same. This cannot be true. The views of the governed are often materially different from those who govern. The science of policy is the knowledge of human nature. A State government will ever be the rival power of the general government. It is therefore highly improper, that the State legislatures should be the paymasters of the members of the national government. All political bodies love power, and it will often be improperly attained.

Judge Ellsworth. If we are so exceedingly jealous of State legislatures, will they not have reason to be equally jealous of us? If I return to my State, and tell them we made such and such regulations for a general government, because we dared not trust you with any extensive powers, will they be satisfied? nay, will they adopt your government? And let it ever be remembered, that, without their approbation, your government is nothing more than a rope of sand.

Mr. Wilson. I am not for submitting the national government to the approbation of the State legislatures. I know that they and the State officers will oppose it. I am for carrying it to the people of each State.

Mr. Rutledge's motion was then put. Four States for the clause; five against; two States divided. New York divided.

The clause, " to be ineligible to any office," &c., came next to be considered.

Mr. Mason moved, that, after the words " two years," be added, "and to be of the age of twenty-five years.

Question put and agreed to. Seven ayes, three noes. New York divided.

Mr. Gorham. I move, that after the words "and under the national government for one year after its expiration," be struck out.

Mr. King for the motion. It is impossible to carry the system of exclusion so far; and in this instance, we refine too much, by going to *utopian* lengths. It is a mere cobweb.

Mr. Butler. We have no way of judging of mankind but by experience. Look at the history of the government of Great Britain, where there is a very flimsy exclusion; does it not ruin their government? A man takes a seat in parliament, to get an office for himself, or friends, or both ; and this is the great source from which flows its great venality and corruption.

Mr. Wilson.   I am for striking out the words moved for.   Strong reasons must induce me to disqualify a good man from office.   If you do, you give an opportunity to the dependent or avaricious man to fill it up, for to them offices are objects of desire.   If we admit there may be cabal and intrigue between the executive and legislative bodies, the exclusion of one year will not prevent the effects of it.   But we ought to hold forth every honorable inducement for men of abilities to enter the service of the public.   This is truly a republican principle.   Shall talents, which entitle a man to public reward, operate as a punishment?   While a member of the legislature, he ought to be excluded from any other office, but no longer.   Suppose a war breaks out, and a number of your best military characters are members ; must we lose the benefit of their services?   Had this been the case in the beginning of the war, what would have been our situation? and what has happened may happen again.

Mr. Madison.   Some gentlemen give too much weight, and others too little, to this subject.   If you have no exclusive clause, there may be danger of creating offices, or augmenting the stipends of those already created, in order to gratify some members, if they were not excluded.   Such an instance has fallen within my own observation.   I am therefore of opinion, that no office ought to be open to a member, which may be created or augmented while he is in the legislature.

Mr. Mason.   It seems as if it was taken for granted, that all offices will be filled by the executive, while I think many will remain in the gift of the legislature.

In either case, it is necessary to shut the door against corruption If otherwise, they may make or multiply offices in order to fill them.   Are gentlemen in earnest, when they suppose that this exclusion will prevent the first characters from coming forward? Are we not struck at seeing the luxury and venality which has already crept in among us? If not checked, we shall have ambassadors to every petty state in Europe ; the little republic of St. Marino not excepted.   We must in the present system remove the temptation.   I admire many parts of the British constitution and government, but I detest their corruption.   Why has the power of the crown so remarkably increased the last century? A stranger, by reading their laws, would suppose it considerably diminished ; and yet, by the sole power of appointing the increased officers of government, corruption pervades every town and village in the kingdom.   If such a restriction should abridge the right of election, it is still necessary, as it will prevent the people from ruining themselves ; and will not the same causes here produce the same effects? I consider this clause as the corner-stone on which our liberties depend ; and if we strike it out we are erecting a fabric for our destruction.

Mr. Gorham.   The corruption of the English government cannot be applied to America.   This evil exists there in the venality of their boroughs : but even this corruption has its advantage, as it gives stability to their government.   We do not know what the effect would be, if members of Parliament were excluded from offices.   The great bulwark of our liberty is the frequency of elections, and their great danger is the septennial parliaments.

Mr. Hamilton.   In all general questions which

become the subjects of discussion, there are always some truths mixed with falsehoods. I confess, there is danger where men are capable of holding two offices. Take mankind in general, they are vicious, — their passions may be operated upon. We have been taught to reprobate the danger of influence in the British government, without duly reflecting how far it was necessary to support a good government. We have taken up many ideas upon trust, and at last, pleased with our own opinions, establish them as undoubted truths. Hume's opinion of the British constitution confirms the remark, that there is always a body of firm patriots, who often shake a corrupt administration. Take mankind as they are, and what are they governed by? Their passions. There may be in every government a few choice spirits, who may act from more worthy motives. One great error is, that we suppose mankind more honest than they are. Our prevailing passions are ambition and interest; and it will ever be the duty of a wise government to avail itself of those passions, in order to make them subservient to the public good; for these ever induce us to action. Perhaps a few men in a State, may, from patriotic motives, or to display their talents, or to reap the advantage of public applause, step forward; but, if we adopt the clause, we destroy the motive. I am, therefore, against all exclusions and refinements, except only in this case; that, when a member takes his seat, he should vacate every other office. It is difficult to put any exclusive regulation into effect. We must, in some degree, submit to the inconvenience.

The question was then put for striking out; four ayes; four noes; three States divided. New York of the number.

Adjourned till to-morrow morning.

SATURDAY, JUNE 23D, 1787.

Met pursuant to adjournment. Present, eleven States.

Mr. Gorham. I move, that the question which was yesterday proposed on the clause, "to be paid out of the national treasury," be now put.

Question put; five ayes; five noes; one State divided. So the clause was lost.

Mr. Pinckney moved, that that part of the clause which disqualifies a person from holding an office in the State, be expunged, because the first and best characters in a State may thereby be deprived of a seat in the national council.

Mr. Wilson. I perceive, that some gentlemen are of opinion to give a bias in favor of State governments. This question ought to stand on the same footing.

Mr. Sherman. By the conduct of some gentlemen, we are erecting a kingdom to act against itself. The legislature ought to be free and unbiassed.

Question put to strike out the words moved for, and carried; eight ayes, three noes.

Mr. Madison then moved, that, after the word "established," be added, "or the emoluments whereof shall have been augmented by the legislature of the United States, during the time they were members thereof, and for one year thereafter."

Mr. Butler. The proposed amendment does not go far enough. How easily may this be evaded. What was the conduct of George the Second to support the pragmatic sanction? To some of the opposers he gave pensions; others offices, and some, to put them out of the House of Commons, he made Lords.

15

The great Montesquieu says, it is unwise to intrust persons with power, which, by being abused, operates to the advantage of those intrusted with it.

Governor Rutledge was against the proposed amendment. No person ought to come to the legislature with an eye to his own emolument in any shape.

Mr. Mason. I differ from my colleague in his proposed amendment. Let me state the practice in the State where we came from. There, all officers are appointed by the legislature. Need I add, that many of their appointments are most shameful. Nor will the check proposed by this amendment be sufficient. It will soon cease to be any check at all. It is asserted, that it will be very difficult to find men sufficiently qualified as legislators without the inducement of emolument. I do believe, that men of genius will be deterred, unless possessed of great virtues. We may well dispense with the first characters when destitute of virtue. I should wish them never to come forward. But if we do not provide against corruption, our government will soon be at an end ; nor would I wish to put a man of virtue in the way of temptation. Evasions and caballing would evade the amendment. Nor would the danger be less, if the executive has the appointment of officers. The first three or four years we might go on well enough ; but what would be the case afterwards ? I will add, that such a government ought to be refused by the people ; and it will be refused.

Mr. Madison. My wish is, that the national legislature be as uncorrupt as possible. I believe all public bodies are inclined, from various motives, to support its members ; but it is not always done from the base motives of venality. Friendship, and a knowledge of the abilities of those with whom they associate, may produce it. If you bar the door against such attachments, you deprive the government of its greatest strength and support. Can you always rely on the patriotism of the members? If this be the only inducement, you will find a great indifferency in filling your legislative body. If we expect to call forth useful characters, we must hold out allurements; nor can any great inconveniency arise from such inducements. The legislative body must be the road to public honor; and the advantage will be greater to adopt my motion, than any possible inconvenience.

Mr. King. The intimate association of offices will produce a vigorous support to your government. To check it would produce no good consequences. Suppose connexions are formed? Do they not all tend to strengthen the government under which they are formed? Let, therefore, preferment be open to all men. We refine otherwise too much; nor is it possible we can eradicate the evil.

Mr. Wilson. I hope the amendment will be adopted. By the last vote it appears, that the convention have no apprehension of danger of State appointments. It is equally imaginary to apprehend any from the national government. That such officers will have influence in the legislature, I readily admit; but I would not therefore exclude them. If any ill effects were to result from it, the bargain can as well be made with the legislature as with the executive. We ought not to shut the door of promotion against the great characters in the public councils, from being rewarded by being promoted. If otherwise, will not these gentlemen be put in the legislatures to prevent them from holding offices, by those who wish to enjoy them themselves?

Mr. Sherman. If we agree to this amendment, our good intentions may be prostrated by changing offices to avoid or evade the rule.

Mr. Gerry. This amendment is of great weight, and its consequences ought to be well considered. At the beginning of the war we possessed more than Roman virtue. It appears to me it is now the reverse. We have more land and stock-jobbers than any place on earth. It appears to me, that we have constantly endeavoured to keep distinct the three great branches of government; but, if we agree to this motion, it must be destroyed, by admitting the legislators to share in the executive, or to be too much influenced by the executive, in looking up to him for offices.

Mr. Madison. This question is certainly of much moment. There are great advantages in appointing such persons as are known. The choice otherwise will be chance. How will it operate on the members themselves? Will it not be an objection to become members when they are to be excluded from office? For these reasons I am for the amendment.

Mr. Butler. These reasons have no force. Characters fit for offices will always be known.

Mr. Mason. It is said, it is necessary to open the door to induce gentlemen to come into the legislature. This door is open, but not immediately. A seat in the House will be the field to exert talents, and when to a good purpose, they will in due time be rewarded.

Mr. Jenifer. Our senators are appointed for five years, and they can hold no other office. This circumstance gives them the greatest confidence of the people.

The question was put on Mr. Madison's amendment, and lost; eight noes; two ayes; one State divided.

Question on the clause as amended before. Carried. Eight ayes, two noes, and one State divided.

The question was next on the latter part of the clause.

Mr. Mason. We must retain this clause; otherwise evasions may be made. The legislature may admit of resignations, and thus make members eligible; places may be promised at the close of their duration, and that a dependency may be made.

Mr. Gerry. And this actually has been the case in Congress; a member resigned to obtain an appointment, and had it failed he would have resumed it.

Mr. Hamilton. The clause may be evaded many ways. Offices may be held by proxy; they may be procured by friends, &c.

Mr. Rutledge. I admit, in some cases, it may be evaded; but this is no argument against shutting the door as close as possible.

The question was then put on this clause, to wit, "and for the space of one year after its expiration," and negatived.

Adjourned to Monday morning.

MONDAY, JUNE 25th, 1787.

Met pursuant to adjournment. Present, eleven States.

Mr. C. Pinckney. On the question upon the second branch of the general legislature, as reported by the committee in the fourth resolve, now under consideration, it will be necessary to inquire into the true situation of the people of this country. Without this, we can form no adequate idea what kind of government will secure their rights and liberties. There is more equality of rank and fortune in America, than in any other country under the sun; and this is likely to continue as long as the unappropriated western lands remain unsettled. They are equal in rights, nor is extreme of poverty to be seen in any part of the Union. If we are thus singularly situated, both as to fortune and rights, it evidently follows, that we cannot draw any useful lessons from the examples of any of the European states or kingdoms; much less can Great Britain afford us any striking institution, which can be adapted to our own situation, unless we indeed intend to establish an hereditary executive, or one for life. Great Britain drew its first rude institutions from the forests of Germany, and with it that of its nobility. These having originally in their hands the property of the state, the crown of Great Britain was obliged to yield to the claims of power, which those large possessions enabled them to assert. The commons were then too contemptible to form part of the national councils. Many parliaments were held, without their being represented; until, in process of time, under the protection of the crown, and forming distinct communities, they obtained some weight in the British government. From such discordant materials, brought casually together, those admirable checks and balances, now so much the boast of the British constitution, took their rise. But will we be able to copy from this original? I do not suppose, that in the confederation there are one hundred gentlemen of sufficient fortunes to establish a nobility; and the equality of others, as to rank, would never admit of the distinctions of nobility. I lay it therefore down as a settled principle, that equality of condition is a leading axiom in our government. It may be said, we must necessarily establish checks, lest one rank of people should usurp the rights of another. Commerce can never interfere with the government, nor give a complexion to its councils. Can we copy from Greece or Rome? Have we their nobles or patricians? With them, offices were open to few. The different ranks in the community formed opposite interests, and produced unceasing struggles and disputes. Can this apply equally to the free yeomanry of America? We surely differ from the whole. Our situation is unexampled; and it is in our power, on different grounds, to secure civil and religious liberty; and when we secure these, we secure every thing that is necessary to establish happiness. We cannot pretend to rival the European nations in their grandeur or power; nor is the situation of any two nations so exactly alike, as that one can adopt the regulations or government of the other. If we have any distinctions, they may be divided into three classes.

1. Professional men.
2. Commercial men.
3. The landed interest.

The latter is the governing power of America, and the other two must ever be dependent on them. Will a national government suit them? No. The three orders have necessarily a mixed interest; and, in that view, I repeat it again, the United States of America compose, in fact, but one order. The clergy and nobility of Great Britain can never be adopted by us. Our government must be made suitable to the people, and we are perhaps the only people in the world who ever had sense enough to appoint delegates to establish a general government. I believe, that the propositions from Virginia, with some amendments, will satisfy the people. But a general government must not be made dependent on the State governments.

The United States include a territory of about one thousand five hundred miles in length, and in breadth about four hundred; the whole of which is divided into States and districts. While we were dependent on the crown of Great Britain, it was in contemplation to have formed the whole into one; but it was found impracticable. No legislature could make good laws for the whole, nor can it now be done. It would necessarily place the power in the hands of the few, nearest the seat of government. State governments must therefore remain, if you mean to prevent confusion. The general negative powers will support the general government. Upon these considerations, I am led to form the second branch differently from the report. Their powers are important, and the number not too large, upon the principle of proportion. I have considered the subject with great attention; and I propose this plan, (reads it,) and if no better plan is proposed, I will then move its adoption.

Mr. Randolph moved, that the fourth resolve be divided, in the same manner as the third resolve.

Mr. Gorham moved the question on the first resolve. Sixteen members from one State will certainly have greater weight than the same number of members from different States. We must, therefore, depart from this rule of apportionment, in some shape or other; perhaps on the plan Mr. Pinckney has suggested.

Mr. Read. Some gentlemen argue, that the representation must be determined according to the weight of each State; that we have heretofore been partners in trade, in which we all put in our respective proportions of stock; that the articles of our copartnership were drawn in forming the confederation; and that, before we make a new copartnership, we must first settle the old business. But, to drop the allusion, we find that the great States have appropriated to themselves the common lands in their respective States. These lands having been forfeited, as heretofore belonging to the King, ought to be applied to the discharge of our public debts. Let this still be done; and then, if you please, proportion the representation, and we shall not be jealous of one another. A jealousy in a great measure owing to the public property being appropriated by individual States; and which, as it has been gained by the united power of the confederation, ought to be appropriated to the discharge of the public debts.

Mr. Gorham. This motion has been agitated often in Congress; and it was owing to the want of power, rather than inclination, that it was not justly settled. Great surrenders have been made by the great States, for the benefit of the confederation.

Mr. Wilson. The question now before us is, whether the second branch of the general legislature shall or shall not be appointed by the State legislatures. In every point of view it is an important question. The magnitude of the object is indeed embarrassing. The great system of Henry the Fourth, of France, aided by the greatest statesmen, is small when compared to the fabric we are now about to erect. In laying the stone amiss, we may injure the superstructure; and what will be the consequence, if the corner-stone should be loosely placed? It is improper, that the State legislatures should have the power contemplated to be given them. A citizen of America may be considered in two points of view; as a citizen of the general government, and as a citizen of the partic ular State in which he may reside. We ought to consider in what character he acts in forming a general government. I am both a citizen of Pennsylvania and of the United States. I must, therefore, lay aside my State connexions, and act for the general good of the whole. We must forget our local habits and attachments. The general government should not depend on the State governments. This ought to be a leading distinction between the one and the other; nor ought the general government to be composed of an assemblage of different State governments. We have unanimously agreed to establish a general government; that the powers of peace, war, treaties, coinage, and regulating of commerce, ought to reside in that government. And if we reason in this manner, we shall soon see the impropriety of admitting the interference of State governments into the general government. Equality of representation can not be established, if the second branch is elected by the State legislatures. When we are laying the foundation of a building, which is to last for ages, and in which millions are interested, it ought to be well laid. If the national government does not act upon State prejudices, State distinctions will be lost. I therefore move, "That the second branch of the legislature of the national government be elected by electors chosen by the people of the United States."

Judge Ellsworth. I think the second branch of the general legislature ought to be elected agreeably to the report. The other way, it is said, will be more the choice of the people. The one mode is as much so as the other. No doubt every citizen of every State is interested in the State governments; and, elect him in whatever manner you please, whenever he takes a seat in the general government, it will prevail in some shape or other. The State legislatures are more competent to make a judicious choice, than the people at large. Instability pervades their choice. In the second branch of the general government we want wisdom and firmness. As to balances, where nothing can be balanced, it is a perfect utopian scheme. But still greater advantages will result in having a second branch endowed with the qualifications I have mentioned. Their weight and wisdom may check the inconsiderate and hasty proceedings of the first branch.

I cannot see the force of the reasoning in attempting to detach the State governments from the general government. In that case, without a standing army, you cannot support the general government, but on the pillars of the State governments. Are the larger States now more energetic than the smaller? Massachusetts cannot support a government at the distance of one hundred miles from her capital, without an army; and how long Virginia and Pennsylvania will support their governments it is difficult to say. Shall we proceed like unskilful workmen, and make use of timber, which is too weak to build a first-rate ship? We know that the people of the States are strongly attached to their own constitutions. If you hold up a system of general government, destructive of their constitutional rights, they will oppose it. Some are of opinion, that if we cannot form a general government so as to destroy State governments, we ought at least to balance the one against the other. On the contrary, the only chance we have to support a general government is to graft it on the State governments. I want to proceed on this ground, as the safest, and I believe no other plan is practicable. In this way, and in this way only, can we rely on the confidence and support of the people.

Dr. Johnson. The State governments must be preserved; but this motion leaves them at the will and pleasure of the general government.

Mr. Madison. I find great differences of opinion in this convention on the clause now under consideration. Let us postpone it in order to take up the eighth resolve, that we may previously determine the mode of representation.

Mr. Mason. All agree that a more efficient government is necessary. It is equally necessary to preserve the State governments, as they ought to have the means of self-defence. On the motion of Mr. Wilson, the only means they ought to have would be destroyed.

The question was put for postponing, in order to take into consideration the eighth resolve, and lost; seven noes; four ayes.

Question on the first clause in the fourth resolve; nine States for; two against it.

The age of the senators (thirty years) agreed to.

Mr. Gorham proposed, that the senators be classed, and to remain four years in office; otherwise great inconveniences may arise, if a dissolution should take place at once.

Governor Randolph. This body must act with firmness. They may possibly always sit, — perhaps to aid the executive. The State governments will always attempt to counteract the general government. They ought to go out in classes; therefore I move, " That they go out of office in fixed proportions of time," instead of the words, " seven years."

Mr. Read moved (though not seconded), that they ought to continue in office during good behaviour.

Mr. Williamson moved, that they remain in office for six years.

Mr. Pinckney. I am for four years. Longer time would give them too great attachment to the States, where the general government may reside. They may be induced, from the proposed length of time, to sell their estates, and become inhabitants near the seat of government.

Mr. Madison. We are proceeding in the same manner that was done when the confederation was first formed. Its original draft was excellent, but in its progress and completion it became so insufficient as to give rise to the present convention. By the vote already taken, will not the temper of the State legislatures transfuse itself into the Senate? Do we create a free government?

Question on Governor Randolph's motion; seven ayes; three noes; one divided.

Motion to fix the term of service at six years; five ayes; five noes; one divided.

Do. for five years; five ayes; five noes; one divided.

The question for four years was not put; and the convention adjourned till to-morrow morning.

TUESDAY, JUNE 26th, 1787.

Met pursuant to adjournment. Present, eleven States.

Mr. Gorham. My motion for four years' continuance, was not put yesterday. I am still of opinion, that classes will be necessary, but I would alter the time. I therefore move, that the senators be elected for six years, and that the rotation be triennial.

Mr. Pinckney. I oppose the time, because of too

long a continuance. The members will by this means be too long separated from their constituents, and will imbibe attachments different from that of the State; nor is there any danger that members, by a shorter duration of office, will not support the interest of the Union, or that the States will oppose the general interest. The State of South Carolina was never opposed in principle to Congress, nor thwarted their views in any case, except in the requisition of money, and then only for want of power to comply; for it was found there was not money enough in the State to pay their requisition.

Mr. Read moved, that the term of "nine years" be inserted in triennial rotation.

Mr. Madison. We are now to determine, whether the republican form shall be the basis of our government. I admit, there is weight in the objection of the gentleman from South Carolina; but no plan can steer clear of objections. That great powers are to be given, there is no doubt; and that those powers may be abused is equally true. It is also probable, that members may lose their attachments to the States which sent them. Yet, the first branch will control them in many of their abuses. But we are now forming a body on whose wisdom we mean to rely, and their permanency in office secures a proper field in which they may exert their firmness and knowledge. Democratic communities may be unsteady, and be led to action by the impulse of the moment. Like individuals, they may be sensible of their own weakness, and may desire the counsels and checks of friends to guard them against the turbulency and weakness of unruly passions. Such are the various pursuits of this life, that, in all civilized countries, the interest of a community will be divided. There will be debtors and creditors, and an unequal possession of property, and hence arise different views and different objects in government. This, indeed, is the ground-work of aristocracy ; and we find it blended in every government, both ancient and modern. Even where titles have survived property, we discover the noble beggar, haughty and assuming.

The man who is possessed of wealth, who lolls on his sofa or rolls in his carriage, cannot judge of the wants or feelings of the day laborer. The government we mean to erect is intended to last for ages. The landed interest, at present, is prevalent ; but, in process of time, when we approximate to the states and kingdoms of Europe ; when the number of landholders shall be comparatively small, through the various means of trade and manufactures, will not the landed interest be overbalanced in future elections, and unless wisely provided against, what will become of your government ? In England, at this day, if elections were open to all classes of people, the property of the landed proprietors would be insecure. An agrarian law would soon take place. If these observations be just, our government ought to secure the permanent interests of the country against innovation. Landholders ought to have a share in the government, to support these invaluable interests, and to balance and check the other. They ought to be so constituted as to protect the minority of the opulent against the majority. The Senate, therefore, ought to be this body ; and to answer these purposes, they ought to have permanency and stability. Various have been the propositions ; but my opinion is, the longer they continue in office, the better will these views be answered.

Mr. Sherman. The two objects of this body are permanency and safety to those who are to be governed. A bad government is the worse for being long. Frequent elections give security and even permanency. In Connecticut, we have existed one hundred and thirty-two years under an annual government ; and, as long as a man behaves himself well, he is never turned out of office. Four years to the Senate is quite sufficient, when you add to it the rotation proposed.

Mr. Hamilton. This question has already been considered in several points of view. We are now forming a republican government. Real liberty is neither found in despotism or the extremes of democracy, but in moderate governments.

Those who mean to form a solid republican government, ought to proceed to the confines of another government. As long as offices are open to all men, and no constitutional rank is established, it is pure republicanism. But, if we incline too much to democracy, we shall soon shoot into a monarchy. The difference of property is already great amongst us. Commerce and industry will still increase the disparity. Your government must meet this state of things, or combinations will, in process of time, undermine your system. What was the tribunitial power of Rome ? It was instituted by the plebeians as a guard against the patricians. But was this a sufficient check ? No. The only distinction which remained at Rome, was, at last, between the rich and the poor. The gentleman from Connecticut forgets, that the democratic body is already secure in a representation. As to Connecticut, what were the little objects of their government before the Revolution ? Colonial concerns merely. They ought now to act on a more extended scale; and dare they do this? Dare they collect the taxes and requisitions of Congress? Such a government may do well, if they do not tax; and this is precisely their situation.

Mr. Gerry. It appears to me, that the American people have the greatest aversion to monarchy; and the nearer our government approaches to it, the less chance have we for their approbation. Can gentlemen suppose, that the reported system can be approved of by them? Demagogues are the great pests of our government, and have occasioned most of our distresses. If four years are insufficient, a future convention may lengthen the time.

Mr. Wilson. The motion is now for nine years, and a triennial rotation. Every nation attends to its foreign intercourse, to support its commerce, to prevent foreign contempt, and to make war and peace. Our Senate will be possessed of these powers, and therefore ought to be dignified and permanent. What is the reason, that Great Britain does not enter into a commercial treaty with us? Because Congress have not the power to enforce its observance. But give them those powers, and give them the stability proposed by the motion, and they will have more permanency than a monarchical government. The great objection of many is, that this duration would give birth to views inconsistent with the interests of the Union. This can have no weight, if the triennial rotation is adopted; and this plan may possibly tend to conciliate the minds of the members of the convention on this subject, which have varied more than on any other question.

16*

The question was then put on Mr. Read's motion, and lost.   Eight noes, three ayes.

The question on five years, and a biennial rotation, was carried.   Seven ayes, four noes.   New York in the minority.

Mr. Pinckney. I move, that the clause for granting stipends be stricken out.

Question put.   Five ayes, six noes.

On the amendment to the question, "to receive a compensation."   Ten ayes, one no.

Judge Ellsworth. I move, that the words, "out of the national treasury," be stricken out, and the words, "the respective State legislatures," be inserted.

If you ask the States what is reasonable, they will comply ; but if you ask of them more than is necessary to form a good government, they will grant you nothing.

Captain Dayton. The members should be paid from the general treasury, to make them independent.

The question was put on the amendment, and lost. Five ayes, six noes.

Mr. Mason. I make no motion, but throw out for the consideration of the convention, whether a person in the second branch ought not to be qualified as to property.

The question was then put on the clause, and lost. Five ayes, six noes.

It was moved to strike out the clause, "to be ineligible to any State office."

Mr. Madison. Congress heretofore depended on State interests.   We are now going to pursue the same plan.

Mr. Wilson. Congress has been ill managed, because particular States controlled the Union.   In this convention, if a proposal is made promising independency to the general government, before we have done with it, it is so modified and changed as to amount to nothing. In the present case, the States may say, although I appoint you for six years, yet, if you are against the State, your table will be unprovided. Is this the way you are to erect an independent government?

Mr. Butler. This second branch I consider as the aristocratic part of our government; and they must be controlled by the States, or they will be too independent.

Mr. Pinckney. The States and general government must stand together. On this plan have I acted throughout the whole of this business. I am therefore for expunging the clause. Suppose a member of this House was qualified to be a State judge, must the State be prevented from making the appointment?

Question put for striking out. Eight ayes, three noes.

The fifth resolve, "that each House have the right of originating bills," was taken into consideration, and agreed to.

Adjourned till to-morrow morning.

WEDNESDAY, JUNE 27th, 1787.

Met pursuant to adjournment. Present, eleven States.

The sixth resolve was postponed, in order to take into consideration the seventh and eighth resolves. The first clause of the seventh was proposed for consideration, which respected the suffrage of each State in the first branch of the legislature.

[Mr. Martin, the Attorney-General from Maryland,

spoke on this subject upwards of three hours. As his arguments were too diffuse, and in many instances desultory, it was not possible to trace him through the whole, or to methodize his ideas into a systematic or argumentative arrangement. I shall therefore only note such points as I conceive merit most particular notice.]

The question is important, said Mr. Martin, and I have already expressed my sentiments on the subject. My opinion is, that the general government ought to protect and secure the State governments. Others, however, are of a different sentiment, and reverse the principle.

The present reported system is a perfect medley of confederated and national government, without example and without precedent. Many, who wish the general government to protect the State governments, are anxious to have the line of jurisdiction well drawn and defined, so that they may not clash. This suggests the necessity of having this line well detailed. Possibly this may be done. If we do this, the people will be convinced that we mean well to the State governments ; and should there be any defects, they will trust a future convention with the power of making further amendments.

A general government may operate on individuals in cases of general concern, and still be federal. This distinction is with the States, as States, represented by the people of those States. States will take care of their internal police and local concerns. The general government has no interest but the protection of the whole. Every other government must fail. We are proceeding in forming this government, as if there were no State governments at all. The States must approve, or you will have none at all. I have never heard of a confederacy having two legislative branches. Even the celebrated Mr. Adams, who talks so much of checks and balances, does not suppose it necessary in a confederacy. Public and domestic debts are our great distress. The treaty between Virginia and Maryland, about the navigation of the Chesapeake and Potomac, is no infraction of the confederacy. The corner-stone of a federal government, is equality of votes. States may surrender this right; but if they do, their liberties are lost. If I err on this point, it is the error of the head, not of the heart.

The first principle of government is founded on the natural rights of individuals, and in perfect equality. Locke, Vattel, Lord Somers, and Dr. Priestley, all confirm this principle. This principle of equality, when applied to individuals, is lost in some degree, when he becomes a member of a society, to which it is transferred; and this society, by the name of state or kingdom, is, with respect to others, again on a perfect footing of equality, — a right to govern themselves as they please. Nor can any other state, of right, deprive them of this equality. If such a state confederates, it is intended for the good of the whole ; and if it again confederate, those rights must be well guarded. Nor can any state demand a surrender of any of those rights; if it can, equality is already destroyed. We must treat as free States with each other, upon the same terms of equality that men originally formed themselves into societies. Vattel, Rutherford, and Locke, are united in support of the position, that states, as to each other, are in a state of nature.

Thus, said Mr. Martin, have I travelled with the most respectable authorities in support of principles, all tending to prove the equality of independent states. This is equally applicable to the smallest as well as the largest states, on the true principles of reciprocity and political freedom.

Unequal confederacies can never produce good effects. Apply this to the Virginia plan. Out of the number ninety, Virginia has sixteen votes, Massachusetts fourteen, Pennsylvania twelve, — in all, forty-two. Add to this a State having four votes, and it gives a majority in the general legislature. Consequently, a combination of these States will govern the remaining nine or ten States. Where is the safety and independency of those States? Pursue this subject further. The executive is to be appointed by the legislature, and becomes the executive in consequence of this undue influence. And hence flows the appointment of all your officers, civil, military, and judicial. The executive is also to have a negative on all laws. Suppose the possibility of a combination of ten States. He negatives a law; it is totally lost, because those States cannot form two thirds of the legislature. I am willing to give up private interest for the public good ; but I must be satisfied first, that it is the public interest ; and who can decide this point? A majority only of the Union.

The Lacedemonians insisted, in the amphictyonic council, to exclude some of the smaller states from a right to vote, in order that they might tyrannize over them. If the plan now on the table be adopted, three States in the Union have the control, and they may make use of their power when they please.

If there exist no separate interests. there is no danger of an equality of votes ; and, if there be danger, the smaller States cannot yield. If the foundation of the existing confederation is well laid, powers may be added. You may safely add a third story to a house where the foundation is good. Read then the votes and proceedings of Congress on forming the confederation. Virginia only was opposed to the principle of equality. The smaller States yielded rights, not the large States. They gave up their claim to the unappropriated lands with the tenderness of the mother recorded by Solomon; they sacrificed affection to the preservation of others. New Jersey and Maryland rendered more essential services during the war than many of the larger States. The partial representation in Congress is not the cause of its weakness, but the want of power. I would not trust a government organized upon the reported plan, for all the slaves of Carolina or the horses and oxen of Massachusetts. Price says, that laws made by one man, or a set of men, and not by common consent, is slavery. And it is so when applied to States, if you give them an unequal representation. What are called human feelings in this instance, are only the feelings of ambition and the lust of power.

Adjourned till to-morrow morning.

THURSDAY, JUNE 28th, 1787.

Met pursuant to adjournment.

Mr. Martin in continuation.

On federal grounds, it is said, that a minority will govern a majority; but, on the Virginia plan, a minority would tax a majority. In a federal government, a majority of States must, and ought to tax. In the local government of States, counties may be unequal; still numbers, not property, govern. What is the government now forming, over States or per-

sons ? As to the latter, their rights cannot be the object of a general government. These are already
secured by their guardians, the State governments.
The general government is, therefore, intended only to
protect and guard the rights of the States, as States.

This general government, I believe, is the first
upon earth which gives checks against democracies or
aristocracies. The only necessary check in a general
government ought to be a restraint to prevent its ab-
sorbing the powers of the State governments. Representation on federal principles can only flow from
State societies. Representation and taxation are ever
inseparable ; not according to the quantum of property, but the quantum of freedom.

Will the representatives of a State forget State
interests? The mode of election cannot change it.
These prejudices cannot be eradicated. Your general
government cannot be just or equal upon the Virginia
plan, unless you abolish State interests. If this cannot be done, you must go back to principles purely
federal.

On this latter ground, the State legislatures and
their constituents will have no interests to pursue different from the general government, and both will be
interested to support each other. Under these ideas
can it be expected, that the people can approve the
Virginia plan ? But it is said, the people, not the State
legislatures, will be called upon for approbation ; with
an evident design to separate the interest of the governors from the governed. What must be the consequence? Anarchy and confusion. We lose the idea
of the powers with which we are intrusted. The
legislatures must approve. By them it must, on your
own plan, be laid before the people. How will such

a government, over so many great States, operate ?
Wherever new settlements have been formed in large
States, they immediately want to shake off their independency.   Why ? Because the government is too
remote for their good.   The people want it nearer
home.

The basis of all ancient and modern confederacies
is the freedom and the independency of the states
composing it.   The states forming the amphictyonic
council were equal, though Lacedemon, one of the
greatest states, attempted the exclusion of three of
the lesser states from this right.   The plan reported,
it is true, only intends to diminish those rights, not to
annihilate them.   It was the ambition and power of
the great Grecian states which at last ruined this respectable council.   The states, as societies, are ever
respectful.   Has Holland or Switzerland ever complained of the equality of the states which compose
their respective confederacies ? Bern and Zurich are
larger than the remaining eleven cantons ; so of many
of the states of Germany ; and yet, their governments
are not complained of.   Bern alone might usurp the
whole power of the Helvetic confederacy, but she is
contented still with being equal.

The admission of the larger States into the confederation, on the principles of equality, is dangerous.
But, on the Virginia system, it is ruinous and destructive.   Still it is the true interest of all the States to
confederate.   It is their joint efforts which must protect and secure us from foreign danger, and give us
peace and harmony at home.

[Here Mr. Martin entered into a detail of the comparative powers of each State, and stated their probable weakness and strength.]

17

At the beginning of our troubles with Great Britain, the smaller States were attempted to be cajoled to submit to the views of that nation, lest the larger States should usurp their rights. We then answered them, Your present plan is slavery, which, on the remote prospect of a distant evil, we will not submit to.

I would rather confederate with any single State, than submit to the Virginia plan. But we are already confederated, and no power on earth can dissolve it but by the consent of all the contracting powers; and four States, on this floor, have already declared their opposition to annihilate it. Is the old confederation dissolved, because some of the States wish a new confederation?

Mr. Lansing. I move, that the word "not" be struck out of the resolve, and then the question will stand on its proper ground; and the resolution will read thus: "That the representation of the first branch be according to the articles of the confederation;" and the sense of the convention on this point will determine the question of a federal or national government.

Mr. Madison. I am against the motion. I confess the necessity of harmonizing, and if it could be shown, that the system is unjust or unsafe, I would be against it. There has been much fallacy in the arguments advanced by the gentleman from Maryland. He has, without adverting to many manifest distinctions, considered confederacies and treaties as standing on the same basis. In the one, the powers act collectively, in the other individually. Suppose, for example, that France, Spain, and some of the smaller states in Europe, should treat on war or peace, or on any other general concern, it would be done on principles of equality; but, if they were to form a plan of general govern-

ment, would they give, or are the greater states obliged to give to the lesser, the same and equal legislative powers? Surely not. They might differ on
this point, but no one can say, that the large states
were wrong in refusing this concession. Nor can the
gentleman's reasoning apply to the present powers of
Congress; for they may, and do, in some cases, affect
property, and, in case of war, the lives of the citizens.
Can any of the lesser States be endangered by an adequate representation? Where is the probability of a
combination? What the inducements? Where is the
similarity of customs, manners, or religion? If there
possibly can be a diversity of interest, it is the case
of the three large States. Their situation is remote,
their trade different. The staple of Massachusetts is
fish, and the carrying trade; of Pennsylvania, wheat
and flour; of Virginia, tobacco. Can States thus
situated in trade, ever form such a combination? Do
we find those combinations in the larger counties in
the different State governments to produce rivalships?
Does not the history of the nations of the earth
verify it? Rome rivalled Carthage, and could not
be satisfied before she was destroyed. The houses
of Austria and Bourbon acted on the same view;
and the wars of France and England have been
waged through rivalship; and let me add, that we,
in a great measure, owe our independency to those
national contending passions. France, through this
motive, joined us. She might, perhaps, with less
expense, have induced England to divide America
between them. In Greece the contention was ever
between the larger states. Sparta against Athens;
and these again, occasionally, against Thebes, were
ready to devour each other. Germany presents the

same prospect, — Prussia against Austria. Do the greater provinces in Holland endanger the liberties of the lesser? And let me remark, that the weaker you make your confederation, the greater the danger to the lesser States. They can only be protected by a strong federal government. Those gentlemen who oppose the Virginia plan do not sufficiently analyze the subject. Their remarks, in general, are vague and inconclusive.

Captain Dayton. On the discussion of this question the fate of the State governments depend.

Mr. Williamson. If any argument will admit of demonstration, it is that which declares, that all men have an equal right in society. Against this position, I have heard, as yet, no argument, and I could wish to hear what could be said against it. What is tyranny? Representatives of representatives, if you give them the power of taxation. From equals take equals, and the remainder is equal. What process is to annihilate smaller States, I know not. But I know it must be tyranny, if the smaller States can tax the greater, in order to ease themselves. A general government cannot exercise direct taxation. Money must be raised by duties and imposts, &c., and this will operate equally. It is impossible to tax according to numbers. Can a man over the mountains, where produce is a drug, pay equal with one near the shore?

Mr. Wilson. I should be glad to hear the gentleman from Maryland explain himself upon the remark of Old Sarum, when compared with the city of London. This he has allowed to be an unjust proportion; as in the one place one man sends two members, and in the other, one million are represented by four members. I would be glad to hear how he applies this to the larger and smaller States in America ; and whether the borough, as a borough, is represented, or the people of the borough.

Mr. Martin rose to explain. Individuals, as composing a part of the whole of one consolidated government, are there represented.

The further consideration of the question was postponed.

Mr. Sherman. In society, the poor are equal to the rich in voting, although one pays more than the other. This arises from an equal distribution of liberty amongst all ranks ; and it is, on the same grounds, secured to the States in the confederation ; for this would not even trust the important powers to a majority of the States. Congress has too many checks, and its powers are too limited. A gentleman from New York thinks a limited monarchy the best government, and no State distinctions. The plan now before us gives the power to four States to govern nine States. As they will have the purse, they may raise troops, and can also make a king when they please.

Mr. Madison. There is danger in the idea of the gentleman from Connecticut. Unjust representation will ever produce it. In the United Netherlands, Holland governs the whole, although she has only one vote. The counties in Virginia are exceedingly disproportionate, and yet the smaller have an equal vote with the greater, and no inconvenience arises.

Governor Franklin read some remarks, acknowledging the difficulties of the present subject. Neither ancient nor modern history, said Governor Franklin, can give us light. As a sparrow does not fall without Divine permission, can we suppose that governments can be erected without his will ? We shall, I am

afraid, be disgraced through little party views. I
move, that we have prayers every morning.

Adjourned till to-morrow morning.

FRIDAY, JUNE 29TH, 1787.

Met pursuant to adjournment. Present, eleven
States.

Dr. Johnson. As the debates have hitherto been
managed, they may be spun out to an endless length ;
and as gentlemen argue on different grounds, they are
equally conclusive on the points they advance, but
afford no demonstration either way.   States are political societies.   For whom are we to form a government ? for the people of America, or for those societies?
Undoubtedly for the latter.   They must, therefore,
have a voice in the second branch of the general government, if you mean to preserve their existence.   The
people already compose the first branch.   This mixture is proper and necessary.   For we cannot form a
general government on any other ground.

Mr. Gorham.   I perceive no difficulty in supposing
a union of interest in the different States.   Massachusetts formerly consisted of three distinct provinces.
They have been united into one, and we do not find
the least trace of party distinctions arising from their
former separation.   Thus it is, that the interest of the
smaller States will unite in a general government.   It
is thus they will be supported.   Jersey, in particular,
situated between Philadelphia and New York, can
never become a commercial State.   It would be her
interest to be divided, and part annexed to New York
and part to Pennsylvania ; or otherwise the whole to
the general government.   Massachusetts cannot long
remain a large State.   The Province of Maine must

soon become independent of her.   Pennsylvania can
never become a dangerous State ; her western country
must, at some period, become separated from her, and
consequently her power will be diminished.   If some
States will not confederate on a new plan, I will remain here, if only one State will consent to confederate with us.

Judge Ellsworth.   I do not despair but that we
shall be so fortunate as to devise and adopt some good
plan of government.

Judge Read.   I would have no objection, if the
government was more national ; but the proposed plan
is so great a mixture of both, that it is best to drop it
altogether.   A State government is incompatible with
a general government.   If it was more national, I
would be for a representation proportionate to population.   The plan of the gentleman from New York is
certainly the best ; but the great evil is, the unjust appropriation of the public lands.   If there was but one
national government, we would be all equally interested.

Mr. Madison.   Some gentlemen are afraid, that
the plan is not sufficiently national, while others apprehend, that it is too much so.   If this point of representation was once well fixed, we would come nearer
to one another in sentiment.   The necessity would
then be discovered of circumscribing more effectually
the State governments, and enlarging the bounds of
the general government.   Some contend, that States
are sovereign, when, in fact, they are only political
societies.   There is a gradation of power in all societies, from the lowest corporation to the highes sovereign.   The States never possessed the essential rights
of sovereignty.   These were always vested in Con-

gress. Their voting as States, in Congress, is no evidence of sovereignty. The State of Maryland voted
by counties; did this make the counties sovereign?
The States, at present, are only great corporations,
having the power of making by-laws, and these are
effectual only if they are not contradictory to the gen·
eral confederation. The States ought to be placed
under the control of the general government; at least
as much so as they formerly were under the King and
British Parliament. The arguments, I observe, have
taken a different turn, and I hope may tend to convince all of the necessity of a strong, energetic government, which would equally tend to give energy to,
and protect the State governments. What was the
origin of the military establishments of Europe? It
was the jealousy which one state or kingdom entertained of another. This jealousy was ever productive
of evil. In Rome, the patricians were often obliged
to excite a foreign war, to divert the attention of the
plebeians from encroaching on the senatorial rights.
In England and France, perhaps, this jealousy may
give energy to their governments, and contribute to
their existence. But a state of danger is like a state
of war, and it unites the various parts of the government to exertion. May not our distractions, however,
invite danger from abroad? If the power is not immediately derived from the people, in proportion to
their numbers, we may make a paper confederacy, but
that will be all. We know the effects of the old confederation, and without a general government this will
be like the former.

Mr. Hamilton. The course of my experience in
human affairs, might, perhaps, restrain me from saying
much on this subject. I shall, however, give birth to

some of the observations I have made during the course of this debate. The gentleman from Maryland has been at great pains to establish positions which are not denied. Many of them, as drawn from the best writers on government, are become almost self-evident principles. But I doubt the propriety of his application of those principles in the present discussion. He deduces from them the necessity, that states, entering into a confederacy, must retain the equality of votes. This position cannot be correct. Facts plainly contradict it. The Parliament of Great Britain asserted a supremacy over the whole empire, and the celebrated Judge Blackstone labors for the legality of it, although many parts were not represented. This parliamentary power we opposed, as contrary to our colonial rights. With that exception, throughout that whole empire, it is submitted to. May not the smaller and greater States so modify their respective rights, as to establish the general interest of the whole, without adhering to the right of equality? Strict representation is not observed in any of the State governments. The Senate of New York are chosen by persons of certain qualifications, to the exclusion of others. The question, after all, is, is it our interest, in modifying this general government, to sacrifice individual rights to the preservation of the rights of an artificial being, called States? There can be no truer principle than this, that every individual of the community at large has an equal right to the protection of government. If, therefore, three States contain a majority of the inhabitants of America, ought they to be governed by a minority? Would the inhabitants of the great States ever submit to this? If the smaller States maintain this principle, through a love of power, will not the larger, from the same motives, be equally tenacious to preserve their power? They are to surrender their rights, for what? For the preservation of an artificial being. We propose a free government. Can it be so, if partial distinctions are maintained? I agree with the gentleman from Delaware, that, if the State governments are to act in the general government, it affords the strongest reason for exclusion. In the State of New York, five counties form a majority of representatives, and yet the government is in no danger, because the laws have a general operation. The small States exaggerate their danger, and on this ground contend for an undue proportion of power. But their danger is increased, if the larger States will not submit to it. Where will they form new alliances for their support? Will they do this with foreign powers? Foreigners are jealous of our increasing greatness, and would rejoice in our distractions. Those who have had opportunities of conversing with foreigners respecting sovereigns in Europe, have discovered in them an anxiety for the preservation of our democratic governments, probably for no other reason but to keep us weak. Unless your government is respectable, foreigners will invade your rights; and to maintain tranquillity, it must be respectable. Even to observe neutrality, you must have a strong government. I confess, our present situation is critical. We have just finished a war, which has established our independency, and loaded us with a heavy debt. We have still every motive to unite for our common defence. Our people are disposed to have a good government, but this disposition may not always prevail. It is difficult to amend confederations; it has been attempted in vain, and it is perhaps a miracle that we are now met. We must, therefore, improve the opportunity, and render the present system as perfect as possible. Their good sense, and above all the necessity of their affairs, will induce the people to adopt it.

Mr. Pierce. The great difficulty in Congress arose from the mode of voting. Members spoke on the floor as State advocates, and were biassed by local advantages. What is federal? No more than a compact between states; and the one heretofore formed is insufficient. We are now met to remedy its defects, and our difficulties are great, but not, I hope, insurmountable. State distinctions must be sacrificed so far as the general government shall render it necessary, — without, however, destroying them altogether. Although I am here as a representative from a small State, I consider myself as a citizen of the United States, whose general interest I will always support.

Mr. Gerry. It appears to me, that the States never were independent; they had only corporate rights. Confederations are a mongrel kind of government, and the world does not afford a precedent to go by. Aristocracy is the worst kind of government, and I would sooner submit to a monarchy. We must have a system that will execute itself.

The question was then put on Mr. Lansing's motion, and lost; four ayes; six noes; one State divided.

Question on the clause; six ayes; four noes; and one State divided.

Judge Ellsworth. I move, that the consideration of the eighth resolve be postponed. Carried; nine ayes; two noes.

I now move the following amendment to the resolve: "that in the second branch each State have an equal vote." I confess, that the effect of this motion is, to make the general government partly federal and partly national. This will secure tranquillity, and still make it efficient ; and it will meet the objections of the larger States. In taxes they will have a proportional weight in the first branch of the general legislature. If the great States refuse this plan, we will be for ever separated. Even in the executive the larger States have ever had great influence. The provinces of Holland ever had it. If all the States are to exist, they must necessarily have an equal vote in the general government. Small communities, when associating with greater, can only be supported by an equality of votes. I have always found in my reading and experience, that in all societies the governors are ever gradually rising into power.

The large States, although they may not have a common interest for combination, yet they may be partially attached to each other for mutual support and advancement. This can be more easily effected than the union of the remaining small States to check it; and ought we not to regard antecedent plighted faith to the confederation already entered into, and by the terms of it declared to be perpetual? And it is not yet obvious to me, that the States will depart from this ground. When in the hour of common danger we united as equals, shall it now be urged by some, that we must depart from this principle when the danger is over? Will the world say that this is just? We then associated as free and independent States, and were well satisfied. To perpetuate that independence, I wish to establish a national legislature, executive, and judiciary, for under these we shall, I doubt not, preserve peace and harmony ; nor should I be surprised (although we made the general government the most perfect in our opinion), that it should hereafter require amendment. But at present this is as far as I possibly can go. If this convention only chalk out lines of a good government we shall do well.

Mr. Baldwin. It appears to be agreed, that the government we should adopt ought to be energetic and formidable ; yet I would guard against the danger of becoming too formidable. The second branch ought not to be elected as the first. Suppose we take the example of the constitution of Massachusetts, as it is commended for its goodness. There the first branch represents the people, and the second its property.

Mr. Madison. I would always exclude inconsistent principles in framing a system of government. The difficulty of getting its defects amended are great and sometimes insurmountable. The Virginia State government was the first which was made, and though its defects are evident to every person, we cannot get it amended. The Dutch have made four several attempts to amend their system without success. The few alterations made in it were by tumult and faction, and for the worse. If there was real danger, I would give the smaller States the defensive weapons. But there is none from that quarter. The great danger to our general government is, the great southern and northern interests of the continent being opposed to each other. Look to the votes in Congress, and most of them stand divided by the geography of the country not according to the size of the States.

Suppose the first branch granted money, may not the second branch, from State views, counteract the first ? In Congress, the single State of Delaware prevented an embargo, at the time that all the other States thought it absolutely necessary for the support of the army.   Other powers, and those very essential, besides the legislative, will be given to the second branch, — such as the negativing all State laws.   I would compromise on this question, if I could do it on correct principles, but otherwise not; if the old fabric of the confederation must be the ground-work of the new, we must fail.

Adjourned till to-morrow morning.

SATURDAY, JUNE 30th, 1787.

Met pursuant to adjournment.   Present, eleven States.

Judge Brearley moved, that the president be directed to write to the executive of New Hampshire, requesting the attendance of its delegates.

Negatived; two ayes; five noes; one State divided.

The discussion of yesterday resumed.

Mr. Wilson.   The question now before us is of so much consequence, that I cannot give it a silent vote.   Gentlemen have said, that, if this amendment is not agreed to, a separation to the north of Pennsylvania may be the consequence.   This neither staggers me in my sentiments or my duty.   If a minority should refuse their assent to the new plan of a general government, and if they will have their own will, and without it, separate the Union, let it be done; but we shall stand supported by stronger and better principles. The opposition to this plan is as twenty-two is to ninety, in the general scale, — not quite a fourth part of the Union.   Shall three fourths of the Union surrender their rights for the support of that artificial being, called State interest?   If we must join issue, I am willing.   I cannot consent that one fourth shall control the power of three fourths.

If the motion is adopted, seven States will control the whole, and the lesser seven compose twenty-four out of ninety. One third must control two thirds; twenty-four overrule sixty-six. For whom do we form a constitution, for men, or for imaginary beings called States, a mere metaphysical distinction? Will a regard to State rights justify the sacrifice of the rights of men? If we proceed on any other foundation than the last, our building will neither be solid nor lasting. Weight and numbers is the only true principle; every other is local, confined, or imaginary. Much has been said of the danger of the three larger States combining together to give rise to monarchy, or an aristocracy. Let the probability of this combination be explained, and it will be found that a rivalship rather than a confederacy will exist among them. Is there a single point in which this interest coincides. Supposing that the executive should be selected from one of the larger States, can the other two be gratified? Will not this be a source of jealousy amongst them, and will they not separately court the interest of the smaller States, to counteract the views of a favorite rival? How can an aristocracy arise from this combination more than amongst the smaller States? On the contrary, the present claims of the smaller States lead directly to the establishment of an aristocracy, which is the government of the few over the many, and the Connecticut proposal removes only a small part of the objection. There are only two kinds of bad governments, — the one which does too much, and therefore oppressive, and the other which does too little, and therefore weak. Congress partakes of the latter, and the motion will leave us in the same situation, and as much fettered as ever we were. The people see its weakness, and would be mortified in seeing our inability to correct it.

The gentleman from Georgia has his doubts how to vote on this question, and wishes some qualification of it to be made. I admit, there ought to be some difference as to the numbers in the second branch ; and, perhaps, there are other distinctions which could, with propriety, be introduced ; such, for example, as the qualifications of the elected, &c. However, if there are leading principles in the system which we adopt, much may be done in the detail. We all aim at giving the general government more energy. The State governments are necessary and valuable. No liberty can be obtained without them. On this question depends the essential rights of the general government and of the people.

Judge Ellsworth. I have the greatest respect for the gentleman who spoke last. I respect his abilities, although I differ from him on many points. He asserts, that the general government must depend on the equal suffrage of the people. But will not this put it in the power of few States to control the rest ? It is a novel thing in politics, that the few control the many. In the British government, the few, as a guard, have an equal share in the government. The House of Lords, although few in number, and sitting in their own right, have an equal share in their legislature. They cannot give away the property of the community, but they can prevent the Commons from being too lavish in their gifts. Where is, or was a confederation ever formed, where equality of voices was not a fundamental principle ? Mankind are apt to go from one extreme to another, and because we have found defects in the confederation, must we therefore pull down the whole fabric, foundation and all, in order to erect a new building totally different from it, without retaining any of its materials? What are its defects? It is said, equality of votes has embarrassed us; but how? Would the real evils of our situation have been cured, had not this been the case? Would the proposed amendment in the Virginia plan, as to representation, have relieved us? I fancy not. Rhode Island has been often quoted as a small State, and by its refusal once defeated the grant of the impost. Whether she was right in so doing is not the question; but was it a federal requisition? And if it was not, she did not, in this instance, defeat a federal measure.

If the larger States seek security, they have it fully in the first branch of the general government. But can we turn the tables, and say that the lesser States are equally secure? In commercial regulations they will unite. If policy should require free ports, they would be found at Boston, Philadelphia, and Alexandria. In the disposition of lucrative offices they would unite. But I ask no surrender of any of the rights of the great States, nor do I plead *duress* in the makers of the old confederation, nor suppose they soothed the danger, in order to resume their rights when the danger was over. No; small States must possess the power of self-defence or be ruined. Will any one say there is no diversity of interests in the States? And if there is, should not those interests be guarded and secured? But if there is none, then the large States have nothing to apprehend from an equality of rights. And let it be remembered, that these remarks are not the result of partial or local views. The State I rep-

18*

resent is respectable, and in importance holds a middle rank.

Mr. Madison. Notwithstanding the admirable and close reasoning of the gentleman who spoke last, I am not yet convinced, that my former remarks are not well founded. I apprehend he is mistaken as to the fact, on which he builds one of his arguments. He supposes, that equality of votes is the principle on which all confederacies are formed. That of Lycia, so justly applauded by the celebrated Montesquieu, was different. He also appeals to our good faith for the observance of the confederacy. We know we have found one inadequate to the purposes for which it was made. Why then adhere to a system which is proved to be so remarkably defective? I have impeached a number of States for the infraction of the confederation, and I have not even spared my own State, nor can I justly spare his. Did not Connecticut refuse her compliance to a federal requisition? Has she paid, for the two last years, any money into the continental treasury? And does this look like government, or the observance of a solemn compact? Experience shows, that the confederation is radically defective; and we must, in a new national government, guard against those defects. Although the large States in the first branch have a weight proportionate to their population, yet, as the smaller States have an equal vote in the second branch, they will be able to control, and leave the larger without any essential benefit. As peculiar powers are intended to be granted to the second branch, such as the negativing State laws, &c., unless the larger States have a proportionate weight in the representation, they cannot be more secure.

Judge Ellsworth. My State has always been

strictly federal; and I can with confidence appeal to your Excellency [the President] for the truth of it, during the war. The muster-rolls will show, that she had more troops in the field than even the State of Virginia. We strained every nerve to raise them, and we neither spared money nor exertions to complete our quotas. This extraordinary exertion has greatly distressed and impoverished us, and it has accumulated our State debts. We feel the effects of it even to this day. But we defy any gentleman to show, that we ever refused a federal requisition. We are constantly exerting ourselves to draw money from the pockets of our citizens, as fast as it comes in; and it is the ardent wish of the State to strengthen the federal government. If she has proved delinquent through inability only, it is not more than others have been, without the same excuse.

Mr. Sherman. I acknowledge there have been failures in complying with the federal requisition. Many States have been defective, and the object of our convention is to amend these defects.

Colonel Davie. I have great objection to the Virginia plan, as to the manner the second branch is to be formed. It is impracticable. The number may, in time, amount to two or three hundred. This body is too large for the purposes for which we intend to constitute it. I shall vote for the amendment. Some intend a compromise. This has been hinted by a member from Pennsylvania; but it still has its difficulties. The members will have their local prejudices. The preservation of the State societies must be the object of the general government. It has been asserted, that we were *one* in war, and *one* in peace. Such we were as States; but every treaty must be the law of the land, as it affects individuals. The formation of the second branch, as it is intended by the motion, is also objectionable. We are going the same round with the old confederation. No plan yet presents sufficient checks to a tumultuary assembly ; and there is none, therefore, which yet satisfies me.

Mr. Wilson. On the present motion, it was not proper to propose another plan. I think the second branch ought not to be numerous. I will propose an expedient. Let there be one member for every one hundred thousand souls, and the smallest States not less than one member each. This would give about twenty-six members. I make this proposal, not because I belong to a large State, but in order to pull down a rotten house, and lay a foundation for a new building. To give additional weight to an old building, is to hasten its ruin.

Governor Franklin. The smaller States, by this motion, would have the power of giving away the money of the greater States. There ought to be some difference between the first and second branches. Many expedients have been proposed, and I am sorry to remark, without effect. A joiner, when he wants to fit two boards, takes off with his plane the uneven parts from each side, and thus they fit. Let us do the same ; we are all met to do something.

I shall propose an expedient. Let the Senate be elected by the States equally ; in all acts of sovereignty and authority, let the votes be equally taken ; the same in the appointment of all officers, and salaries ; but in passing of laws, each State shall have a right of suffrage in proportion to the sums they respectively contribute. Amongst merchants, where a ship has many owners, her destination is determined in that proportion. I have been one of the ministers to France from this country, during the war, and we should have been very glad, if they would have permitted us a vote in the distribution of the money to carry on the war.

Mr. Martin. Mr. Wilson's motion or plan would amount to nearly the same kind of inequality.

Mr. King. The Connecticut motion contains all the vices of the old confederation. It supposes an imaginary evil, — the slavery of State governments. And should this convention adopt the motion, our business here is at an end.

Captain Dayton. Declamation has been substituted for argument. Have gentlemen shown, or must we believe it because it is said, that one of the evils of the old confederation was unequal representation? We, as distinct societies, entered into the compact. Will you now undermine the thirteen pillars that support it?

Mr. Martin. If we cannot confederate on just principles, I will never confederate in any other manner.

Mr. Madison. I will not answer for supporting chimerical objects; but has experience evinced any good in the old confederation? I know it never can answer, and I have therefore made use of bold language against it. I do assert, that a national Senate, elected and paid by the people, will have no more efficiency than Congress; for the States will usurp the general government. I mean, however, to preserve the State rights with the same care as I would trials by jury; and I am willing to go as far as my honorable colleague.

Mr. Bedford. That all the States at present are

equally sovereign and independent, has been asserted from every quarter of this House. Our deliberations here are a confirmation of the position; and I may add to it, that each of them act from interested, and many from ambitious motives. Look at the votes which have been given on the floor of this House, and it will be found that their numbers, wealth, and local views, have actuated their determinations; and that the larger States proceed as if our eyes were already perfectly blinded. Impartiality, with them, is already out of the question. The reported plan is their political creed, and they support it, right or wrong. Even the diminutive State of Georgia has an eye to her future wealth and greatness. South Carolina, puffed up with the possession of her wealth and negroes, and North Carolina, are all, from different views, united with the great States. And these latter, although it is said they can never, from interested views, form a coalition, we find closely united in one scheme of interest and ambition, notwithstanding they endeavour to amuse us with the purity of their principles, and the rectitude of their intentions, in asserting, that the general government must be drawn from an equal representation of the people. Pretences to support ambition, are never wanting. Their cry is, Where is the danger? and they insist, that, although the powers of the general government will be increased, yet it will be for the good of the whole; and, although the three great States form nearly a majority of the people of America, they never will hurt or injure the lesser States. I do not, Gentlemen, trust you. If you possess the power, the abuse of it could not be checked; and what then would prevent your exercising it to our destruction? You gravely allege, that there is no danger of combination, and triumphantly ask, how could combinations be effected? "The larger States," you say, "all differ in productions and commerce; and experience shows, that, instead of combinations, they would be rivals, and counteract the views of one another." This, I repeat, is language calculated only to amuse us. Yes, Sir, the larger States will be rivals, but not against each other; they will be rivals against the rest of the States. But it is urged, that such a government would suit the people, and that its principles are equitable and just. How often has this argument been refuted, when applied to a federal government. The small States never can agree to the Virginia plan; and why then is it still urged? But it is said, that it is not expected that the State governments will approve the proposed system, and that this House must directly carry it to the people for their approbation! Is it come to this, then, that the sword must decide this controversy, and that the horrors of war must be added to the rest of our misfortunes? But what have the people already said? "We find the confederation defective. Go, and give additional powers to the confederation; give to it the imposts, regulation of trade, power to collect the taxes, and the means to discharge our foreign and domestic debts." Can we not, then, as their delegates, agree upon these points? As their ambassadors, can we not clearly grant those powers? Why then, when we are met, must entire, distinct, and new grounds be taken, and a government, of which the people had no idea, be instituted? And are we to be told, if we wont agree to it, it is the last moment of our deliberations? I say, it is indeed the last moment, if we do agree to this assumption of power. The States will never again be entrapped into a

measure like this. The people will say, the small
States would confederate, and grant further powers to
Congress ; but you, the large States, would not.
Then the fault will be yours, and all the nations of
the earth will justify us. But what is to become of
our public debts, if we dissolve the Union ? Where
is your plighted faith ? Will you crush the smaller
States, or must they be left unmolested ? Sooner than
be ruined, there are foreign powers who will take us
by the hand. I say not this to threaten or intimidate,
but that we should reflect seriously before we act. If
we once leave this floor, and solemnly renounce your
new project, what will be the consequence ? You will
annihilate your federal government, and ruin must
stare you in the face. Let us then do what is in our
power, — amend and enlarge the confederation, but
not alter the federal system. The people expect
this, and no more. We all agree in the necessity of a
more efficient government ; and cannot this be done ?
Although my State is small, I know and respect its
rights, as much, at least, as those who have the honor
to represent any of the larger States.

Judge Ellsworth. I am asked by my honorable
friend from Massachusetts, whether by entering into a
national government, I will not equally participate in
national security ? I confess I should ; but I want domestic happiness, as well as general security. A general government will never grant me this, as it cannot
know my wants or relieve my distress. My State is
only as one out of thirteen. Can they, the general
government, gratify my wishes ? My happiness depends as much on the existence of my State government, as a new-born infant depends upon its mother
for nourishment. If this is not an answer, I have no
other to give.

Mr. King. I am in sentiment with those who wish the preservation of State governments; but the general government may be so constituted as to effect it. Let the constitution we are about forming be considered as a commission under which the general government shall act, and as such it will be the guardian of the State rights. The rights of Scotland are secure from all danger and encroachments, although in the Parliament she has a small representation. May not this be done in our general government? Since I am up, I am concerned for what fell from the gentleman from Delaware, — " Take a foreign power by the hand " ! I am sorry he mentioned it, and I hope he is able to excuse it to himself on the score of passion. Whatever may be my distress, I never will court a foreign power to assist in relieving myself from it.

Adjourned till Monday next.

MONDAY, JULY 2D, 1787.

Met pursuant to adjournment. Present, eleven States.

The question was then put on Mr. Ellsworth's motion; five ayes; five noes; one State divided. So the question, as to the amendment, was lost.

Mr. Pinckney. As a professional man, I might say, that there is no weight in the argument adduced in favor of the motion on which we are divided; but candor obliges me to own, that equality of suffrage in the States is wrong. Prejudices will prevail, and they have an equal weight in the larger as in the smaller States. There is a solid distinction as to interest between the southern and northern States. To destroy the ill effects thereof, I renew the motion which I

19

made in the early stage of this business. [See the plan of it before mentioned.]

General Pinckney moved for a select committee, to take into consideration both branches of the legislature.

Mr. Martin. It is again attempted to compromise. You must give each State an equal suffrage, or our business is at an end.

Mr. Sherman. It seems we have got to a point, that we cannot move one way or the other. Such a committee is necessary to set us right.

Mr. Morris. The two branches, so equally poised, cannot have their due weight. It is confessed, on all hands, that the second branch ought to be a check on the first ; for without its having this effect it is perfectly useless. The first branch, originating from the people, will ever be subject to precipitancy, changeability, and excess. Experience evinces the truth of this remark, without having recourse to reading. This can only be checked by ability and virtue in the second branch. On your present system, can you suppose that one branch will possess it more than the others ? The second branch ought to be composed of men of great and established property, — an aristocracy ; men, who from pride will support consistency and permanency ; and to make them completely independent they must be chosen for life, or they will be a useless body. Such an aristocratic body will keep down the turbulency of democracy. But, if you elect them for a shorter period, they will be only a name, and we had better be without them. Thus constituted, I hope they will show us the weight of aristocracy.

History proves, I admit, that the men of large property will uniformly endeavour to establish tyranny.

How then shall we ward off this evil? Give them the second branch, and you secure their weight for the public good. They become responsible for their conduct, and this lust of power will ever be checked by the democratic branch, and thus form a stability in your government. But, if we continue changing our measures by the breath of democracy, who will confide in our engagements? Who will trust us? Ask any person, whether he reposes any confidence in the government of Congress, or that of the State of Pennsylvania, — he will readily answer you, no. Ask him the reason, and he will tell you, it is because he has no confidence in their stability.

You intend also, that the second branch shall be incapable of holding any office in the general government. It is a dangerous expedient. They ought to have every inducement to be interested in your government. Deprive them of this right, and they will become inattentive to your welfare. The wealthy will ever exist; and you never can be safe unless you gratify them as a body, in the pursuit of honor and profit. Prevent them by positive institutions, and they will proceed in some left-handed way. A son may want a place, — you mean to prevent him from promotion. They are not to be paid for their services; they will in some way pay themselves; nor is it in your power to prevent it. It is good policy, that men of property be collected in one body, to give them one common influence in your government. Let vacancies be filled up as they happen, by the executive. Besides, it is of little consequence, on this plan, whether the States are equally represented or not. If the State governments have the division of many of the loaves and fishes, and the general government few, it cannot exist.   This Senate would be one of the bawbles of the general government.   If you choose them for seven years, whether chosen by the people or the States ; whether by equal suffrage, or in any other proportion, how will they be a check? They will still have local and State prejudices.   A government by compact is no government at all.   You may as well go back to your congressional federal government, where, in the characters of ambassadors, they may form treaties for each State.

I avow myself the advocate of a strong government ; still I admit, that the influence of the rich must be guarded ; and a pure democracy is equally oppressive to the lower orders of the community.   This remark is founded on the experience of history.   We are a commercial people, and as such will be obliged to engage in European politics.   Local government cannot apply to the general government.   These latter remarks I throw out only for the consideration of the committee who are to be appointed.

Governor Randolph.   I am in favor of appointing a committee ; but, considering the warmth exhibited in debate on Saturday, I have, I confess, no great hopes, that any good will arise from it.   Cannot a remedy be devised ?   If there is danger to the lesser States, from an unequal representation in the second branch, may not a check be found in the appointment of one executive, by electing him, by an equality of State votes ?   He must have the right of interposing between the two branches, and this might give a reasonable security to the smaller States.   Not one of the lesser States can exist by itself ; and a dissolution of the confederation, I confess, would produce conventions, as well in the larger as in the smaller States.

The principle of self-preservation induces me to seek for a government that will be stable and secure.

Mr. Strong moved to refer the seventh resolve to the same committee.

Mr. Wilson. I do not approve of the motion for a committee. I also object to the mode of its appointment; a small committee is the best.

Mr. Lansing. I shall not oppose the appointment, but I expect no good from it.

Mr. Madison. I have observed, that committees only delay business; and, if you appoint one from each State, we shall have in it the whole force of State prejudices. The great difficulty is to conquer former opinions. The motion of the gentleman from South Carolina can be as well decided here as in committee.

Mr. Gerry. The world at large expect something from us. If we do nothing, it appears to me we must have war and confusion, — for the old confederation would be at an end. Let us see if no concession can be made. Accommodation is absolutely necessary, and defects may be amended by a future convention.

The motion was then put to appoint a committee on the eighth resolve, and so much of the seventh as was not agreed to. Carried; nine States against two.

And, by ballot, the following members were appointed:

Massachusetts,	Mr. Gerry,
Connecticut,	Mr. Ellsworth,
New York,	Mr. Yates,
New Jersey,	Mr. Patterson,
Pennsylvania,	Mr. Franklin,
Delaware,	Mr. Bedford,

Maryland,	Mr. Martin,
Virginia,	Mr. Mason,
North Carolina,	Mr. Davie,
South Carolina,	Mr. Rutledge,
Georgia,	Mr. Baldwin.

The convention then adjourned to Thursday, the 5th of July.

TUESDAY, JULY 3D, 1787.

The grand committee met. Mr. Gerry was chosen chairman.

The committee proceeded to consider in what manner they should discharge the business with which they were intrusted. By the proceedings in the convention, they were so equally divided on the important question of representation in the two branches, that the idea of a conciliatory adjustment must have been in contemplation of the House in the appointment of this committee. But still, how to effect this salutary purpose was the question. Many of the members, impressed with the utility of a general government, connected with it the indispensable necessity of a representation from the States according to their numbers and wealth; while others, equally tenacious of the rights of the States, would admit of no other representation but such as was strictly federal; or, in other words, equality of suffrage. This brought on a discussion of the principles on which the House had divided, and a lengthy recapitulation of the arguments advanced in the House in support of these opposite propositions. As I had not openly explained my sentiments on any former occasion on this question, but constantly, in giving my vote, showed my attachment to the national government on federal principles, I took this occasion to explain my motives. [See a copy of my speech hereunto annexed.*]

These remarks gave rise to a motion of Dr. Franklin, which, after some modification, was agreed to, and made the basis of the following report of the committee.

The committee, to whom was referred the eighth resolution reported from the committee of the whole House, and so much of the seventh as had not been decided on, submit the following report:

That the subsequent propositions be recommended to the convention, on condition that both shall be generally adopted.

That, in the first branch of the legislature, each of the States now in the Union, be allowed one member for every forty thousand inhabitants, of the description reported in the seventh resolution of the committee of the whole House. That each State, not containing that number, shall be allowed one member.

That all bills for raising or apportioning money, and for fixing salaries of the officers of government of the United States, shall originate in the first branch of the legislature, and shall not be altered or amended by the second branch; and that no money shall be drawn from the public treasury, but in pursuance of appropriations to be originated in the first branch.

That, in the second branch of the legislature, each State shall have an equal vote.

---

* It is matter of regret, that this document cannot be found. The principles it contained are perhaps embodied in the letter from Mr. Yates and Mr. Lansing to Governor George Clinton, on their retiring from the convention.

THURSDAY, JULY 5th, 1787.

Met pursuant to adjournment.

The report of the committee was read.

Mr. Gorham. I call for an explanation of the principles on which it is grounded.

Mr. Gerry, the chairman, explained the principles.

Mr. Martin. The one representation is proposed as an expedient for the adoption of the other.

Mr. Wilson. The committee have exceeded their powers.

Mr. Martin proposed to take the question on the whole of the report.

Mr. Wilson. I do not choose to take a leap in the dark. I have a right to call for a division of the question on each distinct proposition.

Mr. Madison. I restrain myself from animadverting on the report, from the respect I bear to the members of the committee. But I must confess, I see nothing of concession in it.

The originating money bills is no concession on the part of the smaller States; for if seven States in the second branch should want such a bill, their interest in the first branch will prevail to bring it forward; it is nothing more than a nominal privilege.

The second branch, small in number and well connected, will ever prevail. The powers of regulating trade, imposts, treaties, &c., are more essential to the community than raising money, and no provision is made for those in the report. We are driven to an unhappy dilemma. Two thirds of the inhabitants of the Union are to please the remaining one third, by sacrificing their essential rights.

When we satisfy the majority of the people, in securing their rights, we have nothing to fear; in any other way, every thing. The smaller States, I hope, will at last see their true and real interest; and I hope, that the warmth of the gentleman from Delaware will never induce him to yield to his own suggestion of seeking for foreign aid.

[At this period, Messrs. Yates and Lansing left the convention, and the remainder of the session was employed to complete the constitution on the principles already adopted. See the revised draft of the constitution, and the constitution of the United States, with all the ratified amendments, as at present existing, in the Appendix.]

☞ The preceding Notes of the late Chief Justice Yates, contained in two hundred and forty-five pages,* of two volumes, were copied by me, literally, from the original manuscript in his handwriting. The several papers referred to did not accompany his notes.

JOHN LANSING, JUN.

---

* The number of pages in the manuscript.

APPENDIX.

RESOLUTIONS

OFFERED BY MR. EDMUND RANDOLPH TO THE CONVENTION,
MAY 29TH, 1787.

1. *Resolved*, That the articles of the confederation ought to be so corrected and enlarged, as to accomplish the objects proposed by their institution, namely, common defence, security of liberty, and general welfare.

2. *Resolved*, therefore, That the right of suffrage, in the national legislature, ought to be proportioned to the quotas of contribution, or to the number of free inhabitants, as the one or the other may seem best, in different cases.

3. *Resolved*, That the national legislature ought to consist of two branches.

4. *Resolved*, That the members of the first branch of the national legislature ought to be elected by the people of the several States, every   for the term of   to be of the age of   years at least; to receive liberal stipends, by which they may be compensated for the devotion of their time to public service; to be ineligible to any office established by a particular State, or under the authority of the United States, (except those peculiarly belonging to the functions of

the first branch,) during the term of service and for the space of   after its expiration ; to be incapable of reëlection for the space of   after the expiration of their term of service ; and to be subject to recall.

5. *Resolved*, That the members of the second branch of the national legislature, ought to be elected by those of the first, out of a proper number of persons nominated by the individual legislatures; to be of the age of   years, at least ; to hold their offices for a term sufficient to insure their independency ; to receive liberal stipends, by which they may be compensated for the devotion of their time to the public service ; and to be ineligible to any office established by a particular State, or under the authority of the United States, (except those peculiarly belonging to the functions of the second branch,) during the term of service ; and for the space of   after the expiration thereof.

6. *Resolved*, That each branch ought to possess the right of originating acts ; that the national legislature ought to be empowered to enjoy the legislative right vested in Congress by the confederation ; and moreover to legislate in all cases to which the separate States are incompetent, or in which the harmony of the United States may be interrupted by the exercise of individual legislation ; to negative all laws passed by the several States, contravening, in the opinion of the national legislature, the articles of union, or any treaty subsisting under the authority of the Union ; and to call forth the force of the Union against any member of the Union failing to fulfil its duty under the articles thereof.

7. *Resolved*, That a national executive be instituted, to be chosen by the national legislature for the

term of   years, to receive punctually, at stated times, a fixed compensation for the services rendered, in which no increase or diminution shall be made, so as to affect the magistracy existing at the time of the increase or diminution; to be ineligible a second time; and that, besides a general authority to execute the national laws, it ought to enjoy the executive rights vested in Congress by the confederation.

8. *Resolved*, That the executive, and a convenient number of the national judiciary, ought to compose a council of revision, with authority to examine every act of the national legislature before it shall operate, and every act of a particular legislature before a negative thereon shall be final; and that the dissent of the said council shall amount to a rejection, unless the act of the national legislature be again passed, or that of a particular legislature be again negatived by   of the members of each branch.

9. *Resolved*, That a national judiciary be established   to hold their offices during good behaviour, and to receive punctually, at stated times, fixed compensations for their services, in which no increase or diminution shall be made, so as to affect the person actually in office at the time of such increase or diminution. That the jurisdiction of the inferior tribunals shall be, to hear and determine, in the first instance, and of the supreme tribunal to hear and determine, in the dernier resort, all piracies and felonies on the high seas; captures from an enemy; cases in which foreigners, or citizens of other States, applying to such jurisdictions, may be interested, or which respect the collection of the national revenue; impeachments of any national officer; and questions which involve the national peace or harmony.

10. *Resolved*, That provision ought to be made for the admission of States, lawfully arising within the limits of the United States, whether from a voluntary junction of government and territory, or otherwise, with the consent of a number of voices in the national legislature less than the whole.

11. *Resolved*, That a republican government, and the territory of each State, (except in the instance of a voluntary junction of government and territory,) ought to be guarantied by the United States to each State.

12. *Resolved*, That provisions ought to be made foɪ the continuance of a Congress, and their authorities and privileges until a given day, after the reform of the articles of union shall be adopted, and for the completion of all their engagements.

13. That provision ought to be made for the amendment of the articles of union, whensoever it shall seem necessary ; and that the assent of the national legislature ought not to be required thereto.

14. *Resolved*, That the legislative, executive, and judiciary powers within the several States, ought to be bound by oath to support the articles of union.

15. *Resolved*, that the amendments which shall be offered to the confederation by the convention, ought, at a proper time or times, after the approbation of Congress, to be submitted to an assembly or assemblies of representatives, recommended by the seveɪal legislatures, to be expressly chosen by the people, to consider and decide thereon.

MR. CHARLES PINCKNEY'S DRAFT OF A FEDERAL GOVERNMENT.

WE the people of the States of New Hampshire, Massachusetts, Rhode Island and Providence Plantations, Connecticut, New York, New Jersey, Pennsylvania, Delaware, Maryland, Virginia, North Carolina, South Carolina, and Georgia, do ordain, declare, and establish the following constitution for the government of ourselves and posterity.

ARTICLE I.

The style of this government shall be The United States of America, and the government shall consist of supreme legislative, executive, and judicial powers.

ARTICLE II.

The legislative power shall be vested in a Congress, to consist of two separate Houses; one to be called the House of Delegates, and the other the Senate, who shall meet on the   day of   in every year.

ARTICLE III.

The members of the House of Delegates shall be chosen every   year by the people of the several States; and the qualification of the electors shall be the same as those of the electors in the several States for their legislature. Each member shall have been a citizen of the United States for   years; shall be of   years of age, and a resident in the State he is chosen for   until a census of the people shall be taken in the manner hereinafter mentioned. The House of Delegates shall consist of   to be chosen from the different States in the following proportions;

for New Hampshire,   for Massachusetts,
for Rhode Island,   for Connecticut,   for
New York,   for New Jersey,   for Pennsylvania,   for Delaware,   for Maryland,
for Virginia,   for North Carolina,   for South
Carolina,   for Georgia,   and the legislature
shall hereafter regulate the number of delegates by
the number of inhabitants, according to the provisions
hereinafter made, at the rate of one for every
thousand. All money bills of every kind shall originate in the House of Delegates, and shall not be altered by the Senate. The House of Delegates shall
exclusively possess the power of impeachment, and
shall choose its own officers; and vacancies therein
shall be supplied by the executive authority of the
State in the representation from which they shall
happen.

ARTICLE IV.

The Senate shall be elected and chosen by the
House of Delegates; which House, immediately after
their meeting, shall choose by ballot   senators
from among the citizens and residents of New Hampshire,   from among those of Massachusetts,
from among those of Rhode Island,   from among
those of Connecticut,   from among those of New
York,   from among those of New Jersey,
from among those of Pennsylvania,   from among
those of Delaware,   from among those of Maryland,   from among those of Virginia,   from
among those of North Carolina,   from among
those of South Carolina, and   from among those
of Georgia. The senators chosen from New Hampshire, Massachusetts, Rhode Island, and Connecticut,

shall form one class; those from New York, New Jersey, Pennsylvania, and Delaware, one class; and those from Maryland, Virginia, North Carolina, South Carolina, and Georgia, one class. The House of Delegates shall number these classes one, two, and three; and fix the times of their service by lot. The first class shall serve for   years; the second for   years; and the third for   years. As their times of service expire, the House of Delegates shall fill them up by elections for   years; and they shall fill all vacancies that arise from death, or resignation, for the time of service remaining of the members so dying or resigning. Each senator shall be   years of age at least; shall have been a citizen of the United States four years before his election; and shall be a resident of the State he is chosen from. The Senate shall choose its own officers.

ARTICLE V.

Each State shall prescribe the time and manner of holding elections by the people for the House of Delegates; and the House of Delegates shall be the judges of the elections, returns, and qualifications of their members.

In each House a majority shall constitute a quorum to do business. Freedom of speech and debate in the legislature shall not be impeached, or questioned, in any place out of it; and the members of both Houses shall, in all cases, except for treason, felony, or breach of the peace, be free from arrest during their attendance on Congress, and in going to and returning from it. Both Houses shall keep journals of their proceedings, and publish them, except on secret occasions; and the yeas and nays may be entered thereon at the

desire of one   of the members present. Neither
House, without the consent of the other, shall adjourn
for more than   days, nor to any place but where
they are sitting.

The members of each House shall not be eligible
to, or capable of holding any office under the Union,
during the time for which they have been respectively
elected, nor the members of the Senate for one year
after. The members of each House shall be paid for
their services by the States which they represent.
Every bill, which shall have passed the legislature,
shall be presented to the President of the United
States for his revision ; if he approves it he shall sign
it ; but, if he does not approve it, he shall return it,
with his objections, to the House it originated in ;
which House, if two thirds of the members present,
notwithstanding the President's objections, agree to
pass it, shall send it to the other House, with the
President's objections ; where, if two thirds of the
members present also agree to pass it, the same shall
become a law ; and all bills sent to the president, and
not returned by him within   days, shall be laws,
unless the legislature by their adjournment, prevent
their return ; in which case they shall not be laws.

ARTICLE VI.

The legislature of the United States shall have the
power to lay and collect taxes, duties, imposts, and
excises ;

To regulate commerce with all nations, and among
the several States ;

To borrow money and emit bills of credit ;

To establish post-offices ;

To raise armies ;

20*

To build and equip fleets ;

To pass laws for arming, organizing, and disciplining the militia of the United States ;

To subdue a rebellion in any State, on application of its legislature ;

To coin money, and regulate the value of all coins, and fix the standard of weights and measures ;

To provide such dock-yards and arsenals, and erect such fortifications, as may be necessary for the United States, and to exercise exclusive jurisdiction therein ;

To appoint a treasurer by ballot ,

To constitute tribunals inferior to the Supreme Court ;

To establish post and military roads ;

To establish and provide for a national university at the seat of the government of the United States ;

To establish uniform rules of naturalization ;

To provide for the establishment of a seat of government for the United States, not exceeding miles square, in which they shall have exclusive jurisdiction ;

To make rules concerning captures from an enemy ;

To declare the law and punishment of piracies and felonies at sea, and of counterfeiting coin, and of all offences against the laws of nations ;

To call forth the aid of the militia, to execute the laws of the Union, enforce treaties, suppress insurrections, and repel invasions ;

And to make all laws for carrying the foregoing powers into execution.

The legislature of the United States shall have the power to declare the punishment of treason, which shall consist only in levying war against the United States, or any of them, or in adhering to their enemies.

No person shall be convicted of treason but by the testimony of two witnesses.

The proportion of direct taxation shall be regulated by the whole number of inhabitants of every description ; which number shall, within   years after the first meeting of the legislature, and within the term of every   year after, be taken in the manner to be prescribed by the legislature.

No tax shall be laid on articles exported from the States ; nor capitation tax, but in proportion to the census before directed.

All laws regulating commerce shall require the assent of two thirds of the members present in each House. The United States shall not grant any title of nobility. The legislature of the United States shall pass no law on the subject of religion ; nor touching or abridging the liberty of the press ; nor shall the privilege of the writ of *habeas corpus* ever be suspended, except in case of rebellion or invasion.

All acts made by the legislature of the United States, pursuant to this constitution, and all treaties made under the authority of the United States, shall be the supreme law of the land ; and all judges shall be bound to consider them as such in their decisions.

ARTICLE VII.

The Senate shall have the sole and exclusive power to declare war, and to make treaties, and to appoint ambassadors and other ministers to foreign nations, and judges of the Supreme Court.

They shall have the exclusive power to regulate the manner of deciding all disputes and controversies now subsisting, or which may arise, between the States respecting jurisdiction or territory.

ARTICLE VIII.

The executive power of the United States shall be vested in a President of the United States of America, which shall be his style; and his title shall be his Excellency. He shall be elected for   years, and shall be reeligible.

He shall, from time to time, give information to the legislature of the state of the Union, and recommend to their consideration the measures he may think necessary. He shall take care that the laws of the United States be duly executed. He shall commission all the officers of the United States; and, except as to ambassadors, other ministers, and judges of the Supreme Court, he shall nominate, and with the consent of the Senate appoint, all other officers of the United States. He shall receive public ministers from foreign nations; and may correspond with the executive of the different States. He shall have power to grant pardons and reprieves, except in impeachments. He shall be Commander-in-chief of the army and navy of the United States, and of the militia of the several States; and shall receive a compensation which shall not be increased or diminished during his continuance in office. At entering on the duties of his office, he shall take an oath faithfully to execute the duties of a President of the United States. He shall be removed from his office on impeachment by the House of Delegates, and conviction in the Supreme Court, of treason, bribery, or corruption. In case of his removal, death, resignation, or disability, the President of the Senate shall exercise the duties of his office until another President be chosen. And in case of the death of the President of the Senate, the Speaker of the House of Delegates shall do so.

ARTICLE IX.

The legislature of the United States shall have the power, and it shall be their duty, to establish such courts of law, equity, and admiralty, as shall be necessary.

The judges of the courts shall hold their offices during good behaviour; and receive a compensation, which shall not be increased or diminished during their continuance in office. One of these courts shall be termed the Supreme Court, whose jurisdiction shall extend to all cases arising under the laws of the United States, or affecting ambassadors, other public ministers, and consuls; to the trial of impeachment of officers of the United States; to all cases of admiralty and maritime jurisdiction. In cases of impeachment, affecting ambassadors and other public ministers, this jurisdiction shall be original; and in all the other cases appellate.

All criminal officers (except in cases of impeachment) shall be tried in the State where they shall be committed. The trials shall be open and public, and be by jury.

ARTICLE X.

Immediately after the first census of the people of the United States, the House of Delegates shall apportion the Senate, by electing for each State, out of the citizens resident therein, one senator for every members such State shall have in the House of Delegates. Each State shall be entitled to have at least one member in the Senate.

ARTICLE XI.

No State shall grant letters of marque and reprisal, or enter into treaty, or alliance, or confederation; nor grant any title of nobility; nor, without the consent of the legislature of the United States, lay any impost on imports; nor keep troops or ships of war in time of peace; nor enter into any compacts with other States or foreign powers, or emit bills of credit, or make any thing but gold, silver, or copper a tender in payment of debts; nor engage in war, except for self-defence when actually invaded, or the danger of invasion is so great as not to admit of a delay until the government of the United States can be informed thereof. And, to render these prohibitions effectual, the legislature of the United States shall have the power to revise the laws of the several States, that may be supposed to infringe the powers exclusively delegated by this constitution to Congress, and to negative and annul such as do.

ARTICLE XII.

The citizens of each State shall be entitled to all the privileges and immunities of citizens in the several States. Any person, charged with crimes in any State, fleeing from justice to another, shall, on demand of the executive of the State from which he fled, be delivered up, and removed to the State having jurisdiction of the offence.

ARTICLE XIII.

Full faith shall be given, in each State, to the acts of the legislature, and to the records and judicial proceedings of the courts and magistrates of every State.

ARTICLE XIV.

The legislature shall have power to admit new States into the Union on the same terms with the original States; provided two thirds of the members present in both Houses agree.

ARTICLE XV.

On the application of the legislature of a State, the United States shall protect it against domestic insurrection.

ARTICLE XVI.

If two thirds of the legislatures of the States apply for the same, the legislature of the United States shall call a convention for the purpose of amending the constitution; or, should Congress, with the consent of two thirds of each House, propose to the States amendments to the same, the agreement of two thirds of the legislatures of the States shall be sufficient to make the said amendments parts of the constitution.

The ratification of the   conventions of States shall be sufficient for organizing this constitution.

PROPOSITIONS

OFFERED TO THE CONVENTION BY THE HONORABLE MR. PAT-
TERSON, JUNE 15TH, 1787.

1. *Resolved*, That the articles of confederation ought to be so revised, corrected, and enlarged, as to render the federal constitution adequate to the ex-

igencies of government, and the preservation of the Union.

2. *Resolved*, That in addition to the powers vested in the United States in Congress, by the present existing articles of confederation, they be authorized to pass acts for raising a revenue, by levying a duty or duties on all goods and merchandise of foreign growth or manufacture, imported into any part of the United States, — by stamps on paper, vellum, or parchment, and by a postage on all letters and packages passing through the general post-office, — to be applied to such federal purposes as they shall deem proper and expedient; to make rules and regulations for the collection thereof; and the same from time to time to alter and amend, in such manner as they shall think proper. To pass acts for the regulation of trade and commerce, as well with foreign nations as with each other; provided, that all punishments, fines, forfeitures, and penalties, to be incurred for contravening such rules and regulations, shall be adjudged by the common law judiciary of the States in which any offence contrary to the true intent and meaning of such rules and regulations shall be committed or perpetrated; with liberty of commencing, in the first instance, all suits or prosecutions for that purpose, in the superior common law judiciary of such State; subject, nevertheless, to an appeal for the correction of all errors, both in law and fact, in rendering judgment, to the judiciary of the United States.

3. *Resolved*, That whenever requisitions shall be necessary, instead of the present rule, the United States in Congress be authorized to make such requisitions in proportion to the whole number of white, and other free citizens and inhabitants of every age,

sex, and condition, including those bound to servitude for a term of years, and three fifths of all other persons not comprehended in the foregoing description, except Indians not paying taxes; that, if such requisitions be not complied with in the time to be specified therein, to direct the collection thereof in the non-complying States; and for that purpose to devise and pass acts directing and authorizing the same; provided, that none of the powers hereby vested in the United States in Congress, shall be exercised without the consent of at least   States; and in that proportion, if the number of confederated States should be hereafter increased or diminished.

4. *Resolved*, That the United States in Congress be authorized to elect a federal executive to consist of   persons, to continue in office for the term of   years; to receive punctually, at stated times, a fixed compensation for the services by them rendered, in which no increase or diminution shall be made, so as to affect the persons composing the executive at the time of such increase or diminution; to be paid out of the federal treasury; to be incapable of holding any other office or appointment during their term of service, and for   years thereafter; to be ineligible a second time, and removable on impeachment and conviction for malpractices or neglect of duty, by Congress, on application by a majority of the executives of the several States. That the executive, besides a general authority to execute the federal acts, ought to appoint all federal officers not otherwise provided for, and to direct all military operations; provided, that none of the persons composing the federal executive shall, on any occasion, take command of

any troops, so as personally to conduct any military enterprise as general, or in any other capacity.

5. *Resolved*, That a federal judiciary be established, to consist of a supreme tribunal, the judges of which to be appointed by the executive, and to hold their offices during good behaviour; to receive punctually, at stated times, a fixed compensation for their services, in which no increase or diminution shall be made, so as to affect the persons actually in office at the time of such increase or diminution. That the judiciary, so established, shall have authority to hear and determine, in the first instance, on all impeachments of federal officers; and, by way of appeal, in the dernier resort, in all cases touching the rights and privileges of ambassadors; in all cases of captures from an enemy; in all cases of piracies and felonies on the high seas; in all cases in which foreigners may be interested, in the construction of any treaty or treaties, or which may arise on any act or ordinance of Congress for the regulation of trade, or the collection of the federal revenue. That none of the judiciary officers shall, during the time they remain in office, be capable of receiving or holding any other office or appointment during their term of service, or for   thereafter.

6. *Resolved*, That the legislative, executive, and judiciary powers within the several States, ought to be bound by oath, to support the articles of union.

7. *Resolved*, That all acts of the United States in Congress assembled, made by virtue and in pursuance of the powers hereby vested in them, and by the articles of the confederation, and all treaties made and ratified under the authority of the United States, shall be the supreme law of the respective States, as far as

those acts or treaties shall relate to the said States, or their citizens ; and that the judiciaries of the several States shall be bound thereby in their decisions, any thing in the respective laws of the individual States to the contrary notwithstanding.

And if any State, or any body of men in any State, shall oppose or prevent the carrying into execution such acts or treaties, the federal executive shall be authorized to call forth the powers of the confederated States, or so much thereof as may be necessary, to enforce and compel an obedience to such acts, or an observance of such treaties.

8. *Resolved*, That provision ought to be made for the admission of new States into the Union.

9. *Resolved*, That provision ought to be made for hearing and deciding upon all disputes arising between the United States and an individual State, respecting territory.

10. *Resolved*, That the rule for naturalization ought to be the same in every State.

11. *Resolved*, That a citizen of one State, committing an offence in another State, shall be deemed guilty of the same offence as if it had been committed by a citizen of the State in which the offence was committed.

COLONEL HAMILTON'S PLAN OF GOVERNMENT.

THE FOLLOWING PAPER WAS READ BY COLONEL HAMILTON, AS CONTAINING HIS IDEAS OF A SUITABLE PLAN OF GOVERNMENT FOR THE UNITED STATES.

1. The supreme legislative power of the United States of America to be vested in two distinct bodies

of men, the one to be called the Assembly, the other the Senate, who together shall form the legislature of the United States, with power to pass all laws whatsoever, subject to the negative hereafter mentioned.

2. The Assembly to consist of persons elected by the people, to serve for three years.

3. The Senate to consist of persons elected to serve during good behaviour; their election to be made by electors chosen for that purpose by the people. In order to this, the States to be divided into election districts. On the death, removal, or resignation of any senator, his place to be filled out of the district from which he came.

4. The supreme executive authority of the United States to be vested in a Governor, to be elected to serve during good behaviour. His election to be made by electors, chosen by electors, chosen by the people, in the election districts aforesaid. His authorities and functions to be as follows:

To have a negative upon all laws about to be passed, and the execution of all laws passed; to have the entire direction of war, when authorized, or begun; to have, with the advice and approbation of the Senate, the power of making all treaties; to have the sole appointment of the heads or chief officers of the departments of finance, war, and foreign affairs; to have the nomination of all other officers, (ambassadors to foreign nations included,) subject to the approbation or rejection of the Senate; to have the power of pardoning all offences, except treason, which he shall not pardon, without the approbation of the Senate.

5. On the death, resignation, or removal of the Governor, his authorities to be exercised by the President of the Senate, until a successor be appointed.

6. The Senate to have the sole power of declaring war; the power of advising and approving all treaties; the power of approving or rejecting all appointments of officers, except the heads or chiefs of the departments of finance, war, and foreign affairs.

7. The supreme judicial authority of the United States to be vested in   judges, to hold their offices during good behaviour, with adequate and permanent salaries. This court to have original jurisdiction in all causes of capture; and an appellative jurisdiction in all causes in which the revenues of the general government, or the citizens of foreign nations are concerned.

8. The legislature of the United States to have power to institute courts in each State, for the determination of all matters of general concern.

9. The governors, senators, and all officers of the United States to be liable to impeachment for mal and corrupt conduct; and, upon conviction, to be removed from office, and disqualified for holding any place of trust or profit. All impeachments to be tried by a court to consist of the chief or senior judge of the superior court of law in each State; provided, that such judge hold his place during good behaviour, and have a permanent salary.

10. All laws of the particular States, contrary to the constitution or laws of the United States, to be utterly void. And the better to prevent such laws being passed, the Governor or President of each State shall be appointed by the general government, and shall have a negative upon the laws about to be passed in the State of which he is Governor or President.

11. No State to have any forces, land or naval; and the militia of all the States to be under the sole and ex-

clusive direction of the United States: the officers of which are to be appointed and commissioned by them.

STATE OF THE RESOLUTIONS

SUBMITTED TO THE CONSIDERATION OF THE HOUSE BY THE HONORABLE MR. RANDOLPH, AS ALTERED, AMENDED, AND AGREED TO, IN COMMITTEE OF THE WHOLE HOUSE.

1. *Resolved,* That it is the opinion of this committee, that a national government ought to be established, consisting of a supreme legislative, judiciary, and executive.

2. *Resolved,* that the national legislature ought to consist of two branches.

3. *Resolved,* That the members of the first branch of the national legislature ought to be elected by the people of the several States, for the term of three years; to receive fixed stipends, by which they may be compensated for the devotion of their time to public service, to be paid out of the national treasury; to be ineligible to any office established by a particular State, or under the authority of the United States, (except those peculiarly belonging to the functions of the first branch,) during the term of service, and, under the national government, for the space of one year after its expiration.

4. *Resolved,* That the members of the second branch of the national legislature ought to be chosen by the individual legislatures; to be of the age of thirty years, at least; to hold their offices for a term sufficient to insure their independency, namely, seven years; to receive fixed stipends, by which they may

be compensated for the devotion of their time to public service, to be paid out of the national treasury ; to be ineligible to any office established by a particular State, or under the authority of the United States, (except those peculiarly belonging to the functions of the second branch,) during the term of service, and, under the national government, for the space of one year after its expiration.

5. *Resolved*, That each branch ought to possess the right of originating acts.

6. *Resolved*, That the national legislature ought to be empowered to enjoy the legislative rights vested in Congress by the confederation ; and, moreover, to legislate in all cases to which the separate States are incompetent, or in which the harmony of the United States may be interrupted, by the exercise of individual legislation ; to negative all laws passed by the several States contravening, in the opinion of the national legislature, the articles of union, or any treaties subsisting under the authority of the Union.

7. *Resolved*, That the right of suffrage in the first branch of the national legislature ought not to be according to the rule established in the articles of confederation, but according to some equitable ratio of representation ; namely, in proportion to the whole number of white and other free citizens and inhabitants, of every age, sex, and condition, including those bound to servitude for a term of years, and three fifths of all other persons not comprehended in the foregoing description, except Indians not paying taxes in each State.

8. *Resolved*, That the rights of suffrage in the second branch of the national legislature ought to be according to the rule established for the first.

9. *Resolved,* That a national executive be instituted to consist of a single person ; to be chosen by the national legislature, for the term of seven years ; with power to carry into execution the national laws ; to appoint to offices in cases not otherwise provided for ; to be ineligible the second time ; and to be removable on impeachment, and conviction of malpractice, or neglect of duty ; to receive a fixed stipend, by which he may be compensated for the devotion of his time to public service, to be paid out of the national treasury.

10. *Resolved,* That the national executive shall have a right to negative any legislative act, which shall not be afterwards passed, unless by two third parts of each branch of the national legislature.

11. *Resolved,* That a national judiciary be established to consist of one supreme tribunal ; the judges of which to be appointed by the second branch of the national legislature ; to hold their offices during good behaviour ; to receive punctually, at stated times, a fixed compensation for their services, in which no increase or diminution shall be made, so as to affect the persons actually in office at the time of such increase or diminution.

12. *Resolved,* That the national legislature be empowered to appoint inferior tribunals.

13. *Resolved,* That the jurisdiction of the national judiciary shall extend to cases which respect the collection of the national revenue ; impeachment of any national officer ; and questions which involve the national peace and harmony.

14. *Resolved,* That provision ought to be made for the admission of States, lawfully arising within the limits of the United States, whether from a voluntary

junction of government and territory, or otherwise, with the consent of a number of voices in the national legislature less than the whole.

15. *Resolved,* That provision ought to be made for the continuance of Congress and their authorities, until a given day after the reform of the articles of union shall be adopted; and for the completion of all their engagements.

16. *Resolved,* That a republican constitution, and its existing laws, ought to be guarantied to each State by the United States.

17. *Resolved,* That provision ought to be made for the amendment of the articles of union, whensoever it shall seem necessary.

18. *Resolved,* That the legislative, executive, and judiciary powers, within the several States, ought to be bound, by oath, to support the articles of union.

19. *Resolved,* That the amendments which shall be offered to the confederation by the convention, ought, at a proper time or times, after the approbation of Congress, to be submitted to an assembly or assemblies of representatives, recommended by the several legislatures, to be expressly chosen by the people to consider and decide thereon.

RESOLUTIONS OF THE CONVENTION

REFERRED, ON THE TWENTY-THIRD AND TWENTY-SIXTH OF JULY, 1787, TO A COMMITTEE OF DETAIL, (MESSRS. RUT-LEDGE, RANDOLPH, GORHAM, ELLSWORTH, AND WILSON,) FOR THE PURPOSE OF REPORTING A CONSTITUTION.

1. *Resolved,* That the government of the United States ought to consist of a supreme legislative, judiciary, and executive.

2. *Resolved,* That the legislature consist of two branches.

3. *Resolved,* That the members of the first branch of the legislature ought to be elected by the people of the several States, for the term of two years; to be paid out of the public treasury; to receive an adequate compensation for their services; to be of the age of twenty-five years at least : to be ineligible and incapable of holding any office under the authority of the United States (except those peculiarly belonging to the functions of the first branch) during the term of service of the first branch.

4. *Resolved,* That the members of the second branch of the legislature of the United States ought to be chosen by the individual legislatures; to be of the age of thirty years at least; to hold their offices for six years, one third to go out biennially; to receive a compensation for the devotion of their time to the public service; to be ineligible to, and incapable of holding any office, under the authority of the United States (except those peculiarly belonging to the functions of the second branch) during the term for which they are elected, and for one year thereafter.

5. *Resolved,* That each branch ought to possess the right of originating acts.

6. *Resolved,* That the national legislature ought to possess the legislative rights vested in Congress by the confederation ; and, moreover, to legislate in all cases for the general interests of the Union, and also in those to which the States are separately incompetent, or in which the harmony of the United States may be interrupted by the exercise of individual legislation.

7. *Resolved,* That the legislative acts of the United States, made by virtue and in pursuance of the arti-

cles of union, and all treaties made and ratified under the authority of the United States, shall be the supreme law of the respective States, as far as those acts or treaties shall relate to the said States, or their citizens and inhabitants ; and that the judiciaries of the several States shall be bound thereby in their decisions, any thing in the respective laws of the individual States to the contrary notwithstanding.

8. *Resolved*, That in the original formation of the legislature of the United States, the first branch thereof shall consist of sixty-five members ; of which number,

New Hampshire shall send	three,
Massachusetts,	"	eight,
Rhode Island,	"	one,
Connecticut,	"	five,
New York,	"	six,
New Jersey,	"	four,
Pennsylvania,	"	eight,
Delaware,	"	one,
Maryland,	"	six,
Virginia,	"	ten,
North Carolina,	"	five,
South Carolina,	"	five,
Georgia,	"	three.

But, as the present situation of the States may probably alter in the number of their inhabitants, the legislature of the United States shall be authorized, from time to time, to apportion the number of representatives ; and in case any of the States shall hereafter be divided, or enlarged by addition of territory, or any two or more States united, or any new States created within the limits of the United States, the legislature of the United States shall possess authority to regulate the number of representatives, in any of the foregoing cases, upon the principle of their number of inhabitants, according to the provision hereafter mentioned, namely, — provided always, that representation ought to be proportioned according to direct taxation. And, in order to ascertain the alteration in the direct taxation, which may be required from time to time by the changes in the relative circumstances of the States : —

9. *Resolved*, That a census be taken within six years from the first meeting of the legislature of the United States, and once within the term of every ten years afterwards, of all the inhabitants of the United States, in the manner and according to the ratio recommended by Congress in their resolution of April 18th, 1783; and that the legislature of the United States shall proportion the direct taxation accordingly.

10. *Resolved*, That all bills for raising or appropriating money, and for fixing the salaries of the officers of the government of the United States, shall originate in the first branch of the legislature of the United States, and shall not be altered or amended by the second branch ; and that no money shall be drawn from the public treasury, but in pursuance of appropriations to be originated by the first branch.

11. *Resolved*, That in the second branch of the legislature of the United States, each State shall have an equal vote.

12. *Resolved*, That a national executive be instituted, to consist of a single person ; to be chosen by the national legislature for the term of seven years ; to be ineligible a second time ; with power to carry into execution the national laws ; to appoint to offices in

cases not otherwise provided for ; to be removable on impeachment and conviction of malpractice or neglect of duty ; to receive a fixed compensation for the devotion of his time to public service, to be paid out of the public treasury.

13. *Resolved*, That the national executive shall have a right to negative any legislative act, which shall not be afterwards passed, unless by two third parts of each branch of the national legislature.

14. *Resolved*, That a national judiciary be established, to consist of one supreme tribunal, the judges of which shall be appointed by the second branch of the national legislature ; to hold their offices during good behaviour ; to receive punctually, at stated times, a fixed compensation for their services, in which no diminution shall be made, so as to affect the persons actually in office at the time of such diminution.

15. *Resolved*, That the national legislature be empowered to appoint inferior tribunals.

16. *Resolved*, That the jurisdiction of the national judiciary shall extend to cases arising under laws passed by the general legislature ; and to such other questions as involve the national peace and harmony.

17. *Resolved*, That provision ought to be made for the admission of States, lawfully arising within the limits of the United States, whether from a voluntary junction of government and territory, or otherwise, with the consent of a number of voices in the national legislature less than the whole.

18. *Resolved*, That a republican form of government shall be guarantied to each State ; and that each State shall be protected against foreign and domestic violence.

19. *Resolved*. That provision ought to be made for

the amendment of the articles of union, whensoever it shall seem necessary.

20. *Resolved,* That the legislative, executive, and judiciary powers, within the several States, and of the national government, ought to be bound by oath to support the articles of union.

21. *Resolved,* That the amendments which shall be offered to the confederation by the convention, ought, at a proper time or times, after the approbation of Congress, to be submitted to an assembly or assemblies of representatives, recommended by the several legislatures, to be expressly chosen by the people, to consider and decide thereon.

22. *Resolved,* That the representation in the second branch of the legislature of the United States consist of two members from each State, who shall vote *per capita.*

23. *Resolved,* That it be an instruction to the committee, to whom were referred the proceedings of the convention for the establishment of a national government, to receive a clause or clauses, requiring certain qualifications of property and citizenship, in the United States, for the executive, the judiciary, and the members of both branches of the legislature of the United States.

DRAFT OF A CONSTITUTION,

REPORTED BY THE COMMITTEE OF FIVE, AUGUST 6TH, 1787.

WE the people of the States of New Hampshire, Massachusetts, Rhode Island and Providence Plantations, Connecticut, New York, New Jersey, Pennsylvania, Delaware, Maryland, Virginia, North Carolina,

South Carolina, and Georgia, do ordain, declare, and establish the following constitution for the government of ourselves and our posterity.

ARTICLE I.

The style of this government shall be, The United States of America."

ARTICLE II.

The government shall consist of supreme legislative, executive, and judicial powers.

ARTICLE III.

The legislative power shall be vested in a Congress, to consist of two separate and distinct bodies of men, a House of Representatives and a Senate; each of which shall, in all cases, have a negative on the other. The legislature shall meet on the first Monday in December in every year.

ARTICLE IV.

Sect. 1. The members of the House of Representatives shall be chosen every second year, by the people of the several States comprehended within this Union. The qualifications of the electors shall be the same, from time to time, as those of the electors in the several States of the most numerous branch of their own legislatures.

Sect. 2. Every member of the House of Representatives shall be of the age of twenty-five years at least; shall have been a citizen of the United States for at least three years before his election; and shall be, at the time of his election, a resident of the State in which he shall be chosen.

Sect. 3. The House of Representatives shall, at its first formation, and until the number of citizens and inhabitants shall be taken in the manner hereinafter described, consist of sixty-five members; of whom three shall be chosen in New Hampshire, eight in Massachusetts, one in Rhode Island and Providence Plantations, five in Connecticut, six in New York, four in New Jersey, eight in Pennsylvania, one in Delaware, six in Maryland, ten in Virginia, five in North Carolina, five in South Carolina, and three in Georgia.

Sect. 4. As the proportions of numbers in the different States will alter from time to time ; as some of the States may hereafter be divided; as others may be enlarged by addition of territory ; as two or more States may be united ; as new States will be erected within the limits of the United States, the legislature shall, in each of these cases, regulate the number of representatives by the number of inhabitants, according to the provisions hereinafter made, at the rate of one for every forty thousand.

Sect. 5. All bills for raising or appropriating money, and for fixing the salaries of the officers of government, shall originate in the House of Representatives, and shall not be altered or amended by the Senate. No money shall be drawn from the public treasury but in pursuance of appropriations that shall originate in the House of Representatives.

Sect. 6. The House of Representatives shall have the sole power of impeachment. It shall choose its Speaker and other officers.

Sect. 7. Vacancies in the House of Representatives shall be supplied by writs of election from the executive authority of the State in the representation from which they shall happen.

ARTICLE V.

Sect. 1. The Senate of the United States shall be chosen by the legislatures of the several States. Each legislature shall choose two members. Vacancies may be supplied by the executive until the next meeting of the legislature. Each member shall have one vote.

Sect. 2. The senators shall be chosen for six years; but, immediately after the first election, they shall be divided, by lot, into three classes, as nearly as may be, numbered one, two, and three. The seats of the members of the first class shall be vacated at the expiration of the second year; of the second class, at the expiration of the fourth year; of the third class, at the expiration of the sixth year; so that a third part of the members may be chosen every second year.

Sect. 3. Every member of the Senate shall be of the age of thirty years at least; shall have been a citizen in the United States for at least four years before his election; and shall be, at the time of his election, a resident of the State from which he shall be chosen.

Sect. 4. The Senate shall choose its own President and other officers.

ARTICLE VI.

Sect. 1. The times and places, and the manner of holding the elections of the members of each House, shall be prescribed by the legislature of each State; but their provisions concerning them may, at any time, be altered by the legislature of the United States.

Sect. 2. The legislature of the United States shall have authority to establish such uniform qualifications

22*

of the members of each House, with regard to property, as to the said legislature shall seem expedient.

Sect. 3. In each House a majority of the members shall constitute a quorum to do business ; but a smaller number may adjourn from day to day.

Sect. 4. Each House shall be the judge of the elections, returns, and qualifications of its own members.

Sect. 5. Freedom of speech and debate in the legislature shall not be impeached or questioned in any court or place out of the legislature ; and the members of each House shall, in all cases, except treason, felony, and breach of the peace, be privileged from arrest during their attendance at Congress, and in going to and returning from it.

Sect. 6. Each House may determine the rules of its proceedings ; may punish its members for disorderly behaviour ; and may expel a member.

Sect. 7. The House of Representatives, and the Senate, when it shall be acting in a legislative capacity, shall keep a journal of their proceedings, and shall, from time to time, publish them ; and the yeas and nays of the members of each House, on any question, shall, at the desire of one fifth part of the members present, be entered on the journal.

Sect. 8. Neither House, without the consent of the other, shall adjourn for more than three days, nor to any other place than that at which the two Houses are sitting. But this regulation shall not extend to the Senate, when it shall exercise the powers mentioned in the   article.

Sect. 9. The members of each House shall be ineligible to, and incapable of holding any office under the authority of the United States, during the time for which they shall respectively be elected ; and the members of the Senate shall be ineligible to, and incapable of holding any such office for one year afterwards.

Sect. 10. The members of each House shall receive a compensation for their services, to be ascertained and paid by the State in which they shall be chosen.

Sect. 11. The enacting style of the laws of the United States shall be, " Be it enacted, and it is hereby enacted, by the House of Representatives, and by the Senate of the United States, in Congress assembled."

Sect. 12. Each House shall possess the right of originating bills, except in the cases before mentioned.

Sect. 13. Every bill, which shall have passed the House of Representatives and the Senate, shall, before it becomes a law, be presented to the President of the United States, for his revision. If, upon such revision, he approve of it, he shall signify his approbation by signing it ; but if, upon such revision, it shall appear to him improper for being passed into a law, he shall return it, together with his objections against it, to that House in which it shall have originated, who shall enter the objections at large on their journal, and proceed to reconsider the bill ; but if, after such reconsideration, two thirds of that House shall, notwithstanding the objections of the President, agree to pass it, it shall, together with his objections, be sent to the other House, by which it shall likewise be reconsidered ; and if approved by two thirds of the other House also, it shall become a law. But, in all such cases, the votes of both Houses shall be determined by yeas and nays ; and the names of the persons voting for or against the bill, shall be entered in the journal of each House respectively. If any bill shall not be returned by the President within seven days after it shall have been presented to him, it shall be a law, unless the legislature, by their adjournment, prevent its return; in which case, it shall not be a law.

ARTICLE VII.

Sect. 1. The legislature of the United States shall have the power to lay and collect taxes, duties, imposts, and excises;

To regulate commerce with foreign nations, and among the several States;

To establish a uniform rule of naturalization throughout the United States;

To coin money;

To regulate the value of foreign coin;

To fix the standard of weights and measures;

To establish post-offices;

To borrow money, and emit bills on the credit of the United States;

To appoint a treasurer by ballot;

To constitute tribunals inferior to the Supreme Court;

To make rules concerning captures on land and water;

To declare the law and punishment of piracies and felonies committed on the high seas, and the punishment of counterfeiting the coin of the United States, and of offences against the law of nations;

To subdue a rebellion in any State, on the application of its legislature;

To make war;

To raise armies;

To build and equip fleets;

To call forth the aid of the militia, in order to execute the laws of the Union ; enforce treaties, suppress insurrections, and repel invasions ; and

To make all laws that shall be necessary and proper for carrying into execution the foregoing powers, and all other powers vested, by this constitution, in the government of the United States, or in any depart-ment or officer thereof.

Sect. 2. Treason against the United States shall consist only in levying war against the United States, or any of them ; and in adhering to the enemies of the United States, or any of them. The legislature of the United States shall have power to declare the punishment of treason. No person shall be convicted of treason, unless on the testimony of two witnesses. No attainder of treason shall work corruption of blood, nor forfeiture, except during the life of the person attainted.

Sect. 3. The proportions of direct taxation shall be regulated by the whole number of white and other free citizens and inhabitants of every age, sex, and condition, including those bound to servitude for a term of years, and three fifths of all other persons not comprehended in the foregoing description (except In-dians not paying taxes) ; which number shall within six years after the first meeting of the legislature, and within the term of every ten years afterwards, be taken in such manner as the said legislature shall direct.

Sect. 4. No tax or duty shall be laid by the legis-lature on articles exported from any State ; nor on the migration or importation of such persons as the several States shall think proper to admit ; nor shall such migration or importation be prohibited.

Sect. 5. No capitation tax shall be laid, unless in

proportion to the census herein before directed to be taken.

Sect. 6. No navigation act shall be passed without the assent of two thirds of the members present in each House.

Sect. 7. The United States shall not grant any title of nobility.

ARTICLE VIII.

The acts of the legislature of the United States made in pursuance of this constitution, and all treaties made under the authority of the United States, shall be the supreme law of the several States, and of their citizens and inhabitants; and the judges in the several States shall be bound thereby in their decisions; any thing in the constitution or laws of the several States to the contrary notwithstanding.

ARTICLE IX.

Sect. 1. The Senate of the United States shall have power to make treaties, and to appoint ambassadors, and judges of the Supreme Court.

Sect. 2. In all disputes and controversies now subsisting, or that may hereafter subsist, between two or more States, respecting jurisdiction or territory, the Senate shall possess the following powers: Whenever the legislature, or the executive authority, or the lawful agent of any State in controversy with another, shall, by memorial to the Senate, state the matter in question, and apply for a hearing, notice of such memorial and application shall be given, by order of the Senate, to the legislature or the executive authority of the other State in controversy. The Senate shall also assign a day for the appearance of the parties, by their agents, before that House. The agents shall be directed to appoint, by joint consent, commissioners or judges to constitute a court for hearing and determining the matter in question. But, if the agents cannot agree, the Senate shall name three persons out of each of the several States ; and from the list of such persons each party shall, alternately, strike out one, until the number shall be reduced to thirteen ; and from that number not less than seven, nor more than nine names, as the Senate shall direct, shall, in their presence, be drawn out by lot ; and the persons whose names shall be so drawn, or any five of them, shall be commissioners or judges to hear and finally determine the controversy ; provided a majority of the judges, who shall hear the cause, agree in the determination. If either party shall neglect to attend at any day assigned, without showing sufficient reasons for not attending, or, being present, shall refuse to strike, the Senate shall proceed to nominate three persons out of each State, and the clerk of the Senate shall strike in behalf of the party absent or refusing. If any of the parties shall refuse to submit to the authority of such court, or shall not appear to prosecute or defend their claim or cause, the court shall nevertheless proceed to pronounce judgment. The judgment shall be final and conclusive. The proceedings shall be transmitted to the President of the Senate, and shall be lodged among the public records for the security of the parties concerned. Every commissioner shall, before he sit in judgment, take an oath, to be administered by one of the judges of the Supreme or Superior Court of the State where the cause shall be tried, " well and truly to hear and determine the matter in question, according to the best of his judgment, without favor, affection, or hope of reward."

Sect. 3. All controversies concerning lands claimed under different grants of two or more States, whose jurisdictions, as they respect such lands, shall have been decided or adjusted subsequent to such grants, or any of them, shall, on application to the Senate, be finally determined, as near as may be, in the same manner as is before prescribed for deciding controversies between different States.

ARTICLE X.

Sect. 1. The executive power of the United States shall be vested in a single person. His style shall be, " The President of the United States of America "; and his title shall be, " His Excellency." He shall be elected by ballot by the legislature. He shall hold his office during the term of seven years; but shall not be elected a second time.

Sect. 2. He shall, from time to time, give information to the legislature of the state of the Union. He may recommend to their consideration such measures as he shall judge necessary and expedient. He may convene them on extraordinary occasions. In case of disagreement between the two Houses, with regard to the time of adjournment, he may adjourn them to such time as he thinks proper. He shall take care, that the laws of the United States be duly and faithfully executed. He shall commission all the officers of the United States; and shall appoint officers in all cases not otherwise provided for by this constitution. He shall receive ambassadors, and may correspond with the supreme executives of the several States. He shall have power to grant reprieves and pardons; but his pardon shall not be pleadable in bar of an impeachment. He shall be Commander-in-chief of the army and navy of the United States, and of the militia of the several States. He shall, at stated times, receive for his services a compensation, which shall neither be increased nor diminished during his continuance in office. Before he shall enter on the duties of his department, he shall take the following oath or affirmation : " I ———— solemnly swear (or affirm), that I will faithfully execute the office of President of the United States of America." He shall be removed from his office on impeachment by the House of Representatives, and conviction in the Supreme Court, of treason, bribery, or corruption. In case of his removal as aforesaid, death, resignation, or disability to discharge the powers and duties of his office, the President of the Senate shall exercise those powers and duties until another President of the United States be chosen, or until the disability of the President be removed.

ARTICLE XI.

Sect. 1. The judicial power of the United States shall be vested in one Supreme Court, and in such inferior courts as shall, when necessary, from time to time, be constituted by the legislature of the United States.

Sect. 2. The judges of the Supreme Court, and of the inferior courts, shall hold their offices during good behaviour. They shall, at stated times, receive for their services a compensation, which shall not be diminished during their continuance in office.

Sect. 3. The jurisdiction of the Supreme Court shall extend to all cases arising under laws passed by the legislature of the United States ; to all cases affecting ambassadors, other public ministers, and consuls ; to the trial of impeachments of officers of the United States ;

23

to all cases of admiralty and maritime jurisdiction; to controversies between two or more States (except such as shall regard territory or jurisdiction); between a State and citizens of another State; between citizens of different States; and between a State, or the citizens thereof, and foreign states, citizens, and subjects. In cases of impeachment, cases affecting ambassadors, other public ministers, and consuls, and those in which a State shall be party, this jurisdiction shall be original. In all the other cases before mentioned, it shall be appellate, with such exceptions and under such regulations as the legislature shall make. The legislature may assign any part of the jurisdiction above mentioned (except the trial of the President of the United States), in the manner and under the limitations which it shall think proper, to such inferior courts as it shall constitute from time to time.

Sect. 4. The trial of all criminal offences, (except in cases of impeachments,) shall be in the State where they shall be committed; and shall be by jury.

Sect. 5. Judgment, in cases of impeachment, shall not extend farther than to removal from office, and disqualification to hold and enjoy any office of honor, trust, or profit under the United States. But the party convicted shall, nevertheless, be liable and subject to indictment, trial, judgment, and punishment, according to law.

ARTICLE XII.

No State shall coin money; nor grant letters of marque and reprisal; nor enter into any treaty, alliance, or confederation; nor grant any title of nobility.

ARTICLE XIII.

No State, without the consent of the legislature of

the United States, shall emit bills of credit, or make any thing but specie a tender in payment of debts; lay impost or duties on imports; nor keep troops or ships of war in time of peace; nor enter into any agreement or compact with another State, or with any foreign power; nor engage in any war, unless it shall be actually invaded by enemies, or the danger of invasion be so imminent as not to admit of a delay until the legislature of the United States can be consulted.

ARTICLE XIV.

The citizens of each State shall be entitled to all privileges and immunities of citizens in the several States.

ARTICLE XV.

Any person charged with treason, felony, or high misdemeanor, in any State, who shall flee from justice, and shall be found in any other State, shall, on demand of the executive power of the State from which he fled, be delivered up and removed to the State having jurisdiction of the offence.

ARTICLE XVI.

Full faith shall be given in each State to the acts of the legislatures, and to the records and judicial proceedings of the courts and magistrates of every other State.

ARTICLE XVII.

New States, lawfully constituted or established within the limits of the United States, may be admitted by the legislature into this government; but to such admission the consent of two thirds of the members present in each House shall be necessary. If a new State shall arise within the limits of any of the present States, the consent of the legislatures of such States shall be also necessary to its admission. If the admission be consented to, the new States shall be admitted on the same terms with the original States. But the legislature may make conditions with the new States concerning the public debt, which shall be then subsisting.

ARTICLE XVIII.

The United States shall guarantee to each State a republican form of government; and shall protect each State against foreign invasions; and, on the application of its legislature, against domestic violence.

ARTICLE XIX.

On the application of the legislatures of two thirds of the States in the Union for an amendment of this constitution, the legislature of the United States shall call a convention for that purpose.

ARTICLE XX.

The members of the legislatures, and the executive and judicial officers of the United States, and of the several States, shall be bound by oath to support this constitution.

ARTICLE XXI.

The ratification of the conventions of   States shall be sufficient for organizing this constitution.

ARTICLE XXII.

This constitution shall be laid before the United States in Congress assembled, for their approbation; and it is the opinion of this convention, that it should be afterwards submitted to a convention chosen in each

State, under the recommendation of its legislature, in order to receive the ratification of such convention.

ARTICLE XXIII.

To introduce this government, it is the opinion of this convention, that each assenting convention should notify its assent and ratification to the United States in Congress assembled ; that Congress, after receiving the assent and ratifications of the conventions of States, should appoint and publish a day, as early as may be, and appoint a place for commencing proceedings under this constitution ; that, after such publication, the legislatures of the several States should elect members of the Senate, and direct the election of members of the House of Representatives; and that the members of the legislature should meet at the time and place assigned by Congress, and should, as soon as may be after their meeting, choose the President of the United States, and proceed to execute this constitution.

CONSTITUTION OF THE UNITED STATES,

AS AMENDED AND ADOPTED IN CONVENTION, SEPTEMBER 17TH, 1787.

WE the people of the United States, in order to form a more perfect union, establish justice, insure domestic tranquillity, provide for the common defence, promote the general welfare, and secure the blessings of liberty to ourselves and our posterity, do ordain and establish this constitution of the United States of America.

ARTICLE I.

Sect. 1. All legislative powers herein granted shall be vested in a Congress of the United States, which shall consist of a Senate and House of Representatives.

Sect. 2. The House of Representatives shall be composed of members chosen every second year by the people of the several States, and the electors in each State shall have the qualifications requisite for electors of the most numerous branch of the State legislature.

No person shall be a representative who shall not have attained to the age of twenty-five years, and been seven years a citizen of the United States, and who shall not, when elected, be an inhabitant of that State in which he shall be chosen.

Representatives and direct taxes shall be apportioned among the several States which may be included within this Union, according to their respective numbers, which shall be determined by adding to the whole number of free persons, including those bound to servitude for a term of years, and excluding Indians not taxed, three fifths of all other persons. The actual enumeration shall be made within three years after the first meeting of the Congress of the United States, and within every subsequent term of ten years, in such manner as they shall by law direct. The number of representatives shall not exceed one for every thirty thousand, but each State shall have at least one representative ; and, until such enumeration shall be made, the State of New Hampshire shall be entitled to choose three, Massachusetts eight, Rhode Island and Providence Plantations one, Connecticut five, New York six, New Jersey four, Pennsylvania eight, Delaware one, Maryland six, Virginia ten, North Carolina five, South Carolina five, and Georgia three.

When vacancies happen in the representation from any State, the executive authority thereof shall issue writs of election to fill such vacancies.

The House of Representatives shall choose their Speaker and other officers; and shall have the sole power of impeachment.

Sect. 3. The Senate of the United States shall be composed of two senators from each State, chosen by the legislature thereof, for six years; and each senator shall have one vote.

Immediately after they shall be assembled in consequence of the first election, they shall be divided as equally as may be into three classes. The seats of the senators of the first class shall be vacated at the expiration of the second year, of the second class at the expiration of the fourth year, and of the third class at the expiration of the sixth year; so that one third may be chosen every second year. And, if vacancies happen by resignation, or otherwise, during the recess of the legislature of any State, the executive thereof may make temporary appointments until the next meeting of the legislature, which shall then fill such vacancies.

No person shall be a senator who shall not have attained to the age of thirty years, and been nine years a citizen of the United States, and who shall not, when elected, be an inhabitant of that State, for which he shall be chosen.

The Vice-President of the United States, shall be President of the Senate, but shall have no vote, unless they be equally divided.

The Senate shall choose their other officers, and

also a president *pro tempore,* in the absence of the Vice-President, or when he shall exercise the office of President of the United States.

The Senate shall have the sole power to try all impeachments. When sitting for that purpose, they shall be on oath or affirmation. When the President of the United States is tried, the chief justice shall preside ; and no person shall be convicted without the concurrence of two thirds of the members present.

Judgment in cases of impeachment shall not extend further than to removal from office, and disqualification to hold and enjoy any office of honor, trust, or profit under the United States ; but the party convicted shall, nevertheless, be liable and subject to indictment, trial, judgment, and punishment, according to law.

Sect. 4. The times, places, and manner of holding elections for senators and representatives, shall be prescribed in each State by the legislature thereof ; but the Congress may, at any time, by law, make or alter such regulations, except as to the places of choosing senators.

The Congress shall assemble at least once in every year ; and such meeting shall be on the first Monday in December, unless they shall by law appoint a different day.

Sect. 5. Each House shall be the judge of the elections, returns, and qualifications of its own members ; and a majority of each shall constitute a quorum to do business ; but a smaller number may adjourn from day to day, and may be authorized to compel the attendance of absent members, in such manner, and under such penalties, as each House may provide.

Each House may determine the rules of its pro-

ceedings ; punish its members for disorderly behaviour, and, with the concurrence of two thirds, expel
a member.

Each House shall keep a journal of its proceedings,
and from time to time publish the same, excepting
such parts as may in their judgment require secrecy ;
and the yeas and nays of the members of either House
on any question shall, at the desire of one fifth of those
present, be entered on the journals.

Neither House, during the session of Congress,
shall, without the consent of the other, adjourn for
more than three days, nor to any other place than that
in which the two Houses shall be sitting.

Sect. 6. The senators and representatives shall receive a compensation for their services, to be ascertained by law, and paid out of the treasury of the United
States. They shall in all cases, except treason, felony, and breach of the peace, be privileged from arrest
during their attendance at the session of their respective Houses, and in going to and returning from the
same , and for any speech or debate in either House,
they shall not be questioned in any other place.

No senator or representative shall, during the time
for which he was elected, be appointed to any civil
office under the authority of the United States, which
shall have been created, or the emoluments whereof
shall have been increased during such time ; and no
person holding any office under the United States,
shall be a member of either House during his continuance in office.

Sect. 7. All bills for raising revenue shall originate
in the House of Representatives ; but the Senate may
propose or concur with amendments as on other bills.

Every bill which shall have passed the House of

Representatives and the Senate shall, before it become
a law, be presented to the President of the United
States. If he approve, he shall sign it; but if not, he
shall return it, with his objections, to that House in
which it shall have originated, who shall enter the
objections at large on their journal, and proceed to reconsider it. If, after such reconsideration, two thirds
of that House shall agree to pass the bill, it shall be
sent, together with the objections, to the other House,
by which it shall likewise be reconsidered, and, if approved by two thirds of that House, it shall become
a law. But in all such cases, the votes of both Houses
shall be determined by yeas and nays; and the names
of the persons voting for and against the bill, shall be
entered on the journal of each House respectively. If
any bill shall not be returned by the President within
ten days (Sundays excepted) after it shall have been
presented to him, the same shall be a law, in like
manner as if he had signed it, unless the Congress, by
their adjournment, prevent its return, in which case it
shall not be a law.

Every order, resolution, or vote to which the concurrence of the Senate and House of Representatives
may be necessary, (except on a question of adjournment,) shall be presented to the President of the United
States; and, before the same shall take effect, shall be
approved by him, or, being disapproved by him, shall
be repassed by two thirds of the Senate and House of
Representatives, according to the rules and limitations
prescribed in the case of a bill.

Sect. 8. The Congress shall have power,

To lay and collect taxes, duties, imposts, and excises; to pay the debts and provide for the common
defence and general welfare of the United States; but

all duties, imposts, and excises shall be uniform throughout the United States.

To borrow money on the credit of the United States;

To regulate commerce with foreign nations, and among the several States, and with the Indian tribes;

To establish an uniform rule of naturalization, and uniform laws on the subject of bankruptcies throughout the United States;

To coin money, regulate the value thereof, and of foreign coin, and fix the standard of weights and measures;

To provide for the punishment of counterfeiting the securities and current coin of the United States;

To establish post-offices and post-roads;

To promote the progress of science and useful arts, by securing, for limited times, to authors and inventors, the exclusive right to their respective writings and discoveries;

To constitute tribunals inferior to the Supreme Court;

To define and punish piracies and felonies committed on the high seas, and offences against the law of nations;

To declare war, grant letters of marque and reprisal, and make rules concerning captures on land or water;

To raise and support armies; but no appropriation of money to that use shall be for a longer term than two years;

To provide and maintain a navy;

To make rules for the government and regulation of the land and naval forces;

To provide for calling forth the militia to execute

the laws of the Union, suppress insurrections, and repel invasions;

To provide for organizing, arming, and disciplining the militia, and for governing such part of them as may be employed in the service of the United States, reserving to the States respectively, the appointment of the officers, and the authority of training the militia, according to the discipline prescribed by Congress;

To exercise exclusive legislation in all cases whatsoever, over such district (not exceeding ten miles square) as may, by cession of particular States, and the acceptance of Congress, become the seat of government of the United States; and to exercise like authority over all places purchased by the consent of the legislature of the State in which the same shall be, for the erection of forts, magazines, arsenals, dockyards, and other needful buildings; and

To make all laws which shall be necessary and proper for carrying into execution the foregoing powers, and all other powers vested by this constitution in the government of the United States, or in any department or office thereof.

Sect. 9. The migration or importation of such persons as any of the States now existing shall think proper to admit, shall not be prohibited by the Congress prior to the year one thousand eight hundred and eight; but a tax or duty may be imposed on such importation not exceeding ten dollars for each person.

The privilege of the writ of *habeas corpus* shall not be suspended, unless when, in cases of rebellion or invasion, the public safety may require it.

No bill of attainder or *ex post facto* law shall be passed.

No capitation or other direct tax shall be laid, unless

in proportion to the census or enumeration herein before directed to be taken.

No tax or duty shall be laid on articles exported from any State. No preference shall be given by any regulation of commerce or revenue to the ports of one State over those of another; nor shall vessels bound to or from one State, be obliged to enter, clear, or pay duties in another.

No money shall be drawn from the treasury, but in consequence of appropriations made by law; and a regular statement and account of the receipts and expenditures of all public money shall be published from time to time.

No title of nobility shall be granted by the United States; and no person holding any office of profit or trust under them, shall, without the consent of the Congress, accept of any present, emolument, office, or title of any kind whatever, from any king, prince, or foreign state.

Sect. 10. No State shall enter into any treaty, alliance, or confederation; grant letters of marque and reprisal; coin money; emit bills of credit; make any thing but gold and silver coin a tender in payment of debts; pass any bill of attainder, *ex post facto* law, or law impairing the obligation of contracts, or grant any title of nobility.

No State shall, without the consent of the Congress, lay any imposts or duties on imports or exports, except what may be absolutely necessary for executing its inspection laws; and the net produce of all duties and imposts, laid by any State on imports or exports, shall be for the use of the treasury of the United States; and all such laws shall be subject to the revision and control of the Congress. No State shall, without the consent of Congress, lay any duty of tonnage, keep troops or ships of war in time of peace, enter into any agreement or compact with another State, or with a foreign power, or engage in war, unless actually invaded, or in such imminent danger as will not admit of delay.

ARTICLE II.

Sect. 1. The executive power shall be vested in a President of the United States of America. He shall hold his office during the term of four years, and together with the Vice-President, chosen for the same term, be elected as follows :

Each State shall appoint, in such manner as the legislature thereof may direct, a number of electors, equal to the whole number of senators and representatives to which the State may be entitled in the Congress ; but no senator or representative, or person holding an office of trust or profit under the United States, shall be appointed an elector.

The electors shall meet in their respective States, and vote by ballot for two persons of whom one at least shall not be an inhabitant of the same State with themselves. And they shall make a list of all the persons voted for, and of the number of votes for each ; which list they shall sign and certify, and transmit sealed to the seat of government of the United States, directed to the President of the Senate. The President of the Senate shall, in the presence of the Senate and House of Representatives, open all the certificates, and the votes shall then be counted. The person having the greatest number of votes shall be the President, if such number be a majority of the whole number of electors appointed ; and, if there be more than one who have such majority, and have an equal number of votes, then the House of Representatives shall immediately choose by ballot one of them for President ; and, if no person have a majority, then from the five highest on the list, the said House shall, in like manner, choose the President. But in choosing the President, the votes shall be taken by States, the representation from each State having one vote ; a quorum for this purpose shall consist of a member or members from two thirds of the States, and a majority of all the States shall be necessary to a choice. In every case, after the choice of the President, the person having the greatest number of votes of the electors, shall be the Vice-President. But, if there should remain two or more who have equal votes, the Senate shall choose from them by ballot, the Vice-President.

The Congress may determine the time of choosing the electors, and the day in which they shall give their votes ; which day shall be the same throughout the United States.

No person except a natural born citizen, or a citizen of the United States at the time of the adoption of this constitution, shall be eligible to the office of President ; neither shall any person be eligible to that office who shall not have attained to the age of thirty-five years, and been fourteen years a resident within the United States.

In case of the removal of the President from office, or of his death, resignation, or inability to discharge the powers and duties of the said office, the same shall devolve on the Vice-President ; and the Congress may by law provide for the case of removal, death, resignation, or inability, both of the President and Vice-

President, declaring what officer shall then act as President; and such officer shall act accordingly, until the disability be removed, or a President shall be elected.

The President shall, at stated times, receive for his services a compensation, which shall neither be increased nor diminished during the period for which he shall have been elected, and he shall not receive within that period any other emolument from the United States, or any of them.

Before he enters on the execution of his office, he shall take the following oath or affirmation:

" I do solemnly swear (or affirm), that I will faithfully execute the office of President of the United States, and will, to the best of my ability, preserve, protect, and defend the Constitution of the United States."

Sect. 2. The President shall be Commander-in-chief of the army and navy of the United States, and of the militia of the several States, when called into the actual service of the United States. He may require the opinion, in writing, of the principal officers in each of the executive departments, upon any subject relating to the duties of the respective offices. And he shall have power to grant reprieves and pardons for offences against the United States, except in cases of impeachment.

He shall have power, by and with the advice and consent of the Senate, to make treaties, provided two thirds of the senators present concur; and he shall nominate, and by and with the advice and consent of the Senate shall appoint ambassadors, other public ministers, and consuls, judges of the Supreme Court, and all other officers of the United States, whose appointments are not herein otherwise provided for, and which shall be established by law. But the Congress may, by law, vest the appointment of such inferior officers as they think proper, in the President alone, in the courts of law, or in the heads of departments.

The President shall have power to fill up all vacancies that may happen during the recess of the Senate, by granting commissions, which shall expire at the end of their next session.

Sect. 3. He shall from time to time give to the Congress information of the state of the Union, and recommend to their consideration such measures as he shall judge necessary and expedient. He may, on extraordinary occasions, convene both Houses, or either of them; and in case of disagreement between them, with respect to the time of adjournment, he may adjourn them to such time as he shall think proper. He shall receive ambassadors and other public ministers. He shall take care, that the laws be faithfully executed; and shall commission all the officers of the United States.

Sect. 4. The President, Vice-President, and all civil officers of the United States, shall be removed from office on impeachment for, and conviction of treason, bribery, or other high crimes and misdemeanors.

ARTICLE III.

Sect. 1. The judicial power of the United States, shall be vested in one Supreme Court, and in such inferior courts as the Congress may from time to time ordain and establish. The judges, both of the supreme and inferior courts, shall hold their offices during good behaviour, and shall, at stated times, receive for their services a compensation, which shall not be diminished during their continuance in office.

Sect. 2. The judicial power shall extend to all cases, in law and equity, arising under this constitution, the laws of the United States, and treaties made, or which shall be made, under their authority; to all cases affecting ambassadors, other public ministers, and consuls; to all cases of admiralty and maritime jurisdiction; to controversies to which the United States shall be a party; to controversies between two or more States; between a State and citizens of another State; between citizens of different States; between citizens of the same State claiming lands under grants of different States, and between a State, or the citizens thereof, and foreign states, citizens, or subjects.

In all cases affecting ambassadors, other public ministers, or consuls, and those in which a State shall be party, the Supreme Court shall have original jurisdiction. In all the other cases before mentioned, the Supreme Court shall have appellate jurisdiction, both as to law and fact, with such exceptions, and under such regulations, as the Congress shall make.

The trial of all crimes, except in cases of impeachment, shall be by jury; and such trial shall be held in the State where the said crimes shall have been committed; but when not committed within any State, the trial shall be at such place or places as the Congress may by law have directed.

Sect. 3. Treason against the United States, shall consist only in levying war against them, or in adhering to their enemies, giving them aid and comfort. No person shall be convicted of treason, unless on the testimony of two witnesses to the same overt act, or on the confession in open court.

The Congress shall have power to declare the punishment of treason; but no attainder of treason shall work corruption of blood, or forfeiture, except during the life of the person attainted.

ARTICLE IV.

Sect. 1. Full faith and credit shall be given in each State to the public acts, records, and judicial proceedings of every other State. And the Congress may, by general laws, prescribe the manner in which such acts, records, and proceedings shall be proved, and the effect thereof.

Sect. 2. The citizens of each State shall be entitled to all privileges and immunities of citizens in the several States.

A person charged in any State with treason, felony, or other crime, who shall flee from justice, and be found in another State, shall, on demand of the executive authority of the State from which he fled, be delivered up to be removed to the State having jurisdiction of the crime.

No person held to service or labor in one State, under the laws thereof, escaping into another, shall, in consequence of any law or regulation therein, be discharged from such service or labor, but shall be delivered up on claim of the party to whom such service or labor may be due.

Sect. 3. New States may be admitted by the Congress into this Union; but no new State shall be formed or erected within the jurisdiction of any other State; nor any State be formed by the junction of two or more States, or parts of States, without the consent of the legislature of the States concerned, as well as of the Congress.

The Congress shall have power to dispose of, and make all needful rules and regulations respecting the territory or other property belonging to the United States; and nothing in this constitution shall be so construed as to prejudice any claims of the United States, or of any particular State.

Sect. 4. The United States shall guarantee to every State in this Union a republican form of government, and shall protect each of them against invasion; and, on application of the legislature, or of the executive, (when the legislature cannot be convened,) against domestic violence.

ARTICLE V.

The Congress, whenever two thirds of both Houses shall deem it necessary, shall propose amendments to this constitution; or, on the application of the legislatures of two thirds of the several States, shall call a convention for proposing amendments; which, in either case, shall be valid to all intents and purposes, as part of this constitution, when ratified by the legislatures of three fourths of the several States, or by conventions in three fourths thereof, as the one or the other mode of ratification may be proposed by the Congress; provided, that no amendment which may be made prior to the year one thousand eight hundred and eight, shall in any manner affect the first and fourth clauses in the ninth section of the first article; and that no State, without its consent, shall be deprived of its equal suffrage in the Senate.

ARTICLE VI.

All debts contracted, and engagements entered into, before the adoption of this constitution, shall be as valid against the United States under this constitution, as under the confederation.

This constitution, and the laws of the United States which shall be made in pursuance thereof, and all treaties made, or which shall be made under the authority of the United States, shall be the supreme law of the land; and the judges in every State shall be bound thereby; any thing in the constitution or laws of any State to the contrary notwithstanding.

The senators and representatives before mentioned, and the members of the several State legislatures, and all executive and judicial officers, both of the United States and of the several States, shall be bound by oath or affirmation, to support this constitution; but no religious test shall ever be required as a qualification to any office of public trust under the United States.

ARTICLE VII.

The ratification of the conventions of nine States shall be sufficient for the establishment of this constitution between the States so ratifying the same.

Done in convention, by the unanimous consent of the States present, the seventeenth day of September, in the year of our Lord one thousand seven hundred and eighty-seven, and of the independence of the United States of America, the twelfth. In witness whereof, we have hereunto subscribed our names.

GEORGE WASHINGTON, President,
AND Deputy from Virginia.

New Hampshire.	Massachusetts.
John Langdon,	Nathaniel Gorham,
Nicholas Gilman.	Rufus King.

CONNECTICUT.
William Samuel Johnson,
Roger Sherman.

NEW YORK.
Alexander Hamilton.

NEW JERSEY.
William Livingston,
David Brearley,
William Patterson,
Jonathan Dayton.

PENNSYLVANIA.
Benjamin Franklin,
Thomas Mifflin,
Robert Morris,
George Clymer,
Thomas Fitzsimons,
Jared Ingersoll,
James Wilson,
Gouverneur Morris.

DELAWARE.
George Read,
Gunning Bedford, Jun.

John Dickinson,
Richard Bassett,
Jacob Broom.

MARYLAND.
James M'Henry,
Daniel of St. Thos. Jenifer,
Daniel Carroll.

VIRGINIA.
John Blair,
James Madison, Jun.

NORTH CAROLINA.
William Blount,
Richard Dobbs Spaight,
Hugh Williamson.

SOUTH CAROLINA.
John Rutledge,
Charles C. Pinckney,
Charles Pinckney,
Pierce Butler.

GEORGIA.
William Few,
Abraham Baldwin.

Attest, WILLIAM JACKSON, *Secretary.*

IN CONVENTION,

Monday, September 17th, 1787.

PRESENT, The States of New Hampshire, Massachusetts, Connecticut, Mr. Hamilton from New York, New Jersey, Pennsylvania, Delaware, Maryland, Virginia, North Carolina, South Carolina, and Georgia:

Resolved, That the preceding Constitution be laid

before the United States in Congress assembled, and that it is the opinion of this convention, that it should afterwards be submitted to a convention of delegates chosen in each State by the people thereof, under the recommendation of its legislature, for their assent and ratification; and that each convention assenting to, and ratifying the same, shall give notice thereof to the United States in Congress assembled.

Resolved, That it is the opinion of this convention, that, as soon as the conventions of nine States shall have ratified this Constitution, the United States in Congress assembled should fix a day on which electors should be appointed by the States which shall have ratified the same, and a day on which the electors should assemble to vote for the President, and the time and place for commencing proceedings under this Constitution. That, after such publication, the electors should be appointed, and the senators and representatives elected. That the electors should meet on the day fixed for the election of the President, and should transmit their votes, certified, signed, sealed, and directed, as the Constitution requires, to the secretary of the United States in Congress assembled; that the senators and representatives should convene at the time and place assigned; that the senators should appoint a President of the Senate, for the sole purpose of receiving, opening, and counting the votes for President; and that, after he shall be chosen, the Congress, together with the President, should, without delay, proceed to execute this Constitution.

By the unanimous order of the convention,

GEO. WASHINGTON, President.

WILLIAM JACKSON, *Secretary.*

IN CONVENTION.

September 17th, 1787.

Sir,

We have now the honor to submit to the consideration of the United States in Congress assembled, that constitution which has appeared to us the most advisable.

The friends of our country have long seen and desired, that the power of making war, peace, and treaties; that of levying money and regulating commerce, and the correspondent executive and judicial authorities, should be fully and effectually vested in the general government of the Union; but the impropriety of delegating such extensive trusts to one body of men is evident. Hence results the necessity of a different organization.

It is obviously impracticable, in the federal government of these States, to secure all rights of independent sovereignty to each, and yet provide for the interest and safety of all; individuals entering into society, must give up a share of liberty to preserve the rest. The magnitude of the sacrifice must depend as well on situation and circumstance as on the object to be obtained. It is at all times difficult to draw with precision the line between those rights which must be surrendered, and those which may be reserved; and on the present occasion this difficulty was increased by a difference among the several States as to their situation, extent, habits, and particular interests.

In all our deliberations on this subject, we kept steadily in our view, that which appears to us the greatest interest of every true American, the consolidation of our Union, in which is involved our prosperity, felicity, safety, perhaps our national existence. This important consideration, seriously and deeply impressed on our minds, led each State in the convention to be less rigid on points of inferior magnitude, than might have been otherwise expected; and thus the constitution, which we now present, is the result of a spirit of amity, and of that mutual deference and concession, which the peculiarity of our political situation rendered indispensable.

That it will meet the full and entire approbation of every State is not perhaps to be expected; but each will doubtless consider, that, had her interests alone been consulted, the consequences might have been particularly disagreeable or injurious to others; that it is liable to as few exceptions as could reasonably have been expected, we hope and believe; that it may promote the lasting welfare of that country so dear to us all, and secure her freedom and happiness, is our most ardent wish. With great respect, we have the honor to be, Sir, your Excellency's most obedient and humble servants,

GEO. WASHINGTON, President.

By unanimous order of the convention.

His Excellency the President of Congress.

THE UNITED STATES, IN CONGRESS ASSEMBLED,

Friday, September 28th, 1787.

Present, New Hampshire, Massachusetts, Connecticut, New York, New Jersey, Pennsylvania, Delaware, Virginia, North Carolina, South Carolina, and Georgia; and from Maryland, Mr. Ross.

25

Congress having received the report of the convention lately assembled in Philadelphia;

Resolved, unanimously, That the said report, with the resolutions and letter accompanying the same, be transmitted to the several legislatures, in order to submit to a convention of delegates, chosen in each State by the people thereof, in conformity to the resolves of the convention, made and provided in that case.

CHARLES THOMPSON, *Secretary.*

AMENDMENTS

TO THE CONSTITUTION OF THE UNITED STATES.

ARTICLE I.

Congress shall make no law respecting an establishment of religion, or prohibiting the free exercise thereof; or abridging the freedom of speech, or of the press; or the right of the people peaceably to assemble, and to petition the government for a redress of grievances.

ARTICLE II.

A well-regulated militia being necessary to the security of a free state, the right of the people to keep and bear arms shall not be infringed.

ARTICLE III.

No soldier shall, in time of peace be quartered in any house, without the consent of the owner; nor in time of war, but in a manner to be prescribed by law.

ARTICLE IV.

The right of the people to be secured in their persons, houses, papers, and effects, against unreasonable searches and seizures, shall not be violated, and no warrants shall issue, but upon probable cause, supported by oath or affirmation, and particularly describing the place to be searched, and the persons or things to be seized.

ARTICLE V.

No person shall be held to answer for a capital, or otherwise infamous crime, unless on a presentment or indictment of a grand jury, except in cases arising in the land or naval forces, or in the militia, when in actual service, in time of war, or public danger; nor shall any person be subject for the same offence to be twice put in jeopardy of life or limb; nor shall be compelled, in any criminal case, to be witness against himself; nor be deprived of life, liberty, or property, without due process of law; nor shall private property be taken for public use, without just compensation.

ARTICLE VI.

In all criminal prosecutions, the accused shall enjoy the right to a speedy and public trial, by an impartial jury of the State and district wherein the crime shall have been committed; which district shall have been previously ascertained by law, and to be informed of the nature and cause of the accusation; to be confronted with the witnesses against him; to have compulsory process for obtaining witnesses in his favor; and to have the assistance of counsel for his defence.

ARTICLE VII.

In suits at common law, where the value in controversy shall exceed twenty dollars, the right of trial by jury shall be preserved; and no fact tried by a jury shall be otherwise reexamined in any court of the United States, than according to the rules of the common law.

ARTICLE VIII.

Excessive bail shall not be required; nor excessive fines imposed; nor cruel and unusual punishments inflicted.

ARTICLE IX.

The enumeration, in the Constitution, of certain rights shall not be construed to deny or disparage others, retained by the people.

ARTICLE X.

The powers not delegated to the United States by the Constitution, nor prohibited by it to the States, are reserved to the States respectively, or to the people.

ARTICLE XI.

The judicial power of the United States shall not be construed to extend to any suit in law or equity, commenced or prosecuted against one of the United States by citizens of another State, or by citizens or subjects of any foreign state.

ARTICLE XII.

The electors shall meet in their respective States, and vote by ballot for President and Vice-President, one of whom at least shall not be an inhabitant of the same State with themselves; they shall name in their ballots the person voted for as President, and in distinct ballots the person voted for as Vice-President, and they shall make distinct lists of all persons voted for as President, and of all persons voted for as Vice-President, and of the number of votes for each, which lists they shall sign and certify, and transmit sealed to the seat of the government of the United States, directed to the President of the Senate; the President of the Senate shall, in the presence of the Senate and House of Representatives, open all the certificates, and the votes shall then be counted; the person having the greatest number of votes for President, shall be the President, if such number be a majority of the whole number of electors appointed; and, if no person have such majority, then from the persons having the highest numbers not exceeding three on the list of those voted for as President, the House of Representatives shall choose immediately, by ballot, the President. But in choosing the President, the votes shall be taken by States, the representation from each State having one vote; a quorum for this purpose shall consist of a member or members from two thirds of the States, and a majority of all the States shall be necessary to a choice. And, if the House of Representatives shall not choose a President whenever the right of choice shall devolve upon them, before the fourth day of March next following, then the Vice-President shall act as President, as in case of the death or other constitutional disability of the President.

The person having the greatest number of votes as Vice-President, shall be the Vice-President, if such number be a majority of the whole number of electors appointed, and if no person have a majority, then from the two highest numbers on the list, the Senate shall choose the Vice-President; a quorum for the purpose shall consist of two thirds of the whole number of senators, and a majority of the whole number shall be necessary to a choice.

But no person constitutionally ineligible to the office of President shall be eligible to that of Vice-President.

ADVERTISEMENT,

Published by the Department of State as an Introduction to the Journal of the Convention assembled at Philadelphia, Monday, May 14th, and dissolved Monday, September 17th, 1787.

The first volume of the late edition of the laws of the United States, compiled under the direction of the late secretary of state and attorney-general, contains a succinct historical review of the successive public measures, which led to the present organization of the North American Union, from the assembling of the Congress of the colonies, on the 5th of September, 1774, to the adoption of the Constitution of the United States, and of the subsequent amendments to it, now in force.

The following resolution of the old Congress, adopted on the 21st of February, 1787, contains the authority by which the convention which formed the Constitution was convoked :

" Whereas, there is provision in the articles of confederation and perpetual union, for making alterations therein, by the assent of a Congress of the United States, and of the legislatures of the several States; and, whereas, experience hath evinced, that there are defects in the present confederation, as a mean to remedy which, several of the States, and particularly the State of New York, by express instructions to their delegates in Congress, have suggested a convention for the purposes expressed in the following resolution ; and such convention appearing to be the most probable mean of establishing in these States a firm national government,

" *Resolved*, That in the opinion of Congress, it is expedient, that on the second Monday in May next, a convention of delegates, who shall have been appointed by the several States, be held at Philadelphia, for the sole and express purpose of revising the articles of confederation, and reporting to Congress and the several legislatures, such alterations and provisions therein, as shall, when agreed to in Congress, and confirmed by the States, render the federal constitution adequate to the exigencies of government, and the preservation of the Union."

The day appointed by this resolution for the meeting of the convention was the second Monday in May; but the 25th of that month was the first day upon which a sufficient number of members appeared to constitute a representation of a majority of the States. They then elected George Washington their President, and proceeded to business.

On the 29th of May, Mr. Edmund Randolph presented to the convention fifteen resolutions, and Mr. C. Pinckney laid before them the draft of a federal government, which were referred to a committee of the whole; which debated the resolutions, from day to day, until the 13th of June, when the committee of the whole reported to the convention a series of nineteen resolutions, founded upon those which had been proposed by Mr. Randolph.

On the 15th of June, Mr. Patterson submitted to the convention his resolutions, which were referred to a committee of the whole, to whom were also recommitted the resolutions reported by them on the 13th.

On the 19th of June, the committee of the whole reported, that they did not agree to Mr. Patterson's propositions, but reported again the resolutions which had been reported before.

The convention never afterwards went into committee of the whole; but, from the 19th of June till the 23d of July, were employed in debating the nineteen resolutions reported by the committee of the whole on the 13th of June; some of which were occasionally referred to grand committees of one member from each State, or to select committees of five members.

After passing upon the nineteen resolutions, it was on the 23d of July resolved, " That the proceedings of the convention for the establishment of a national government, except what respects the supreme executive, be referred to a committee, for the purpose of reporting a constitution conformably to the proceedings aforesaid."

This committee, consisting of five members, and called in the journal "the committee of detail," was appointed on the 24th of July, and with the proceedings of the convention, the propositions submitted to the convention by Mr. Charles Pinckney, on the 29th of May, and by Mr. Patterson, on the 15th of June, were referred to them.

On the 26th of July, a resolution respecting the executive, and two others, offered for the consideration of the convention, were referred to the committee of detail ; and the convention adjourned till Monday, the 6th of August, when the committee reported a constitution for the establishment of a national government. This draft formed the general text of debate from that time till the 8th of September ; many additional resolutions being, in the course of the deliberations, proposed, and referred to and reported upon by the same committee of detail, or other committees of eleven, (a member from each State,) or of five:

On the 8th of September, a committee of five was appointed "to revise the style of, and arrange, the articles agreed to by the House."

On the 12th of September, this committee reported the constitution as revised and arranged, and the draft of a letter to Congress. It was ordered, that printed copies of the reported constitution should be furnished to the members, and they were brought in the next day.

On the 17th of September, 1787, the convention dissolved itself, by an adjournment without day, after transmitting the plan of constitution which they had prepared to Congress, to be laid before conventions, delegated by the people of the several States, for their assent and ratification.

The last act of the convention, was a resolution, that their journal and other papers should be deposited with their president, to be retained by him, subject to the order of the Congress, if ever formed under the constitution.

On the 19th of March, 1796, President Washington deposited in the department of state three manuscript volumes; one containing, in one hundred and fifty-three pages, the journal of the federal convention of 1787; one, the journal of the proceedings of the same convention, while in committee of the whole, in twenty-eight pages; and one, three pages of lists of yeas and nays on various questions debated in the convention; and, after an interval of eight blank pages, five other pages of like yeas and nays. There were also two loose sheets and one half sheet of similar yeas and nays; a printed draft of the constitution, as reported on the 6th of August, 1787, with erasures and written interlineations of amendments afterwards adopted; two sheets containing copies of the series of resolutions offered to the convention by Mr. Edmund Randolph, in different stages of amendment, as reported by the committee of the whole; and seven other papers of no importance in relation to the proceedings of the convention.

The volume containing the journal of the convention, was in an incomplete state. The journal of Friday, September 14th, and a commencement of that of Saturday, September 15th, filled three fourths of the one hundred and fifty-third page; then terminated abruptly, and were, with the exception of five lines, crossed out with a pen. President Madison, to whom application for that purpose was made, has furnished, from his own minutes, the means of completing the journal, as now published.

The yeas and nays were not inserted in the journals, but were entered partly in a separate volume, and partly on loose sheets of paper. They were taken, not individually, but by States. Instead of publishing them as they appear in the manuscript, they are now given immediately after each question upon which they were taken.

General Joseph Bloomfield, executor of David Brearley, one of the members of the convention, transmitted to the department of state several additional papers, which are included in this publication.

The paper purporting to be Colonel Hamilton's plan of a constitution, is not noticed in the journals. It was not offered by him for discussion, but was read by him as part of a speech, observing, that he did not mean it as a proposition, but only to give a more correct view of his ideas.

The return of the members in the several States, appears to have been an estimate used for the purpose of apportioning the number of members to be admitted from each of the States to the House of Representatives.

In order to follow with clear understanding the course of proceedings of the convention, particular attention is required to the following papers, which, except the third, successively formed the general text of their debates.

1. May 29th, 1787. The fifteen resolutions offered by Mr. Edmund Randolph to the convention, and by them referred to a committee of the whole.

2. June 13th. Nineteen resolutions reported by this committee of the whole, on the 13th, and again on the 19th of June, to the convention.

3. July 26th. Twenty-three resolutions adopted and elaborated by the convention, in debate upon the above nineteen, reported from the committee of the whole ; and on the 23d and 26th of July referred, together with the plan of Mr. C. Pinckney, and the propositions of Mr. Patterson, to a committee of five, to report a draft of a constitution.

4. August 6th. The draft of a plan of constitution reported by this committee to the convention ; and debated from that time till the 12th of September.

5. September 13th. Plan of constitution brought in by a committee of revision, appointed on the 8th of September, consisting of five members, to revise the style and arrange the articles agreed to by the convention.

The second and fourth of these papers, are among those deposited by President Washington, at the department of state.

The first, fourth, and fifth, are among those transmitted by General Bloomfield.

The third is collected from the proceedings of the convention, as they are spread over the journal from June 19th to July 26th.

This paper, together with the plan of Mr. C. Pinckney, a copy of which has been furnished by him, and the propositions of Mr. Patterson, included among the papers forwarded by General Bloomfield, comprise the materials, upon which the first draft was made of the constitution, as reported by the committee of detail, on the 6th of August.

To the journal, acts, and proceedings of the convention, are added in this publication, the subsequent proceedings of the Congress of the confederation, upon the constitution, reported as the result of their labors; and the acts of ratification by the conventions of the several States of the Union, by virtue of which it became the supreme law of the land; and also the amendments to it, which have been since adopted and form a part of the constitution. It was thought, that this supplement would be, if not essential, at least well adapted to carry into full effect the intentions of Congress in directing the publication; by presenting at one view the rise, progress, and present condition of the Constitution of the United States.

Department of State, October, 1819.

LIST OF THE MEMBERS

OF THE FEDERAL CONVENTION WHICH FORMED THE CONSTITUTION OF THE UNITED STATES.

From			Attended.
N. Hampshire,	1.	John Langdon,	July 23, 1787
		John Pickering,	
	2.	Nicholas Gilman,	July 23, "
		Benjamin West,	
Massachusetts,		*Francis Dana,*	
		Elbridge Gerry,	May 29, "
	3.	Nathaniel Gorham,	May 28, "
	4.	Rufus King,	May 25, "
		Caleb Strong,	May 28, "
Rhode Island,		[No appointment.]	
Connecticut,	5.	Wm. Sam. Johnson,	June 2, "
	6.	Roger Sherman,	May 30, "
		Oliver Ellsworth,	May 29, "
New York,		Robert Yates,	May 25, "
	7.	Alexander Hamilton,	May 25, "
		John Lansing,	June 2, "
New Jersey,	8.	Wm. Livingston,	June 5, "
	9.	David Brearley,	May 25, "
		William C. Houston,	May 25, "
	10.	William Patterson,	May 25, "
		John Nielson,	
		Abraham Clark,	
	11.	Jonathan Dayton,	June 21, "
Pennsylvania,	12.	Benjamin Franklin,	May 28, "
	13.	Thomas Mifflin,	May 28, "
	14.	Robert Morris,	May 25, "
	15.	George Clymer,	May 28, "
	16.	Thos. Fitzsimons,	May 25, "
	17.	Jared Ingersoll,	May 28, "

From		Attended.
Pennsylvania,	18. James Wilson,	May 25, 1787
	19. Gouverneur Morris,	May 25, "
Delaware,	20. George Read,	May 25, "
	21. Gunning Bedford, Jr.	May 28, "
	22. John Dickinson,	May 28, "
	23. Richard Bassett,	May 25, "
	24. Jacob Broom,	May 25, "
Maryland,	25. James M'Henry,	May 29, "
	26. Daniel of St. Thomas Jenifer,	June 2, "
	27. Daniel Carroll,	July 9, "
	John Francis Mercer,	Aug. 6, "
	Luther Martin,	June 9, "
Virginia,	28. George Washington,	May 25, "
	Patrick Henry, (declined.)	
	Edmund Randolph,	May 25, "
	29. John Blair,	May 25, "
	30. James Madison, Jr.	May 25, "
	George Mason,	May 25, "
	George Wythe,	May 25, "
	James M'Clurg, (in the room of P. Henry)	May 25, "
N. Carolina,	*Richard Caswell*, (resigned.)	
	Alexander Martin,	May 25, "
	William R. Davie,	May 25, "
	31. Wm. Blount, (in the room of R. Caswell)	June 20, "
	Willie Jones, (declined.)	
	32. Richard D. Spaight,	May 25, "
	33. Hugh Williamson, (in the room of W. Jones,)	May 25, "
S. Carolina,	34. John Rutledge,	May 25, "
	35. Charles C. Pinckney,	May 25, "

From		Attended.
S. Carolina,	36. Charles Pinckney,	May 25, 1787.
	37. Pierce Butler,	May 25, "
Georgia,	38. William Few,	May 25, "
	39. Abraham Baldwin,	June 11, "
	William Pierce,	May 31, "
	George Walton,	
	William Houston,	June 1, "
	Nathaniel Pendleton.	

Those with numbers before their names signed
the Constitution,   -   -   -   -   **39**
Those in italics never attended,   -   -   **10**
Members who attended, but did not sign the
Constitution,   -   -   -   -   -   **16**
                               —
                             65

LETTER

FROM THE HONORABLE ROBERT YATES, AND THE HONORABLE
JOHN LANSING, JUN., ESQUIRES, TO THE GOVERNOR OF
NEW YORK, CONTAINING THEIR REASONS FOR NOT SUB-
SCRIBING TO THE FEDERAL CONSTITUTION.

Sir,

We do ourselves the honor to advise your Excellency, that, in pursuance of concurrent resolutions of
the honorable Senate and Assembly, we have, together
with Mr. Hamilton, attended the convention, appointed
for revising the articles of confederation, and reporting
amendments to the same.

It is with the sincerest concern we observe, that, in
the prosecution of the important objects of our mission,

we have been reduced to the disagreeable alternative of either exceeding the powers delegated to us, and giving our assent to measures which we conceive destructive to the political happiness of the citizens of the United States, or opposing our opinions to that of a body of respectable men, to whom those citizens had given the most unequivocal proofs of confidence. Thus circumstanced, under these impressions, to have hesitated would have been to be culpable ; we, therefore, gave the principles of the constitution, which has received the sanction of a majority of the convention, our decided and unreserved dissent ; but we must candidly confess, that we should have been equally opposed to any system, however modified, which had in object the consolidation of the United States into one government.

We beg leave briefly to state some cogent reasons which, among others, influenced us to decide against a consolidation of the States. These are reducible into two heads.

1st. The limited and well-defined powers under which we acted, and which could not, on any possible construction, embrace an idea of such magnitude, as to assent to a general constitution, in subversion of that of the State.

2d. A conviction of the impracticability of establishing a general government, pervading every part of the United States, and extending essential benefits to all.

Our powers were explicit, and confined to the sole and express purpose of revising the articles of confederation, and reporting such alterations and provisions therein, as shall render the federal constitution adequate to the exigencies of government and the preservation of the Union.

From these expressions we were led to believe, that a system of consolidated government could not, in the remotest degree, have been in contemplation of the legislature of this State; for that so important a trust as the adopting measures which tended to deprive the State government of its most essential rights of sovereignty, and to place it in a dependent situation, could not have been confided by implication; and the circumstance, that the acts of the convention were to receive a State approbation in the last resort, forcibly corroborated the opinion, that our powers could not involve the subversion of a constitution, which, being immediately derived from the people, could only be abolished by their express consent, and not by a legislature, possessing authority vested in them for its preservation. Nor could we suppose, that, if it had been the intention of the legislature to abrogate the existing confederation, they would, in such pointed terms, have directed the attention of their delegates to the revision and amendment of it, in total exclusion of every other idea.

Reasoning in this manner, we were of opinion, that the leading feature of every amendment ought to be the preservation of the individual States, in their uncontrolled constitutional rights; and that, in reserving these, a mode might have been devised of granting to the confederacy the moneys arising from a general system of revenue, the power of regulating commerce, and enforcing the observance of foreign treaties, and other necessary matters of less moment.

Exclusive of our objections originating from the want of power, we entertained an opinion, that a general government, however guarded by declarations of rights, or cautionary provisions, must unavoidably, in a short time, be productive of the destruction of the civil liberty of such citizens as could be effectually coerced by it; by reason of the extensive territory of the United States, the dispersed situation of its inhabitants, and the insuperable difficulty of controlling or counteracting the views of a set of men, (however unconstitutional and oppressive their acts might be,) possessed of all the powers of government; and who, from their remoteness from their constituents, and necessary permanency of office, could not be supposed to be uniformly actuated by an attention to their welfare and happiness; that, however wise and energetic the principles of the general government might be, the extremities of the United States could not be kept in due submission and obedience to its laws, at the distance of many hundred miles from the seat of government; that if the general legislature was composed of so numerous a body of men as to represent the interests of all the inhabitants of the United States, in the usual and true ideas of representation, the expense of supporting it would become intolerably burdensome; and that, if a few only were vested with a power of legislation, the interests of a great majority of the inhabitants of the United States must necessarily be unknown; or if known, even in the first stages of the operations of the new government, unattended to.

These reasons were, in our opinion, conclusive against any system of consolidated government. To that recommended by the convention, we suppose most of them very forcibly apply.

It is not our intention to pursue this subject further than merely to explain our conduct in the discharge of the trust which the honorable the legislature reposed in us. Interested, however, as we are, in common with our fellow citizens, in the result, we cannot forbear to declare, that we have the strongest apprehensions, that a government so organized as that recommended by the convention, cannot afford that security to equal and permanent liberty, which we wished to make an invariable object of our pursuit.

We were not present at the completion of the new constitution; but, before we left the convention, its principles were so well established, as to convince us, that no alteration was to be expected to conform it to our ideas of expediency and safety. A persuasion, that our further attendance would be fruitless and unavailing, rendered us less solicitous to return.

We have thus explained our motives for opposing the adoption of the national constitution, which we conceived it our duty to communicate to your Excellency, to be submitted to the consideration of the honorable legislature.

We have the honor to be, with the greatest respect, your Excellency's most obedient and very humble servants,

ROBERT YATES,
JOHN LANSING, Jun.

His Excellency Governor Clinton.

A LETTER

OF HIS EXCELLENCY EDMUND RANDOLPH, ESQUIRE, ON THE
FEDERAL CONSTITUTION, ADDRESSED TO THE HONORABLE
THE SPEAKER OF THE HOUSE OF DELEGATES, VIRGINIA.

Richmond, October 10th, 1787

Sir,

The constitution, which I enclosed to the General
Assembly in a late official letter, appears without my
signature. This circumstance, although trivial in its
own nature, has been rendered rather important to
myself at least, by being misunderstood by some, and
misrepresented by others. As I disdain to conceal the
reasons for withholding my subscription, I have always
been, still am, and ever shall be, ready to proclaim
them to the world. To the legislature, therefore, by
whom I was deputed to the federal convention, I beg
leave now to address them ; affecting no indifference
to public opinion, but resolved not to court it by an
unmanly sacrifice of my own judgment.

As this explanation will involve a summary, but
general review of our federal situation, you will pardon me, I trust, although I should transgress the usual
bounds of a letter.

Before my departure for the convention, I believed,
that the confederation was not so eminently defective
as it had been supposed. But, after I had entered into
a free communication with those who were best informed of the condition and interest of each State ;
after I had compared the intelligence derived from
them, with the properties which ought to characterize
the government of our Union, I became persuaded,
that the confederation was destitute of every energy,
which a constitution of the United States ought to
possess.

For the objects proposed by its institution were, that it should be a shield against foreign hostility, and a firm resort against domestic commotion; that it should cherish trade, and promote the prosperity of the States under its care.

But these are not among the attributes of our present Union. Severe experience under the pressure of war, — a ruinous weakness manifested since the return of peace; and the contemplation of those dangers, which darken the future prospect, have condemned the hope of grandeur and of safety under the auspices of the confederation.

In the exigencies of war, indeed, the history of its effects is but short; the final ratification having been delayed until the beginning of the year 1781. But, however short, this period is distinguished by melancholy testimonies of its inability to maintain in harmony, the social intercourse of the States, to defend Congress against encroachments on their rights, and to obtain by requisitions, supplies to the federal treasury, or recruits to the federal armies. I shall not attempt an enumeration of the particular instances; but leave to your own remembrance and the records of Congress, the support of the assertions.

In the season of peace too, not many years have elapsed; and yet each of them has produced fatal examples of delinquency, and sometimes of pointed opposition to federal duties. To the various remonstrances of Congress I appeal, for a gloomy, but unexaggerated narrative of the injuries which our faith, honor, and happiness have sustained by the failure of the States.

But these evils are past; and some may be led by an honest zeal to conclude, that they cannot be re-

peated.   Yes, sir, they will be repeated as long as the
confederation exists, and will bring with them other
mischiefs springing from the same source, which cannot be yet foreseen in their full array of terror.

If we examine the constitution and laws of the several States, it is immediately discovered, that the law
of nations is unprovided with sanctions in many cases,
which deeply affect public dignity and public justice.
The letter, however, of the confederation does not
permit Congress to remedy those defects, and such an
authority, although evidently deducible from its spirit,
cannot, without violation of the second article, be assumed.   Is it not a political phenomenon, that the
head of the confederacy should be doomed to be
plunged into war, from its wretched impotency to
check offences against this law; and sentenced to
witness, in unavailing anguish, the infraction of their
engagements to foreign sovereigns?

And yet, this is not the only grievous point of
weakness.   After a war shall be inevitable, the requisitions of Congress for quotas of men or money, will
again prove unproductive and fallacious.   Two causes
will always conspire to this baneful consequence.

1. No government can be stable, which hangs on
human inclination alone, unbiassed by coercion; and
2. from the very connexion between States bound
to proportionate contributions, jealousies and suspi-
cions naturally arise, which at least chill the ardor, if
they do not excite the murmurs of the whole.   I do
not forget, indeed, that, by one sudden impulse, our
part of the American continent has been thrown into
a military posture, and that, in the earlier annals of
the war, our armies marched to the field on the mere
recommendations of Congress.   But ought we to argue

from a contest, thus signalized by the magnitude of its stake, that, as often as a flame shall be hereafter kindled, the same enthusiasm will fill our legions, or renew them, as they may be filled by losses?

If not, where shall we find protection? Impressions, like those, which prevent a compliance with requisitions of regular forces, will deprive the American republic of the services of militia. But let us suppose that they are attainable, and acknowledge, as I always shall, that they are the natural support of a free government. When it is remembered, that in their absence agriculture must languish, that they are not habituated to military exposures and the rigor of military discipline, and that the necessity of holding in readiness successive detachments, carries the expense far beyond that of enlistments, this resource ought to be adopted with caution.

As strongly too am I persuaded, that the requisitions for money will not be more cordially received. For besides the distrust, which would prevail with respect to them also, besides the opinion, entertained by each State, of its own liberality and unsatisfied demands against the United States, there is another consideration not less worthy of attention, — the first rule for determining each quota of the value of all lands granted or surveyed, and of the buildings and improvements thereon. It is no longer doubted, that an equitable, uniform mode of estimating that value, is impracticable; and, therefore, twelve States have substituted the number of inhabitants under certain limitations, as the standard according to which money is to be furnished. But, under the subsisting articles of the Union, the assent of the thirteenth State is necessary, and has not yet been given. This does of itself lessen the hope of procuring a revenue for federal uses; and the miscarriage of the impost almost rivets our despondency.

Amidst these disappointments, it would afford some consolation, if, when rebellion shall threaten any State, an ultimate asylum could be found under the wing of Congress. But it is at least equivocal, whether they can intrude forces into a State, rent asunder by civil discord, even with the purest solicitude for our federal welfare, and on the most urgent entreaties of the State itself. Nay, the very allowance of this power would be pageantry alone, from the want of money and of men.

To these defects of congressional power, the history of man has subjoined others, not less alarming. I earnestly pray, that the recollection of common sufferings, which terminated in common glory, may check the sallies of violence, and perpetuate mutual friendship between the States. But I cannot presume, that we are superior to those unsocial passions, which under like circumstances have infested more ancient nations. I cannot presume, that through all time, in the daily mixture of American citizens with each other, in the conflicts for commercial advantages, in the discontents which the neighbourhood of territory has been seen to engender in other quarters of the globe, and in the efforts of faction and intrigue; thirteen distinct communities under no effective superintending control (as the United States confessedly now are, notwithstanding the bold terms of the confederation), will avoid a hatred to each other, deep and deadly.

In the prosecution of this inquiry, we shall find the general prosperity to decline under a system thus unnerved. No sooner is the merchant prepared for foreign ports, with the treasures which this new world kindly offers to his acceptance, than it is announced to him, that they are shut against American shipping, or opened under oppressive regulations. He urges Congress to a counter-policy, and is answered only by a condolence on the general misfortune. He is immediately struck with the conviction, that, until exclusion shall be opposed to exclusion, and restriction to restriction, the American flag will be disgraced. For who can conceive, that thirteen legislatures, viewing commerce under different regulations, and fancying themselves discharged from every obligation to concede the smallest of their commercial advantages for the benefit of the whole, will be wrought into a concert of action in defiance of every prejudice? Nor is this all; let the great improvements be recounted, which have enriched and illustrated Europe; let it be noted, how few those are, which will be absolutely denied to the United States, comprehending within their boundaries the choicest blessings of climate, soil, and navigable waters; then let the most sanguine patriot banish, if he can, the mortifying belief, that all these must sleep, until they shall be roused by the vigor of a national government.

I have not exemplified the preceding remarks by minute details; because they are evidently fortified by truth, and the consciousness of the United States of America. I shall, therefore, no longer deplore the unfitness of the confederation to secure our peace; but proceed, with a truly unaffected distrust of my own opinions, to examine what order of powers the government of the United States ought to enjoy? How they ought to be defended against encroachments? Whether they can be interwoven in the confederation, without an alteration of its very essence, or must be lodged in new hands? Showing, at the same time, the convulsions which seem to await us, from a dissolution of the Union or partial confederacies.

To mark the kind and degree of authority, which ought to be confided to the government of the United States, is no more than to reverse the description which I have already given of the defects of the confederation.

From thence it will follow, that the operations of peace and war will be clogged without regular advances of money, and that these will be slow indeed, if dependent on supplication alone. For what better name do requisitions deserve, which may be evaded or opposed without the fear of coercion? But, although coercion is an indispensable ingredient, it ought not to be directed against a State, as a State; it being impossible to attempt it except by blockading the trade of the delinquent, or carrying war into its bowels. Even if these violent schemes were eligible, in other respects, both of them might perhaps be defeated by the scantiness of the public chest; would be tardy in their complete effect, as the expense of the land and naval equipments must be first reimbursed; and might drive the proscribed State into the desperate resolve of inviting foreign alliances. Against each of them lie separate, unconquerable objections. A blockade is not equally applicable to all the States, they being differently circumstanced in commerce and in ports; nay, an excommunication from the privilege of the Union would be vain, because every regulation or prohibition may be easily eluded under the rights of American citizenship, or of foreign nations. But how shall we speak of the intrusion of troops? Shall we arm citizens against citizens, and habituate them to shed kindred blood? Shall we risk the inflicting of wounds which will generate a rancour never to be subdued? Would there be no room to fear, that an army accustomed to fight for the establishment of authority, would salute an emperor of their own? Let us not bring these things into jeopardy. Let us rather substitute the same process by which individuals are compelled to contribute to the government of their own States. Instead of making requisitions to the legislatures, it would appear more proper, that taxes should be imposed by the federal head, under due modifications and guards; that the collectors should demand from the citizens their respective quotas, and be supported as in the collection of ordinary taxes.

It follows too, that, as the general government will be responsible to foreign nations, it ought to be able to annul any offensive measure, or enforce any public right. Perhaps among the topics on which they may be aggrieved or complain, the commercial intercourse, and the manner in which contracts are discharged, may constitute the principal articles of clamor.

It follows too, that the general government ought to be the supreme arbiter for adjusting every contention among the States. In all their connexions, therefore, with each other, and particularly in commerce, which will probably create the greatest discord, it ought to hold the reins.

It follows too, that the general government ought to protect each State against domestic as well as external violence.

And lastly, it follows, that, through the general government alone, can we ever assume the rank to which we are entitled by our resources and situation.

Should the people of America surrender these powers, they can be paramount to the constitutions and
ordinary acts of legislation, only by being delegated
by them. I do not pretend to affirm, but I venture to
believe, that, if the confederation had been solemnly
questioned in opposition to our constitution, or even
to one of our laws, posterior to it, it must have given
way. For never did it obtain a higher ratification,
than a resolution of assembly in the daily form.

This will be one security against encroachment.
But another not less effectual is, to exclude the individual States from any agency in the national government, as far as it may be safe, and their interposition
may not be absolutely necessary.

But now, Sir, permit me to declare, that, in my humble judgment, the powers by which alone the blessings of a general government can be accomplished,
cannot be interwoven in the confederation, without a
change in its very essence, or, in other words, that the
confederation must be thrown aside. This is almost
demonstrable, from the inefficacy of requisitions, and
from the necessity of converting them into acts of
authority. My suffrage, as a citizen, is also for additional powers. But to whom shall we commit these
acts of authority, these additional powers? To Congress? When I formerly lamented the defects in the
jurisdiction of Congress, I had no view to indicate any
other opinion, than that the federal head ought not to
be so circumscribed. For, free as I am at all times to
profess my reverence for that body, and the individuals who compose it, I am yet equally free to make
known my aversion to repose such a trust in a tribunal so constituted. My objections are not the visions
of theory, but the result of my own observations in

America, and of the experience of others abroad. 1.
The legislative and executive are concentred in the
same persons. This, where real power exists, must
eventuate in tyranny. 2. The representation of the
States bears no proportion to their importance. This
is an unreasonable subjection of the will of the majority to that of the minority. 3. The mode of election,
and the liability of being recalled, may too often render the delegates rather partisans of their own States
than representatives of the Union. 4. Cabal and intrigue must consequently gain an ascendency in a
course of years. 5. A single house of legislation will
sometimes be precipitate, perhaps passionate. 6. As
long as seven States are required for the smallest, and
nine for the greatest votes, may not foreign influence
at some future day insinuate itself, so as to interrupt
every active exertion ? 7. To crown the whole, it is
scarce within the verge of possibility, that so numerous an assembly should acquire that secrecy, despatch,
and vigor, which are the test of excellence in the executive department.

My inference from these facts and principles, is,
that the new powers must be deposited in a new body,
growing out of a consolidation of the Union, as far as
the circumstances of the States will allow. Perhaps,
however, some may meditate its dissolution, and others, partial confederacies.

The first is an idea awful indeed, and irreconcil-
able with a very early, and hitherto uniform conviction, that without union we must be undone. For,
before the voice of war was heard, the pulse of the
then colonies was tried, and found to beat in unison.
The unremitted labor of our enemies was to divide,
and the policy of every Congress to bind us together.

But in no example was this truth more clearly displayed, than in the prudence with which independence was unfolded to the sight, and in the forbearance to declare it, until America almost unanimously called for it. After we had thus launched into troubles never before explored, and in the hour of heavy distress, the remembrance of our social strength not only forbade despair, but drew from Congress the most illustrious repetition of their settled purpose to despise all terms short of independence.

Behold, then, how successful and glorious we have been, while we acted in fraternal concord. But let us discard the illusion, that by this success, and this glory, the crest of danger has irrecoverably fallen. Our governments are yet too youthful to have acquired stability from habit. Our very quiet depends upon the duration of the Union. Among the upright and intelligent, few can read without emotion the future fate of the States, if severed from each other. Then shall we learn the full weight of foreign intrigue. Then shall we hear of partitions of our country. If a prince, inflamed by the lust of conquest, should use one State as the instrument of enslaving others; if every State is to be wearied by perpetual alarms, and compelled to maintain large military establishments; if all questions are to be decided by an appeal to arms, where a difference of opinion cannot be removed by negotiation; in a word, if all the direful misfortunes which haunt the peace of rival nations, are to triumph over the land, for what have we to contend? why have we exhausted our wealth? why have we basely betrayed the heroic martyrs of the federal cause?

But dreadful as the total dissolution of the Union is to my mind, I entertain no less horror at the thought of partial confederacies. I have not the least ground for supposing, that an overture of this kind would be listened to by a single State; and the presumption is, that the politics of a greater part of the States flow from the warmest attachment to an union of the whole. If, however, a lesser confederacy could be obtained by Virginia, let me conjure my countrymen well to weigh the probable consequences, before they attempt to form it.

On such an event, the strength of the Union would be divided in two, or perhaps three parts. Has it so increased since the war as to be divisible, and yet remain sufficient for our happiness?

The utmost limit of any partial confederacy, which Virginia could expect to form, would comprehend the three southern States, and her nearest northern neighbour. But they, like ourselves, are diminished in their real force, by the mixture of an unhappy species of population.

Again may I ask, whether the opulence of the United States has been augmented since the war? This is answered in the negative, by a load of debt, and the declension of trade.

At all times must a southern confederacy support ships of war and a soldiery? As soon would a navy move from the forest, and an army spring from the earth, as such a confederacy, indebted, impoverished in its commerce, and destitute of men, could, for some years at least, provide an ample defence for itself.

Let it not be forgotten, that nations, which can enforce their rights, have large claims against the United States, and that the creditor may insist on payment from any of them. Which of them would probably be the victim? The most productive, and the most exposed. When vexed by reprisals or war, the southern States will sue for alliance on this continent or beyond sea. If for the former, the necessity of an union of the whole is decided; if for the latter, America will, I fear, react the scenes of confusion and bloodshed exhibited among most of those nations, which have, too late, repented the folly of relying on auxiliaries.

Two or more confederacies cannot but be competitors for power. The ancient friendship between the citizens of America being thus cut off, bitterness and hostility will succeed in its place; in order to prepare against surrounding danger, we shall be compelled to vest somewhere or other power approaching near to military government.

The annals of the world have abounded so much with instances of a divided people being a prey to foreign influence, that I shall not restrain my apprehensions of it, should our Union be torn asunder. The opportunity of insinuating it will be multiplied in proportion to the parts into which we may be broken.

In short, Sir, I am fatigued with summoning up to my imagination the miseries which will harass the United States, if torn from each other, and which will not end until they are superseded by fresh mischiefs under the yoke of a tyrant.

I come, therefore, to the last, and perhaps only refuge in our difficulties, a consolidation of the Union, as far as circumstances will permit. To fulfil this desirable object, the Constitution was framed by the federal convention. A quorum of eleven States, and the only member from a twelfth, have subscribed it; Mr. Mason of Virginia, Mr. Gerry of Massachusetts, and myself, having refused to subscribe.

Why I refused, will, I hope, be solved to the satisfaction of those who know me, by saying, that a sense of duty commanded me thus to act. It commanded me, Sir; for believe me, that no event of my life ever occupied more of my reflection. To subscribe, seemed to offer no inconsiderable gratification, since it would have presented me to the world as a fellow-laborer with the learned and zealous statesmen of America.

But it was far more interesting to my feelings, that I was about to differ from three of my colleagues; one of whom is, to the honor of the country which he has saved, embosomed in their affections, and can receive no praise from the highest lustre of language; the other two of whom, have been long enrolled among the wisest and best lovers of the commonwealth ; and the unshaken and intimate friendship of all of whom, I have ever prized, and still do prize, as among the happiest of all acquisitions. I was no stranger to the reigning partiality for the members who composed the convention, and had not the smallest doubt, that from this cause, and from the ardor for a reform of government, the first applauses, at least, would be loud and profuse. I suspected too, that there was something in the human breast, which for a time would be apt to construe a temperateness in politics, into an enmity to the Union. Nay, I plainly foresaw, that, in the dissensions of parties, a middle line would probably be interpreted into a want of enterprise and decision. But these considerations, how seducing soever, were feeble opponents to the suggestions of my conscience. I was sent to exercise my judgment, and to exercise it was my fixed determination ; being instructed by even an imperfect acquaintance with mankind, that self-approbation is the only true reward which a political

career can bestow, and that popularity would have
been but another name for perfidy, if, to secure it,
I had given up the freedom of thinking for myself.

It would have been a peculiar pleasure to me, to
have ascertained before I left Virginia, the temper and
genius of my fellow citizens, considered relatively to
a government so substantially differing from the confederation as that which is now submitted. But this
was, for many obvious reasons, impossible; and I was
thereby deprived of what I thought the necessary
guides.

I saw, however, that the confederation was tottering from its own weakness, and that the sitting of the
convention was a signal of its total insufficiency. I
was, therefore, ready to assent to a scheme of government which was proposed, and which went beyond
the limits of the confederation, believing, that without
being too extensive, it would have preserved our tranquillity, until that temper and that genius should be
collected.

But when the plan which is now before the General
Assembly was on its passage through the convention,
I moved, that the State conventions should be at liberty to amend, and that a second general convention
should be holden to discuss the amendments which
should be suggested by them. This motion was
in some measure justified by the manner in which
the confederation was forwarded originally, by Congress to the State legislatures, in many of which
amendments were proposed, and those amendments
were afterwards examined in Congress. Such a motion was doubly expedient here, as the delegation of
so much more power was sought for. But it was

negatived. I then expressed my unwillingness to sign. My reasons were the following:

1. It is said in the resolutions which accompany the Constitution, that it is to be submitted to a convention of delegates, chosen in each State by the people thereof, for their assent and ratification. The meaning of these terms is allowed universally to be, that the convention must either adopt the Constitution in the whole, or reject it in the whole, and is positively forbidden to amend. If therefore, I had signed, I should have felt myself bound to be silent as to amendments, and to endeavour to support the Constitution without the correction of a letter. With this consequence before my eyes, and with a determination to attempt an amendment, I was taught by a regard for consistency, not to sign.

2. My opinion always was, and still is, that every citizen of America, let the crisis be what it may, ought to have a full opportunity to propose, through his representatives, any amendment which, in his apprehension, tends to the public welfare. By signing, I should have contradicted this sentiment.

3. A constitution ought to have the hearts of the people on its side. But if at a future day it should be burdensome, after having been adopted in the whole, and they should insinuate, that it was in some measure forced upon them, by being confined to the single alternative of taking or rejecting it altogether, under my impressions, and with my opinions, I should not be able to justify myself, had I signed.

4. I was always satisfied, as I have now experienced, that this great subject would be placed in new lights and attitudes by the criticism of the world; and that no man can assure himself how a constitution will

work for a course of years, until at least he shall have heard the observations of the people at large. I also fear more from inaccuracies in a constitution, than from gross errors in any other composition; because our dearest interests are to be regulated by it; and power, if loosely given, especially where it will be interpreted with great latitude, may bring sorrow in its execution. Had I signed with these ideas, I should have virtually shut my ears against the information which I ardently desired.

5. I was afraid, that if the Constitution was to be submitted to the people, to be wholly adopted or wholly rejected by them, they would not only reject it, but bid a lasting farewell to the Union. This formidable event I wished to avert, by keeping myself free to propose amendments, and thus, if possible, to remove the obstacles to an effectual government. But it will be asked, whether all these arguments were not well weighed in the convention. They were, Sir, with great candor. Nay, when I called to mind the respectability of those, with whom I was associated, I almost lost confidence in these principles. On other occasions, I should cheerfully have yielded to a majority; on this, the fate of thousands yet unborn enjoined me not to yield until I was convinced.

Again, may I be asked, why the mode pointed out in the Constitution for its amendment, may not be a sufficient security against its imperfections, without now arresting it in its progress? My answers are: 1. That it is better to amend while we have the Constitution in our power, while the passions of designing men are not yet enlisted, and while a bare majority of the States may amend, than to wait for the uncertain assent of three fourths of the States. 2. That a bad feature in government becomes more and more fixed every day. 3. That frequent changes of a constitution, even if practicable, ought not to be wished, but avoided as much as possible. And 4. That, in the present case, it may be questionable, whether, after the particular advantages of its operation shall be discerned, three fourths of the States can be induced to amend.

I confess, that it is no easy task to devise a scheme which shall be suitable to the views of all. Many expedients have occurred to me, but none of them appear less exceptionable than this; that, if our convention should choose to amend, another federal convention be recommended; that in that federal convention the amendments proposed by this or any other State be discussed; and if incorporated in the Constitution or rejected, or if a proper number of the other States should be unwilling to accede to a second convention, the Constitution be again laid before the same State conventions, which shall again assemble on the summons of the executives, and it shall be either wholly adopted or wholly rejected, without a further power of amendment. I count such a delay as nothing in comparison with so grand an object; especially too as the privilege of amending must terminate after the use of it once.

I should now conclude this letter, which is already too long, were it not incumbent on me, from having contended for amendments, to set forth the particulars which I conceive to require correction. I undertake this with reluctance, because it is remote from my intentions to catch the prejudices or prepossessions of any man. But, as I mean only to manifest, that I have not been actuated by caprice, and now to explain every objection at full length would be an immense labor, I shall content myself with enumerating certain heads, in which the constitution is most repugnant to my wishes.

The two first points are the equality of suffrage in the Senate, and the submission of commerce to a mere majority in the legislature, with no other check than the revision of the President. I conjecture, that neither of these things can be corrected; and particularly the former, without which we must have risen perhaps in disorder.

But I am sanguine in hoping, that, in every other justly obnoxious cause, Virginia will be seconded by a majority of the States. I hope that she will be seconded, 1. In causing all ambiguities of expression to be precisely explained. 2. In rendering the President ineligible after a given number of years. 3. In taking from him the power of nominating to the judiciary offices, or of filling up vacancies which may there happen during the recess of the Senate, by granting commissions which shall expire at the end of their next sessions. 4. In taking from him the power of pardoning for treason, at least before conviction. 5. In drawing a line between the powers of Congress and individual States; and in defining the former, so as to leave no clashing of jurisdictions, nor dangerous disputes; and to prevent the one from being swallowed up by the other, under cover of general words and implication. 6. In abridging the power of the Senate to make treaties supreme laws of the land. 7. In incapacitating the Congress to determine their own salaries. And, 8. In limiting and defining the judicial power.

The proper remedy must be consigned to the wisdom of the convention ; and the final step which Virginia shall pursue, if her overtures shall be discarded, must also rest with them.

You will excuse me, Sir, for having been thus tedious. My feelings and duty demanded this exposition ; for through no other channel could I rescue my omission to sign from misrepresentation, and in no more effectual way could I exhibit to the General Assembly an unreserved history of my conduct.

I have the honor, Sir, to be, with great respect, your most obedient servant,

EDMUND RANDOLPH.

BIOGRAPHICAL SKETCH.

CHIEF JUSTICE YATES, the subject of the following memoir, was born on the 27th day of January, 1738, in the city of Schenectady, in this State. At the age of sixteen, he was sent by his parents to the city of New York, where he received a classical education, and afterwards studied the law with William Livingston, Esquire, a celebrated barrister in that metropolis, and father of Brockholst Livingston, Esquire, one of the judges of the Supreme Court of the United States. On the completion of his studies he was admitted to the bar, and soon after fixed his residence in the city of Albany, where in due time he received the degrees of solicitor and counsellor in the Court of Chancery. He soon became eminent in his profession, and, on account of his incorruptible integrity, was known by the appellation of the *honest lawyer.* At the age of twenty-seven, he married Miss Jane Van Ness, of Columbia county. On the prospect of a rupture between this country and Great Britain, his open and avowed principles as a Whig brought him into political notice, and several well written essays, which were the productions of his pen, contributed in no small degree to establish his reputation as a writer in defence of the rights and liberties of his country. He has already

28*

held a seat as a member of the corporation of the city of Albany, and as attorney and counsel to that board; and he was soon after appointed a member of the Committee of Public Safety, a body of men who were invested with almost inquisitorial powers, and who had justly become the dread and scourge of that class of men called Tories. By the exertions of Chief Justice Yates, the proceedings of that tribunal were tempered with moderation, and the patriotic zeal of the community confined within its proper and legitimate sphere of action. We find him not long afterwards holding a seat in the Provincial Congress of his own State, and, during the recess of that body, performing the complicated and arduous duties of chairman of a committee for the organization and direction of military operations against the common enemy.

In the year 1777, the constitution of this State was adopted, and Chief Justice Yates was an active and distinguished member of the convention that framed that instrument. During the same year he received, without solicitation, the appointment of a judge of the Supreme Court, at a time when an extensive and lucrative practice as a lawyer, held out to him strong inducements to decline its acceptance. Regardless, however, of private interest, he entered upon the duties of that office rendered at the time peculiarly delicate and dangerous. He sat upon the bench, as a writer has expressed it, " with a halter about his neck," exposed to punishment as a rebel, had our efforts for emancipation proved abortive; nor were these the least of his dangers. For in counties ravaged or possessed by the enemy, or by secret domestic foes watching every opportunity to ruin or betray their country, he was sometimes obliged to hold his courts.

But no dangers could appal, nor fears deter him from a faithful and honest performance of the functions of his office. He was particularly distinguished for his impartiality in the trials of state criminals, and he was not unfrequently obliged to abate the intemperate zeal or ill-judged patriotism of the juries who were to decide upon the fate of unfortunate prisoners. On one occasion he sent a jury from the bar four times successively to reconsider a verdict of conviction which they had pronounced most unwarrantably against the accused, merely because they suspected he was a Tory, though without any proof that could authorize the verdict. As the accused had become very obnoxious to the great body of the Whigs, the legislature were inflamed, and seriously contemplated calling Chief Justice Yates before them to answer for his conduct. But he was alike indifferent to censure or applause in the faithful and independent exercise of his judicial duties, and the legislature at length prudently dropped the affair. His salary during the war was very small, and hardly sufficient for the support of himself and family. Indeed, before the scale of depreciation of continental money had been settled, he received one year's salary in that money at its nominal value, the whole of which was just sufficient (as he humorously observed) " to purchase a pound of green tea for his wife." He was often urged to unite with some of his friends in speculating on forfeited estates during the war, by which he might easily have enriched himself and his connexions without censure or suspicion ; and although such speculations were common, yet he would not consent to become wealthy upon the ruin of others. " No," said he, " I will sooner die a beggar than own a foot of land acquired by such means." In September, 1776, George Clinton, afterwards executive of this State, anxious to receive the cooperation of Chief Justice Yates in certain measures then deemed important and necessary, addressed him a letter, of which the following is an extract: " We have at last arrived at a most important crisis, which will either secure the independence of our country or determine that she shall still remain in a state of vassalage to Great Britain. I know your sentiments on this subject, and I am extremely happy to find that they agree so exactly with mine. But as we are called upon to act, as well as to think, your talents and exertions in the common cause cannot be spared." With such men as John Jay, Dr. Franklin, Chancellor Livingston, General Philip Schuyler, and Alexander Hamilton, he was in habits of intimacy and friendship. And to his relatives and more particular friends, Abraham Yates, Jun., former mayor of Albany, and Colonel Christopher Yates, the father of Joseph C. Yates, Esquire, the present judge of the Supreme Court, he was endeared by every tie of affection and esteem. These two last-named gentlemen were well known for their exertions in defence of their country, during the revolutionary war; the former more particularly as the writer of certain spirited publications under the signatures of *Sidney* and *Roughhewer*.

After the conclusion of the revolutionary war, he was chosen, together with General Hamilton and Chancellor Lansing, to represent his native State in the convention that formed the Constitution of the United States; and to his labors in that convention we are indebted for the preservation of some of the most important debates that ever distinguished any age or country.* He was also a member of the convention subsequently held in this State, to whom that Constitution was submitted for adoption and ratification. His political opinions were open and unreserved. He was opposed to a consolidated national government, and friendly to a confederation of the States preserving their integrity and equality as such. Although the form of government eventually adopted, was not, in all its parts agreeable to his views and wishes, still in all his discussions, and especially in his judicial capacity, he deemed it a sacred duty to inculcate entire submission to, and reverence for, that Constitution. In the first charge which he delivered to a grand jury, immediately after its adoption, he used the following language: "The proposed form of government for the Union has at length received the sanction of so many of the States as to make it the supreme law of the land, and it is not therefore any longer a question, whether or not its provisions are such as they ought to be in all their different branches. We, as good citizens, are bound implicitly to obey them, for the united wisdom of America has sanctioned and confirmed the act, and it would be little short of treason against the republic to hesitate in our obedience and respect to the Constitution of the United States of America. Let me therefore exhort you, Gentlemen, not only in your capacity as grand jurors, but in your more durable and equally respectable character as citi-

* Chief Justice Yates, though often solicited, refused during his life, to permit his notes of those debates to be published, not only because they were originally not written for the public eye, but because he conceived himself under honorable obligations to withhold their publication. These notes, after his death, fell into the hands of his widow, who disposed of them, and they are thus become public.

zens, to preserve inviolate this charter of our national
rights and safety, a charter second only in dignity and
importance to the Declaration of our Independence.
We have escaped, it is true, by the blessing of Divine
Providence, from the tyranny of a foreign foe, but let
us now be equally watchful in guarding against worse
and far more dangerous enemies, — domestic broils
and intestine divisions." Soon after this period he
filled the important trust of commissioner to treat with
the States of Massachusetts and Connecticut, on the
subject of territory, and to settle certain claims of his
native State against the State of Vermont. In 1790,
he received the appointment of chief justice of the
State of New York, and was twice supported for the
office of governor, to which latter office he was on
one occasion elected by a majority of votes ; but, on
account of some real or supposed inaccuracy in some
of the returns, he did not receive the certificate of his
election.

In January, 1798, having completed his sixtieth
year, and with it, the constitutional term of his office,
he retired from the bench of which for twenty-one
years he had been its ornament and pride ; and resumed the practice of the law. So highly did the
legislature estimate his former services and usefulness,
that it was proposed in that body to fix an annual
allowance or stipend on him for life, and the proposition actually passed the Senate, but was laid aside in
the Assembly, as being supposed to savor too much of
the monarchical regulation called *pensions*. Determined, however, to provide for an old and faithful
public servant, who had worn out his better days for
the good of his country, the legislature appointed him
a commissioner to settle disputed titles to lands in the

military tract, and this appointment he held till nearly the close of his life, when the law creating it ceased by its own limitation. On the 9th day of September, 1801, he finished his mortal career, "full of honors and full of years," placing a firm reliance on the merits of an atoning Saviour, and the goodness of a merciful God. He left a widow and four children, two of whom only are now living, a son and daughter, the former of whom is the present secretary of this State.

Chief Justice Yates died poor. He had always been indifferent to his own private interest, for his benevolent and patriotic feelings could not be regulated nor restrained by the cold calculations of avarice or gain. No man in this State was more esteemed than himself. He never had, it is believed, in the whole course of his life, a personal enemy, and the tears of the widow, the orphan, the destitute, and oppressed, followed him to his grave. He was emphatically the honest man and the upright judge. His talents were of the higher order, and his manners were plain, attractive, and unassuming. His opinions at *nisi prius* were seldom found to be incorrect, and on the bench of the Supreme Court he was distinguished for a clear, discriminating mind, that readily arrived at the true merits of the case before him. It may be safely affirmed, that no single individual ever filled so many high and responsible stations with greater credit to himself, and honor to the State. His memory will be cherished as long as virtue is esteemed and talents respected, and his epitaph is written in the hearts of his fellow citizens, and in the history of his country.

Printed in the United States
42342LVS00002B/492

9 781410 203632